A
Advances
N
in Nursing
S
Science Series

Advances in Methods of Inquiry for Nursing

D1043707

Peggy L. Chinn, RN, PhD, FAAN

Editor, *Advances in Nursing Science*
Associate Dean for Academics
Faculty Associate,
Center for Human Caring
University of Colorado School of Nursing
Denver, Colorado

An Aspen Publication®
Aspen Publishers, Inc.
Gaithersburg, Maryland
1994

Library of Congress Cataloging-in-Publication Data

Advances in methods of inquiry for nursing / [edited by] Peggy L.
Chinn.
p. cm.—(Advances in nursing science series)
Includes bibliographical references and index.
ISBN 0-8342-0595-5
1. Nursing—Research. 2. Nursing—Philosophy. I. Chinn, Peggy L.
II. Series.
[DNLM: 1. Nursing Research—methods. 2. Philosophy, Nursing. WY
20.5 A2445 1994]
RT81.5.A39 1994
610.73'072—dc20
DNLM/DLC
for Library of Congress
94-4853
CIP

Aspen Publishers, Inc., grants permission for photocopying for limited personal or internal
use. This consent does not extend to other kinds of copying, such as copying for general
distribution, for advertising or promotional purposes, for creating new collective works,
or for resale. For information, address Aspen Publishers, Inc., Permissions Department,
200 Orchard Ridge Drive, Suite 200, Gaithersburg, Maryland 20878.

Editorial Resources: Ruth Bloom

Library of Congress Catalog Card Number: 94-4853
ISBN: 0-8342-0595-5
Series ISBN: 0-8342-0576-9

Printed in the United States of America

1 2 3 4 5

Table of Contents

Preface

Unlike the other volumes in this series, this volume contains original articles that were initially prepared to be considered for publication in *Advances in Nursing Science,* Volume 16, No. 2. The numbers of manuscripts that were submitted and subsequently reviewed favorably for that issue of the journal far exceeded what the journal could accommodate, attesting to the importance of methodological developments in the discipline. Each of the articles contained herein was reviewed by three members of the *ANS* board of review, and met the criteria for publication in *ANS,* as judged by at least two of the three reviewers recommending publication. Subsequent to the review, each of these authors made revisions based on the comments and suggestions of the reviewers, yielding improved readability and clarity.

As the contents of this book and the companion issue of *ANS* demonstrate, nursing inquiry has grown and developed far beyond the strictly traditional boundaries of science. The manner in which new approaches to scholarship are judged by the community of scholars depends in part on the principles on which the scholarship of the discipline is founded. At the same time, new approaches to method serve to stretch the limits around which the principles of scholarship are formed and reformed.

It seems clear to me that while there is growing consensus that the strictly traditional forms of inquiry grounded on notions of causality are not wholly adequate to address some of nursing's pressing problems, this consensus in no way moves to the extreme position of dismissing these traditional forms of inquiry. The debates that once raged in the discipline over which form of inquiry is "best," or most worthy, have given way to substantive discussion of a wide array of methodological developments and the evidence of their adequacy to address the problems of the discipline or to inform the knowledge of the discipline. These substantive discussions have in turn provided insight concerning the principles on which scholarship can be judged as worthy to contribute to our social, professional, and disciplinary growth.

Principles of scholarship that I believe are emerging involve the art of inquiry, which in fact brings into focus some of the fundamental purposes for which the "enterprise of scholarship" exists. As humans, we are capable of envisioning new possibilities, of creating ideas and things that would not exist were it not for our marvelous capacity for creativity. The traditional scientific model derives its potential to a large degree from an implicit dependence on the creativity, flexibility, and openness of the scientist. The very questions posed in the traditional scientific model reflect a creative process that opens the door for exploring something new and different. Likewise, newly evolving methods of inquiry that grow out of philosophy, the arts, and the humanities, rely heavily on the artistic talent, the creativity, and the skill of performance of the inquirer. The evolving methods require their own specification of the "rules of conduct" that apply to the method or approach, but these "rules of conduct" are themselves part of the artistic endeavor—that process that creates something refined out of the rough, the raw, the undeveloped.

If we build on the fundamental principle of creative potential where all forms of inquiry are concerned, then we can abandon allegiance to method for method's sake. Instead, as new methodologic approaches are explored, developed, and implemented, we can ask questions that pertain to the art of the inquiry, such as, "what potential is emerging here that would not exist otherwise?" and "does this approach inform the discipline concerning the meaning or the nature of human health experience?" Essentially, these questions, and others like them, bring to the foreground a principle of creativity, a principle of the meaning of human potential. Worthy scholarship and methods of inquiry need not be bound by preconceived rules of conduct, which in fact are seldom adequate in and of themselves even in the traditional model of science. Rather, worthy scholarship can be judged based on principles that pertain to the art of inquiry: the integrity of the method, the skill of application or performance, and the creative potential that it engenders. As we continue to develop discourse in the discipline that recognizes and develops creativity in the discipline of nursing, nursing will increasingly reflect creativity in our practice, in our education, and in our scholarship. It is my hope that this book contributes substantially to this discourse.

— Peggy L. Chinn, RN, PhD, FAAN
Editor
Advances in Nursing Science

Writing As Inquiry in Qualitative Nursing Research: Elaborating the Web of Meaning

Jeanne Merkle Sorrell, DAEd
Associate Professor
College of Nursing and Health Science
George Mason University
Fairfax, Virginia

The author proposes that the writing process is a powerful tool for inquiry in qualitative nursing research. First, theories and research related to "writing to think" are presented, focusing on how the writing process involves the hand, eye, and brain to relate language to thought. Next, three characteristics of writing as a mode of inquiry in qualitative nursing research are presented: (1) writing as method, (2) writing as narrative, and (3) writing related to language forms. Finally, the author presents implications for qualitative nursing research when writing is used as a mode of inquiry.

> Writing, like life itself, is a voyage of discovery.
> —Henry Miller

VYGOTSKY[1] OBSERVED that writing is elaborating the web of meaning. As a writer calls forth thoughts and attempts to shape them into a written text, complex and recursive patterns are elicited. The writer moves back and forth between thinking and writing, writing and thinking, creating a web-like pattern that may reshape initial ideas into a new meaning that surprises even the writer.

This conceptualization of writing, in which the process of writing intertwines with the process of thinking, has important implications for nursing inquiry. Writing can be a powerful mode of inquiry in nursing research, especially qualitative research, where the written word is closely aligned with interpretive meaning. How, then, can writing be used as inquiry in qualitative nursing research? To answer this question, the author

- presents theories and research from the discipline of composition to relate writing to thinking;
- discusses characteristics of writing as a mode of inquiry in qualitative nursing research; and

The author wishes to acknowledge the contributions of Mary Silva, PhD, in the review of this manuscript.

- identifies implications for the use of writing as inquiry in qualitative nursing research.

THEORIES AND RESEARCH ON WRITING TO THINK

One of the most important findings that emerges from a comprehensive review of research on composition is the predominant focus for many years on the written *product,* rather than the writing *process.*[2,3] A new interest in the writing process began in the late 1960s, as researchers in composition began to analyze what writers do when they write, not what they ought to do. Researchers began to formulate theories of writing to explain how writing informs thinking.[4]

This focus on the writing process has led to a new awareness of the relationship between writing and thinking, and how writing may enhance inquiry and the assimilation of information in a variety of disciplines. Theorists such as Vygotsky[1] have suggested that higher cognitive functions, such as analysis and synthesis, seem to develop most fully with the support system of language, particularly written language. Researchers in composition have identified important relationships between the hand, eye, and brain that influence the inquiry process involved in writing.

Hand–Eye–Brain Research

Emig[5] theorized that writing fosters analysis and synthesis, thus helping to connect experiences of our past, present, and future to make meaning. In classic research that integrated research from fields of biology and physiology, Emig formulated a theory that depicts the writing process as a cycle of reinforcement and feedback involving hand, eye, and brain.

The hand is an integral part of the literal act of writing, whether engaged in writing with a pencil, pen, typewriter, or word processor. Hemingway illustrates the importance of this point: After an automobile accident in which he thought he might lose the use of his right arm, he feared that he would have to give up writing.[6(p111)] Emig[6] identified specific ways in which writing with the hand may be related to thinking:

- The process of writing mobilizes the thinker from a passive, inactive state into a physical engagement with the writing.
- The active process of writing reinforces and stimulates analytic processes in the left hemisphere of the brain.
- Writing helps to slow down the thinking process, allowing for the unexpected to emerge.

The eye is viewed as a critical component of the writing process. An example of how central the sense of vision is to the act of writing was expressed by Jean-Paul Sartre. As Sartre suffered progressive loss of vision, resulting in functional blindness, he stated, "Without the ability to read or write, I no longer have even the slightest possibility of being actively engaged as a writer: my occupation as a writer is completely destroyed. . . . In a sense, it robs me of all reason for existing."[7(p4)]

Emig[6] describes the participation of the eye in three phases of the writing process: (1) prewriting, (2) writing, and (3) revision. In prewriting, which takes place as one is thinking, but not yet writing, the eye is viewed as the major sense modality for presenting experience to the brain. In the phase involving the physical act of writing, the eye coordinates with the hand and brain. Finally, in the revision of writing, the eye is used to scan, rescan, and review what has been written.

In considering the relative importance of the eye as a sense modality in the writing process, the question arises: Can other sense modalities provide comparable data to the brain to use in writing? When an interviewer asked Sartre why he could not use a tape recorder as an alternative to reading in his process of writing, he answered, "I think there is an enormous difference between speaking and writing. One rereads what one writes. But one might read it slowly or quickly: in other words, you do not know how long you will have to spend deliberating over a sentence . . . If I listen to a tape recorder, the listening time is determined by the speed at which the tape turns and not by my own needs."[7(p6)]

Thus, the individual rhythm and pace that the eye makes possible in reading and rereading what one has written appears to be an important characteristic of writing to think.

Emig[6] reviews research related to blind sculptors and writers, noting that James Thurber and John Milton did not become blind until mid-life, and that even Helen Keller had sight the first 18 months of her life. Results of an international writing contest for the blind indicated that the writing of those who were congenitally blind had a strikingly barren quality.[6] It appears that the ability to see for at least some point in one's life seems directly related to the ability to transform *perceived* elements into coherent wholes symbolized in writing.

The brain integrates important functions related to perception, motor ability, linguistic competence, and cognition—all components of the writing process. Current research suggests that specialized functions and interdependence of the two brain hemispheres affect the processing of information that is involved with writing.

Rico[8] states that the dual nature of the brain allows us to structure parts of a whole, even if the whole does not yet exist. Once one begins writing, a natural collaboration occurs between the two halves of the brain. Rico describes the writing process as nucleus words leading to clustering, clustering leading to an internal pattern awareness, and pattern awareness resulting in a trial web formed through writing. The trial web embodies a design or perception of pattern and meaning. The cluster itself is in the external world, accessible to the senses and visible on paper, but the process of pattern awareness occurs in the right hemisphere, inaccessible to the logic of the left hemisphere. From trial web to writing is like a camera zooming in for a close-up. As one writes, the trial web crystalizes into a shape with increasingly sharp detail. Through revision of the writing, the trial vision continues to evolve as a dynamic interplay is created between the two brain hemispheres, between a global and local focus. The local detail sheds new light on the global possibility of the trial vision; the global vision generates new details. It is this recursive process, integrating hand, eye, and brain and moving between trial web, writing, and revision, that helps to elaborate the relationship between language and thought.

Relationship of Language and Thought

From her seminal research that used recorded think-aloud data from eight 12th-grade students, Emig[9] identified specific correlations between writing and thinking and concluded that writing is a complex process—one that is often underconceptualized and oversimplified. In the years following Emig's study, researchers further explored writing as a mode of learning with writers of various ages and backgrounds.[10-12] As a result of this research focusing on the relationship of language and thought, prior assumptions of the writing process have been challenged. Researchers no longer view the writing process as a simple recording of an already formulated thought. Planning what one will write and the writing itself are not necessarily linearly related. Thus, language is not an end in itself, but a tool that the writer uses to come to understanding.[13]

Research focusing on the relationship of language to thought has expanded in recent years,[14-16] providing further support for the premise that the process of writing enhances thinking. In fact, Fulwiler states that "no other thinking process helps us develop a line of inquiry or a mode of thought as completely"[17(p5)] as does writing. Our ability to know and understand appears to be dependent, at least in some aspects, on our ability to process internally information received in isolated parts from external sources and to give this information coherent, verbal shape. We come to know and understand information by processing, and one way of processing is to write to ourselves and others.

WRITING AS INQUIRY IN QUALITATIVE NURSING RESEARCH

An understanding of research and theories from composition leads to a new awareness of how writing may enhance inquiry in qualitative nursing research. Qualitative research methods are receiving increased attention as valuable modes of inquiry for nursing studies. In qualitative studies, researchers "emphasize the dynamic, holistic, and individual aspects of the human experience and attempt to capture those aspects in their entirety, within the context of those who are experiencing them."[18(p25)] Thus, an important characteristic of this qualitative research process is the ability to capture sometimes vague, shadowy, disconnected perceptions of human experience and transform them into coherent wholes symbolized in writing. In the process of this activity, the researcher/writer may find that "writing, like life itself, is a voyage of discovery."

Little attention has been devoted, however, to the influence of the writing process on inquiry in qualitative research. After completion of a nursing research study, results are usually "written up" into a "research report." In this approach, writing is conceived of as a reporting process; the activity of doing the research is separated from the activity of publicly reporting the research. This conceptualization ignores a valuable method of inquiry: the use of the writing process itself as a method of inquiry to inform nursing research.

To illustrate how writing can be used as a method of inquiry in qualitative nursing research, the following characteristics of writing as a mode of inquiry will be discussed:

- writing as method,
- writing as narrative, and
- writing as language.

Writing As Method in Qualitative Nursing Research

Barthes[19] raises the question of the relationship between research and writing. Barthes argues that researchers often become so preoccupied with issues of "method" that they discount the important role that writing plays in research. As a result, the processes of research and writing remain, for the most part, methodologically separated.

One reason for this separation may be that researchers and writers evolve their practices from different epistemological approaches: science in contrast with art. The term *researcher* calls forth an image of a person concerned with method, whereas the term *author* is seen as a lover of text.

Van Manen[20] notes that in the human sciences, writing is closely fused with reflection and with the activity of research itself. In discussing writing as method, Van Manen notes that writing fixes thought on paper, externalizing what until that point may have been internal. Writing serves to distance us from the closeness of a lived involvement with an experience. As we stare at what we have written, our objectified thinking stares back at us, prompting a recursive pattern of reflection that is integral to the research process.

In qualitative research, this interrelationship between writing and reflection is powerful. For scholars such as Husserl, Heidegger, Sartre, and Merleau-Ponty, the activities of researching and reflecting, and reading and writing, were indistinguishable.[20] Sartre, a phenomenologist whose writing was intricately involved with his research, found that advancing age and decreasing vision made writing, as well as research, very difficult. At age 70, Sartre wrote, "The only point to my life was writing. I would write out what I had been thinking about beforehand, but the essential moment was that of the writing itself. I still think, but because writing has become impossible for me, the real activity of thought has in some way been suppressed."[7(p5)]

Phenomenological nursing research is an example of one type of qualitative research in which the process of writing serves an integral role. Phenomenology has been called a method without techniques. But for a phenomenological researcher, writing *is* inquiry. The methodology of hermeneutic phenomenology, specifically, is more a carefully cultivated thoughtfulness than a technique. Researchers need to be able to listen to the way the things of the world speak to them. This methodology requires a sensitivity to subtle undertones of language, to the way language speaks when it allows things themselves to speak. Creating a phe-nomenological text is the object of the research process.[20]

Skillful writing and rewriting can be used to create depth in a phenomenological text. The achievement of this depth involves the construction, through writing, of successive, multiple layers of meaning, thus shining light on certain truths while retaining an essential sense of ambiguity.[7,21] The process of writing and rewriting in this sense is reminiscent of the aesthetic activity of creating an art object. In the creation of the text, researchers are, at different stages of the writing process, sepa-rated from what they know and distanced from lived experiences. At the same time, however, the process of creating the layered text allows researchers to reflect on daily experience and connects them more closely with what they do know.

Research related to the reasoning process suggests that one reasons by challeng-ing and altering premises while thinking through a problem.[22] This reasoning process is an integral part of qualitative research, as one abandons assumptions in the process of inquiry and identifies new questions. Reasoning and writing are directly related in the inquiry process; together they reach beyond anything al-ready known—to discovery. In using writing to capture the meaning of a lived experience, the text assumes a life of its own, giving shape, appearance, and body to shadowy thoughts.

Writing As Narrative in Qualitative Nursing Research

Bateson said, "Storytelling is fundamental to the human search for mean-ing."[23(p34)] The story connects persuasively with human experience, and the story form has become a popular method for presenting aspects of qualitative research. The word *narrative* is derived from the Latin *gnoscere* meaning *to know.*[20] Schol-ars from a variety of academic disciplines increasingly are viewing the narrative as an important, but too often undervalued mode of thought.[24]

This appreciation for the value of narrative as inquiry has also received increas-ing attention in nursing research.[25-29] Storytelling has always been a colorful back-drop in nursing, as nurses regaled each other with humorous or poignant narratives of their nursing experiences. Only recently, however, have these stories been brought to the forefront of nursing inquiry to explore how they may inform the development of competency, expertise, and understanding in nursing practice.

Narratives in nursing research

The term *story* is often associated with literature, not science. Consequently, as a nurse moves through the educational process that molds a nurse researcher, the richly textured stories that form such a colorful part of an early nursing career may be reduced to dryly condensed, structured "scientific" presentations. It appears that the further the nurse moves up the educational ladder, the less time is provided for relaxed, storytelling reflection.

Perhaps, at times, a focus on theories has diverted nurse researchers from an appreciation for the value of the narrative in the inquiry process. Intent on identifying theoretical frameworks for nursing research, it is easy to miss the questions that lie embedded in the "untheoretical" stories of human experience. Coles[30] notes that the word *theory* is derived from the Greek *theamai,* meaning *I behold.* In this sense, theory is an unfolding of a vison in one's mind, similar to what is seen in the theater. The unfolding narrative of a lived life, although not a direct confirmation of a particular theory, does enlarge and clarify the researcher's gaze.

In reflecting on the role of the narrative in qualitative nursing research, it appears appropriate to consider how the type of narrative may relate to inquiry. Van Manen,[21] in discussing the narrative in research, distinguishes between the *story* and *anecdote.* He views the anecdote as an especially significant type of narrative in that formulating anecdotes may go beyond everyday storytelling.

Anecdotal narrative serves as an important mode of qualitative inquiry. We learn from anecdotes. This special kind of mini-story is often derived from an oral tradition. For many years, biographers and historians have realized that anecdotes lend a unique, authentic characterization to a specific person or time. As a research method, however, the use of anecdotes sometimes has been viewed by researchers as "unscientific." It is, of course, inappropriate to generalize on the basis of mere anecdotal evidence, but empirical generalization is not the aim in qualitative research. The anecdote is valuable for other than factual–empirical reasons. Anecdotes tell something particular while addressing the general or the universal.[21] The ability to begin to look outward can come from looking at one's own tradition.[23]

Benner[31] has noted the lack of systematic observation of knowledge gleaned from nurse clinicians' practice, and the need to study the traditions that have informed the development of nursing practice. Benner[32] describes "knowing *that*" and "knowing *how*" as two different kinds of knowledge. One acquires many skills, such as riding a bicycle, without the "knowing that" based on accepted theories. In her research, Benner asked nurse clinicians to present clinical situations that stood out in their minds. The nurses' exemplars that formed the narratives in her qualitative study shed light on the "growing edges of clinical knowledge."[32(pxxi)] Although Benner used oral interviews to call forth narratives about nursing practice, other researchers have noted that written narratives are also an effective mode of inquiry.[30,33]

The written narrative

It is important to consider, then, how the writing process relates to the use of narrative as a mode of inquiry. One consideration is how the inquiry process is affected when research subjects/participants/informants write out the narratives themselves rather than tell their stories orally. A second consideration is how the researcher's written text of the narrative that has unfolded in listening affects the interpretive process. Few researchers have focused on these questions, but an understanding of the nature of the writing process suggests the importance of the written narrative as a mode of inquiry in qualitative nursing research.

Writing can empower the nurse researcher with embodied knowledge to help understand the experiences of everyday life that influence nursing practice. In order to bring forth the fullness and ambiguity of a lived experience that is expressed in a narrative, a complex process of writing, thinking, and rewriting is needed.

Composition researchers[6,12] refer to a "governing gaze" that often guides, and limits, perceptions. We see what we expect to see. Nurse researchers are trained to look for and formulate research "problems," and often come with preconceived notions of what matters, what does not matter, what should be stressed, and what should be overlooked in identifying these problems. The written narrative can help to alter the nurse researcher's gaze, to encourage the researcher to put aside tentatively the perceived need to formulate "problems." The writer/researcher is encouraged to look beyond the obvious, to search out aspects of "dailiness" that are important elements of the human experience.

In this sense, writing decenters the human ego. The writing process helps to decontextualize thought from practice and helps nurse researchers to see what they know and what they do not know. By using writing to slow thinking, the researcher holds off the rush to interpret the obvious. Writing helps to distance us from what we know yet makes us shape what we do know. In the process, we come face to face with questions intimately related to the human experience.

For nurse researchers, then, the written narrative is a valuable mode of inquiry. The task of composing the narrative text can be, in itself, a voyage of discovery.

Writing the Language of Qualitative Nursing Research

When the writing process is used as a mode of inquiry, it is important to consider how the use of specific language forms may enhance the inquiry process in relation to textual representation of qualitative nursing research. Three aspects of language will be considered here: (1) the use of metaphor, (2) the influence of silence, and (3) the value of poetic expression.

The metaphor offers a unique form of language for creating meaning in the qualitative research text.[6,20] The metaphor is not merely a device used for decoration or embellishment but is a rhetorical form that can help to convey meaning of a shadowy idea that is difficult to describe. In a qualitative research text, the writer attempts to use language that is common and connecting, and yet evokes thought. In this sense, the metaphor is a *medium* for perception and understanding—a unique lens that helps us to see past the shadows of an idea. Sontag notes that metaphor is the "spawning ground of most kinds of understanding, including scientific understanding, and expressiveness."[34(p5)] Thus, metaphors cannot be translated or paraphrased into perfectly equivalent literary terms. Instead, the metaphor represents a unique form of language that possesses special powers as a mode of written expression.[6] Van Manen said, "By way of metaphor, language can take us beyond the content of the metaphor toward the original region where language speaks through silence."[20(p49)]

Silence is an integral part of the composition of a qualitative research text. When the researcher sits down to write, there is a fundamental aloneness in the attempt to create meaning on the blank page.[13] One struggles to discover what one knows, so that one can know what to say. At the beginning, there is a blank page; at the end, there is writing that has detached itself from the writer and found its own meaning. Between these two points, until meaning emerges, there is silence.

Van Manen[20] notes that silence is not merely the absence of speech or language but is the truth that lies just beyond the words, on the other side of language. Van Manen describes three types of silence that operate in the composing of qualitative research texts: (1) literal silence, (2) epistemological silence, and (3) ontological silence. Literal silence is the absence of speaking directly through the writing. The writer attempts, instead of "overwriting," to create a unique quality in the writing that leaves certain meanings unsaid. In this sense, the silence of spaces may be as important as the words. Epistemological silence is encountering the "unspeakable." We sense that we know more than we can tell, and we struggle to articulate this knowing. Finally, there is ontological silence. Ontological silence represents "the silence of Being or Life itself,"[20(p114)] when the writer realizes that even at the moment of greatest insight, one returns to a "dumb"-founding, fulfilling silence. Thus, the use of silence in textual representation of the research creates a meaning that transcends words.

Phenomenological research, specifically, is sometimes referred to as a "poetizing" activity.[20(p13)] In poetic writing, language functions as art.[17] Just as painters do not merely paint colors they have seen but use color on the canvas to see, so qualitative researchers do not merely write down words to photograph what is in their heads but use words to move toward understanding. The phenomenological researcher attempts to create a text that speaks evocatively of the essence of a lived experience; in some instances, this meaning may best be conveyed through poetry. Heidegger viewed the highest level of thinking to be poetry.[35] In the process of inquiry in qualitative research, poetry may, at times, speak most authentically.

Little focus has been given in nursing literature to consideration of how different language forms contribute to the process of inquiry in qualitative nursing research. Benner[26] believes that in nurses' efforts to "legitimize" themselves, they may lose their voice of humanism; nurses too often limit writing to a rational, technical style, in which it is impossible to reflect the richness of nursing practice.

As qualitative research assumes an increasingly important focus in nursing studies, we must consider the importance of language forms such as metaphor, silence, and poetry in textual representation of research. With awareness of the influence of these language forms, as well as others, on the process of inquiry, researchers need a forum for presenting their research in nontraditional forms. For example, the format of doctoral dissertations should not constrain qualitative researchers by prescribing a technical, "scientific" rendering of the research. For the qualitative researcher, the review of literature is a dialogue, more than a reporting; references may be used not so much for justification or authenticity, but for pointing in a certain direction and for connecting. Professional research journals also must provide space for the poetic and metaphoric language that often comprises the richly layered texts of qualitative research.

Different language forms contain their own kinds of meaning; as writers create form from chaos, the forms themselves evoke understanding. Nurse researchers need to build an interpretive language of nursing practice through the textual representation of qualitative research, so that the writing gives an authentic voice to interpretation.

IMPLICATIONS FOR THE USE OF WRITING AS INQUIRY IN QUALITATIVE NURSING RESEARCH

New conceptualizations of the writing process suggest that writing functions as a unique mode of inquiry in qualitative nursing research. Based on theories and research that relate the writing process to inquiry, the following strategies for using writing to elaborate meaning are suggested:

1. Incorporate recursive aspects of the writing process, characterized by prewriting, writing, and revision, into the nursing research process as a means to foster inquiry.
2. Use the reflective nature of the writing process, such as writing one's "wonderings" in a research journal, to help make connections between shadowy ideas that can inform ways of knowing in nursing.
3. Explore interdisciplinary approaches to the use of writing as method in qualitative nursing research.
4. Integrate the writing process, such as use of stories and anecdotes, into conceptualizations of the nursing curriculum revolution identified by the National League for Nursing.[36]
5. Enhance textual representation of meaning in qualitative nursing research through awareness of the unique value of different language forms, such as metaphor, silence, and poetry.

•   •   •

The writing of qualitative research is giving voice to interpretation. In the process, the writer often undertakes a voyage of discovery. Bateson[23] tells a story of a Chinese artist painting a landscape. As the artist is almost finished with the painting, a drop of ink falls on the white background. The observers gasp, fearing the scroll is ruined. Without hesitating, the artist takes a fine brush and transforms the spot of fallen ink into a fly hovering in the foreground of the landscape. With a deft stroke, an ability to see beyond the obvious, and an innate understanding of the interpretive process, the artist created a new meaning for the whole.

This story illustrates how the creative process of hand, eye, and brain combine to create meaning. According to Murray, "For most writers the act of putting words on paper is not the recording of discovery, but the very act of exploration itself."[13(p3)] As we search for knowledge embedded in nursing practice, we can reach beyond our governing gaze to formulate research texts that convey new understandings of human experience. The writing process itself helps us to make meaning in these texts. As we write, we think, creating a web of meaning that leads to discovery.

REFERENCES

1. Vygotsky LS. *Thought and Language*. Cambridge, Mass: MIT Press; 1962.
2. Humes A. Research on the composing process. *Rev Educ Res.* 1983;53(2):201–216.
3. Schumacher GM. Reflections on the origins of writing: new perspectives on writing research. *Written Communication.* 1986;3:47–63.
4. Holdskom D, Reed LJ, Porter EJ, Rubin DL. *Research Within Reach: Oral and Written Communication. A Research-guided Response to the Concerns of Educators.* St. Louis, Mo: Mid-continent Regional Educational Laboratory; 1984.
5. Emig JA. Writing as a mode of learning. *College Composition and Communication.* 1977;28:122–133.
6. Emig JA. *The Web of Meaning.* Upper Montclair, NJ: Boynton/Cook; 1983.
7. Sartre JP. *Life/Situations. Essays Written and Spoken.* New York, NY: Pantheon Books; 1977.
8. Rico GL. *Writing the Natural Way.* Los Angeles, Calif: Tarcher; 1983.
9. Emig JA. *The Composing Processes of Twelfth Graders.* Urbana, Ill: National Council of Teachers of English; 1971.
10. Perl A. The composing processes of unskilled college writers. *Research in the Teaching of English.* 1979;13:317–336.
11. Pianko S. A description of the composing processes of college freshman writers. *Research in the Teaching of English.* 1979;13:5–22.
12. Sommers N. Revision strategies of student writers and experienced adult writers. *College Composition and Communication.* 1980;31:378–388.
13. Murray DM. *Learning by Teaching: Selected Articles on Writing and Teaching.* Montclair, NJ: Boynton/Cook; 1982.
14. Bennett WJ. *What Works: Research about Teaching and Learning.* Washington, DC: US Department of Education; 1986.
15. Allen DG, Bowers B, Diekelmann N. Writing to learn: a reconceptualization of thinking and writing in the nursing curriculum. *J Nurs Educ.* 1989;28(1):6–11.
16. Thaiss C. *Write to the Limit.* Fort Worth, Tex: Holt, Rinehart & Winston; 1991.
17. Fulwiler T. *Teaching with Writing.* Upper Montclair, NJ: Boynton/Cook; 1987.
18. Polit DF, Hungler BP. *Nursing Research: Principles and Methods.* 4th ed. Philadelphia, Pa: Lippincott; 1991.
19. Barthes R. *The Rustle of Language.* New York, NY: Hill and Wang; 1986.
20. Van Manen M. *Researching Lived Experience: Human Science for an Action Sensitive Pedagogy.* London, Ontario, Canada: University of Western Ontario; 1990.
21. Van Manen M. By the light of anecdote. *Phenomenology + Pedagogy.* 1989;7:232–253.
22. Howard VA, Barton, JH. *Thinking on Paper.* New York, NY: William Morrow; 1986.
23. Bateson MC. *Composing a Life.* New York, NY: Plume; 1990.
24. DiPardo A. *Narrative Knowers, Expository Knowledge: Discourse as a Dialectic.* Berkeley, Calif: Center for the Study of Writing; 1989.
25. Benner P. The role of experience, narrative, and community in skilled ethical comportment. *ANS.* 1991;14(2):1–21.

26. Benner P. Writers tell nursing's stories. *Am Nurse.* January 1991:27, 31–32.
27. Heinrich KT. Create a tradition. Teach nurses to share stories. *J Nurs Educ.* 1992;31(3):141–143.
28. Parker RS. Nurses stories: the search for a relational ethic of care. *ANS.* 1990;13(1):31–40.
29. Sandelowski M. Telling stories: narrative approaches in qualitative research. *Image.* 1991;23(3):161–166.
30. Coles R. *The Call of Stories.* Boston, Mass: Houghton Mifflin; 1989.
31. Benner P. Uncovering the knowledge embedded in clinical practice. *Image.* 1983;15(2):36–41.
32. Benner P. *From Novice to Expert. Excellence and Power in Clinical Nursing Practice.* Menlo Park, Calif: Addison-Wesley; 1984.
33. Rico G. *Pain and Possibility: Writing Your Way Through Personal Crisis.* New York, NY: Tarcher/Perigee; 1991.
34. Sontag S. *AIDS and Its Metaphors.* New York, NY: Farrar, Straus and Giroux; 1988.
35. Presented at the Nursing Institute for Heideggerian Hermeneutical Studies, University of Wisconsin/Madison School of Nursing, June 1–12, 1992.
36. *Curriculum Revolution: Redefining the Student–Teacher Relationship.* New York, NY: National League for Nursing; 1990.

Representations of Action: Reorienting Field Studies in Nursing Practice

Mary Ellen Purkis, RN, PhD
Assistant Professor
School of Nursing
University of Victoria
Victoria, British Columbia
Canada

The article gives critical attention to current utilization and representation of field studies in the nursing literature. The claim that field studies are undertaken in order to generate knowledge for practice is challenged through a critical examination of recently reported field studies. A concept of action is advanced that reorients the concept as one relevant to nursing practice as well as the conduct of research. The relationship between field studies, the performance of nursing as action, and the accomplishment of nursing and research as practice are addressed. It is argued that the position taken by the researcher in relation to the field plays a crucial part in producing valid and relevant findings in practice-based research.

PORTER[1] HAS RECENTLY leveled some criticism against writers of nursing research who do not acknowledge their presence in the documented findings. Porter's criticism suggests that research is being conducted at some distance from the researcher: either physical distance or abstract distance. While one might raise the question of intent here—that is, whether authors are actively attempting to be objective or whether their presence is merely obfuscated by falling back on a naive realism—the crucial point for Porter is that "truths" generated from research in which the researcher's presence is not acknowledged are presented in the literature as though they were "pure" or uncontaminated by such presence. While this criticism holds for all forms of research, the position I wish to advance here is that it is within that portion of the literature that aims at describing the field of nursing, whether in descriptive or explanatory ways, that the author's presence is so crucial to the representation made of practice. I will argue that the researcher's presence is not only inescapable in field studies but that the researcher's presence is what underpins the authority of field studies in practice-based disciplines such as nursing.

The paper arises from a particular framework for addressing social action. Taking written, documented evidence of studies claiming to represent nursing as the material for the study, the social action framework must be capable of explicating the effects of language on representations of "reality." For instance, if a study seeks to present a version of nursing as a combination of actions, for the consumption and reflection of individuals with an interest in understanding nursing as an organized activity, not only does the content of the study involve a sense of action but so too does the interpretive act of consuming and reflecting on the study. The paper is framed by a perspective on social action that takes the effects of language as constitutive of action. This constitutive effect of language must be understood as one involving a power relation. An exploration of field studies, then, means remaining alert to the notion of power.

Power is not, however, understood to reside in the person of the researcher, nor the person of the nurse, nor the person of the client. Within the context of this article, power is understood as displaced from its common-sense position, which takes it as largely "possessed" by specified individuals. Power is understood as an *effect* that is exercised through language. And so, again, we return to the significance of an attention to language, whether that of the researcher in his or her descriptions or explanations of nursing actions or in the representation of action that such descriptions or explanations form.

This understanding of power and its effects on representations of action reflects a significant departure from that commonly found in nursing research. I want to reiterate that I take action as a common feature of both nursing and research; that is, they are both practice disciplines. Within this article, action represents the object of concern. Here, action is understood first as the organized conduct of social actors recognized in research studies as "nurses" and second as the organized conduct of social actors who may or may not acknowledge their presence as "researchers" but who, nonetheless, authorize representations of nursing. It is in this sense that I will examine studies of nursing in order to reorient action (as "nursing" and as "research") in relation to the act of representing forms of reality.

CONCEPTUALIZING ACTION

Conceptualizations of action represent a central challenge for nursing research. The way in which action is conceptualized influences not only the type of research engaged in but also the very approach to the field of study. For example, Melia[2] stated over a decade ago that "there is an implicit, if not explicit, pressure put upon researchers in nursing to provide answers which can form the basis of action."[2(p328)] Here, Melia suggests that actions engaged in by nurses are informed by knowledge produced by researchers. As a researcher, Melia's statement reflects a response from a "position":[3-4] a position of responsibility to produce answers for practice questions. Picking up the notion of power as an effect of language, the "pressure" referred to here by Melia represents an *effect* of trends influencing the production of nursing research in 1982, trends that remain potent today. Rather than pressure being exerted on researchers by practitioners as Melia's statement suggests, I would argue that researchers have incorporated the concept of pressure into their discourse to account for their own position within the discipline. Pressure to provide answers is understood within the context of this article as a linguistic device widely employed in the literature for legitimating research efforts, that is, in response to an approach to the field of study where research is understood as fulfilling a "need" to inform practice.

While Melia's construction of the relation between practice and research is recognized as widely held, the basis of the construction is now thrown into question. The central concern in this article is answering the question "how can practice be approached and conceptualized so that what actors do, whether as nurses or as researchers, is represented in ways that are valid representations of action?" I will argue that a reorientation of field studies can be accomplished through a critical examination of the relationship between the researcher and the field. Present ethnographic studies— that is, studies of the field of nursing—conducted under the auspices of "informing nursing practice" will be examined in an effort to determine where the researcher locates himself or herself with regard to the site of practice. It will be argued that the position taken by the researcher in relation to the field of practice plays a crucial part in the production of valid and relevant findings in practice research.

ETHNOGRAPHIC STUDIES OF NURSING PRACTICE

Nursing research has reached the point where it is ceasing to be apologetic for using qualitative methods to answer its questions. The move to qualitative studies has a long but perhaps not entirely impressive history in nursing research. A reading of recent compendia of qualitative studies[5-7] immediately suggests two major points that continue to plague the interpretive tradition within nursing studies. First is the purpose for which qualitative research is undertaken. Tied up with the problematics of purpose but treated separately in the literature is how the researcher can relate to the field of study.[8,9] While receiving increasing publicity but little critical debate, these problems can be addressed together by asking the following question: Upon what terms will the researcher relate himself or herself to the field? This question will be explored in the following sections.

The Problem of Purpose

Field studies of nursing practice have tended, for the most part, to be descriptive in nature. The following "rationalization" for conducting field studies represents a common theme in the literature. Field studies in nursing practice are frequently legitimated by having, as their purpose, the "discovery of new information about clients in various situations: The more nurses know about their clients and families and how they experience situations, the better able they will be to care for them."[10(p277)] The image here is one of unknown waters, uncharted territory. The practice of nursing is not questioned. Rather, nursing is characterized as actions aimed at discrete "problems," few of which have yet been explored by researchers. Research is undertaken in order to make these discrete problems available as clear targets on which practicing nurses can focus.

The problems associated with such an approach to the field can best be illustrated with reference to a particular study. Drawing on the example of a collaborative project conducted under the auspices of a "field study," Boyle describes the steps involved in setting up the study.[10] As a collaborative project, the study involved seeking input from a variety of sources, including practitioners, educators, and students. The aim of this (primarily) educational experience focused on "solving clinical problems encountered in community health nursing practice."[10(p278)] In line with the educational model informing the study, the practitioners formulated the problem, the educators conceptualized it as a research project, and the students carried out the field work. The research process is subordinated to the educational process, firmly announcing the field of interest as the educational institution, not, as Boyle implies, the practice setting.

A group of community health nurses were asked "what kind of clients were 'difficult' "[10(p278)] in their practice setting. The population identified as problematic was pregnant teenagers. Teenage pregnancy was formulated by the community health nurses as a problem by drawing on an economic discourse of costs.[10] The nurses claimed that costs to the teenager's family and society at large legitimated teenage pregnancy as a problem because of the propensity of this group to have high-risk pregnancies.

Unfortunately, having identified this problem within a field of practice, the researchers then turned their gaze toward the life-world of "key informants,"[10] that is, teenagers who were or had been pregnant. The researchers only returned to the site of the problem, the nurses working at the community health clinic, at a later date. Returning to the community health clinic, the researchers were then armed with knowledge, packaged as results of their field study into teenage pregnancy. The researchers had fulfilled the remit of ethnography as characterized by Boyle, which was to ascertain "new information about clients in various situations."[10(p277)]

I would argue that this example of a field study represents a failure to understand the nature of the ethnographic field. The field is, after all, the situated context within which pregnant teenagers come to be constituted as "problematic" subjects for nursing care. Having started out on the right foot, Boyle and her associates quickly make a wrong turn as soon as they leave the field behind in search of "knowledge for better practice," particularly as this "knowledge" is treated by the researchers as though it arises in a location entirely apart from practice. It is important to reiterate here that the constitution of "problems" (such as teenage pregnancy) is understood in this article as an effect of power exercised through language. Pregnant teenagers are constituted as a problem by the nurses in the clinic. Rather than seeking innocuous information about this population, the researchers, I would argue, might have been further ahead to have remained in the field and made an attempt to understand how pregnant teenagers are problems for community health nurses.

Boyle's account of the purpose of the field study was framed with a reference to the "experience"[10] of clients and families. Boyle suggests that the object of field research should be to define how people "experience situations"[10(p277)] in order that nurses can improve the care of these people. As a second, widely observed trend that authors claim to address in field studies, experience is, I would argue, more in line with studies of a phenomenological concern. Studies that point to an interest in the experiences of women undergoing hysterectomy,[11] the experience of husbands whose wives are receiving chemotherapy,[12] the child's view of care during chemotherapy,[13] relying exclusively on interview material, clearly point to the individual as a site of interest for the researcher. Locating the research problem within the subjective experience of respondents is accompanied by substantial problems of accessing understanding via accounts given to the researcher.[3,14] Such problems are endemic to the phenomenological project and are not lessened by researchers who examine these accounts without the advantage of a critical position. All too frequently, nurse researchers take an unnecessarily naive position with regard to accounts from research participants. Relying solely on reasons given by research respondents for understandings regarding the nature of reality, nurse researchers must overcome significant difficulties in substantiating these "findings" empirically. This position has been argued in some recent literature that examines practice critically.[1,15–16]

The position adopted in this article is that the problem of empirical substantiation arises through the production of accounts by researchers seeking to attribute knowledge, understanding, and action in the absence of empirical cross-checks. If subjectively generated accounts are treated as knowledgeable action in their own right, a position adopted by theorists such as Giddens[3,14] and Garfinkel,[17] and if actors' accounts represent only one aspect of a triangulated account of action, then such accounts are no longer problematic in the same way they are in phenomenological studies. Accounts of action provided by individuals participating in practice relationships can be triangulated by observational accounts generated by the researcher. Field studies are strengthened in this way because the possibility exists to apply critical methods to the research materials. The importance of considering the relationship between the researcher and the field is raised again to the extent that the researcher's presence in this relation is entirely interlaced in the formulation of interpretations and representations made about the field.

The Effort to Validate Knowledge Outside the Practice Relationship

In advocating a move away from the site of the practice relationship where difficulties are constituted, Boyle demonstrates an unacknowledged view of nursing practice as an objective reality. For Boyle, nursing lacks only a sufficiently detailed knowledge base on which practice can be objectively applied with predictable results. Such a perspective seeks to legitimate knowledge about nursing practice outside of the context within which it is constituted as a reality.

The failure to acknowledge the social construction of institutionalized actions such as nursing goes some way toward explaining the exhaustive lengths entered into by researchers to address the concept of validity in qualitative research. The overriding concern with identifying the many and varied ways in which qualitative research results are equally as valid as those achieved through quantitative means reflects the remnants of an apologia for qualitative designs. More so, however, it reflects the nascent state of debate regarding the relationship between the researcher and the field.

As demonstrated above, the focus of much so-called ethnographic research has been on the development of knowledge for practice. Thus, there has been a concern with obtaining representative samples[18,19] and with the influence of the researcher on the population under study.[8–9,20]

A concern with specifying "units of analysis" for ethnographic research have led Aamodt to state that these are the linguistic expressions that have " 'made it' in the written and oral communication systems of nursing."[13(p48)] However, this is to suggest that viability of language expressions takes precedence over their situated meaning, again attending to the emphasis on practice as "objective reality."

Researchers are advised to "get close"[10(p276)] to the identified study population. Getting close involves studying the population and analyzing results within the natural setting.[10] When treated in this way, the field takes on near-magical properties where the field, and not the researcher, is taken as inducing more valid and reliable results. The researcher is treated here as additional; consideration is given only to maximizing his or her relationship with the field.

Methods advocated to maximize this relationship are addressed by Brink.[20] She suggests that security of interpretation can be maximized by seeking the expert assistance of a "judge panel"[20(p171)] when making decisions about key informants. Interpretation is also said to be secured with the longitudinal nature of ethnographic studies.[20] This is to suggest that if the advice of the experts is followed, and a specified period of time is spent in the field, valid results will ensue. The concern underpinning such a view is, however, with securing valid interpretations by drawing on supportive structures located *external* to the field. As such, it fails to come to grips with the central issue of interpretation.

Brink's advice for increasing validity can be understood as an attempt to remedy that which is central and, I would argue, the only legitimate basis for validation within the ethnographic project: the reflexive relationship between the researcher and the field. Brink exemplifies and reproduces the very suspicions that have marginalized interpretive studies in nursing to date. How can the question "how much is enough?" be answered outside of the context of a particular field study? Will 2 interviews be enough, or are 50 required? Will 2 years of observation necessarily lead to greater security on which interpretations are made than 6 months of observation? Remedial answers to such questions introduce more problems rather than allay concerns of those who are already suspicious of interpretive studies.

SEEKING RESOLUTION TO ISSUES OF VALIDITY WITHIN THE FIELD

Setting aside such remedial solutions as simplistic, the discussion turns now toward exploring the possibilities for validating interpretations inherent in research materials derived from a particular field of study. Issues of validity will be addressed from *within* the interpretive paradigm rather than offering remedies arising from and attending to discourses of other, incommensurable paradigms. The question raised here is simply, what can be said about nursing that situates it as a discrete activity for study?

Talk as an Outcome of Nursing Practice

This question can be approached from within the parameters of the present state of research examining nursing practice. What has been missed in current theorizing about nursing practice is an adequate account of how nursing is constructed as a social reality. Therefore, the question regarding what can be said about nursing practice must be framed in such a way that it takes account of how members, engaged in interaction, construct nursing through social mechanisms.

Power as exercise through language comes forward again here. Nursing does not just happen. Nursing is recognizable patterns of action that are made to happen by members engaged in encounters with others through the strategic deployment of discursive strategies. Nursing actions can be located within specifiable, contextual boundaries, as it is these very boundaries, as structures in Giddens'[3] sense, that are drawn on to constitute nursing. These structures are recursively reproduced through the ongoing and daily actions contributing to the doing of nursing.

Language is clearly central to such an understanding of the constitution of nursing practice. Benner's[21] work signals a new and promising shift in nursing research to investigate this aspect of practice. Wolf[22-23] has examined ritualistic aspects of language in nursing practice such as those used by nurses while caring for the deceased and in making change-of-shift reports. Seeking merely to make these rituals visible, however, Wolf fails to push her interpretations far enough to examine how these rituals constitute action and affect the conduct of nurses and patients in their respective positions within institutions of care.

Two recent studies have sought to extend present understandings of the relation between language and practice. Tilley[24] and May[25-27] have drawn on accounts of practice in order to explore this relation between language and understanding of practice.

Taking psychiatric admission wards as the field, Tilley's concern was to understand the process of reality negotiation operating between nurses and patients. All patients included in the study had been diagnosed as neurotic and were admitted to the particular wards for treatment within this context. Tilley's study exemplifies a much more critical stance toward accounts generated from nurses and patients than that typically demonstrated in descriptive accounts of nursing work. Taking a critical position toward the field, Tilley identifies "topics and resources for the work of understanding each other."[24(p315)] Here, practice is understood as being accomplished through the use of everyday resources but constructed in particular ways that constitute action recognizable as "nursing" and "patient" actions.

Tilley's interpretations of the work of psychiatric nurses and patients to negotiate "reality" is based on what he describes as "second order accounts,"[24(p316)] interpretations of events not directly witnessed by the researcher. In this way, Tilley incorporates distance into the analytic project. The ensuing relationship between researcher and the field has important implications for the position developed in this paper. While Tilley frequently acknowledges the influence of power in the constitution of reality as part of the research framework, he demonstrates a reluctance to suggest in what ways power affects the constitution of knowledge in practice. The nurse and patient individually were asked to account for the encounter which, as an experience, had been incorporated into the "horizon of under-standings"[28(p302)] within which the account then arises. Tilley's decision not to directly record interactions necessarily impinges on his ability to comment on the experiences, which are then accounted for in his interviews with the respondents of the study.

Tilley is concerned to demonstrate that methods used to gather research materials could themselves be put to beneficial use to improve practice. He suggests that giving nurses the opportunity to "produce accounts in which they took their own work as a topic for further explanation"[24(p324)] may contribute in a significant way to the development of understanding about nursing practice. Here, a conceptual link can be demonstrated between Tilley's work and that of Benner.[21] Both suggest that in the process of providing accounts of encounters with patients, the experience of that encounter can be shared to illuminate how practice is accomplished. The implication here is that not only the nurse who gives the account herself understands practice more fully but that others who hear the account are taken to understand practice more fully because the account has been made available: it has been "present-ed."

Noting an "unwillingness to bring 'self' more into practice"[24(p325)] on the part of nurses whose accounts were sought for the study, Tilley suggests that through the process of "talk," this situation might be rectified. Significantly, this special form of talk is to be "conducted outside the current framework of accountability."[24(p325)] By encouraging talk among nursing staff, Tilley suggests that the knowledge generated in the practice relationship might be clarified and that the power relations operating within the relationship might be recognized. The unspoken implication of this process is that nurses would cease to employ power in their relations with patients. Such a position has been widely criticized by Foucault[29] and Lyotard,[4] so these assumptions must, therefore, be questioned.

I would question the possibility that the sort of understanding work Tilley refers to could take place "outside the current framework of accountability." Although accounts and forms of accountability might be changed by individual(s) charged with the responsibility of drawing these accounts out from staff, to assume that one could easily step outside present accountability structures is to theorize inadequately the process of accountability and the interpenetration of accountability by structures of domination, legitimation, and signification.[3,30] Tilley's solution suggests that the slate could be wiped clean. This would leave nurses with no space within which to formulate accounts of practice. They would be unable to make their accounts of practice count. The point raised here is that accountability structures are deeply embedded in members' methods for "going on" in day-to-day encounters.[3] I would argue that it is neither desirable nor possible to suggest that such structures be set aside. It is from the embeddedness of accountability structures that members achieve the space for authorizing accounts, and so, they represent ways of validating representations made of nursing action.

This is not to suggest that analyzing interview transcripts, in the absence of observational cross-checks of the account given by the nurse, cannot still provide illuminating evidence of intricate processes underpinning members' understanding of practice. Tilley's study offers ample evidence of this sort, as does May's[25–27] study where he investigated ways in which nursing practices act to constitute patients as subjects of care. He undertook a critical, textual analysis demonstrating the ways in which patients are constructed as subjects of nursing care in nurses' accounts of practice.

Drawing on Foucault's historical study of the "clinical gaze,"[31] May puts forward the "therapeutic gaze,"[26(p591)] as an extension of the clinical gaze "formulated to reassemble or reconstitute the patient as a human subject."[26(p591)] May theorizes the nurse–client relationship as encounters made problematic through application of the therapeutic gaze. It might be useful here to recall the point made above regarding Boyle's study of community health nurses. In line with May's point, I argued there that pregnant teenagers have been made problematic through the application of a therapeutic gaze.

I would argue, however, that it may be an effect of taking accounts given by nurses in the absence of observation of their practice, a method that again introduces distance into the relation between researcher and field, that leads May to describe the *effect* of the therapeutic gaze to be one of "fixing" what is known about an individual. Although nurses may account for their care as resulting from their ability to fix problems requiring solutions, missing from such accounts of practice are the observational cross-checks that can extend the analysis into the accomplishment of "fixing" as a nursing action. What I would advance for consideration here is that, in order for the account to count, the person giving the account will privilege certain aspects over others. This is not to suggest that the person giving an account is attempting to deceive. Rather, accounts, as social accomplishments, rely on a certain amount of fixity in order to stand *as accounts*. The point to be made from this is that by understanding accounts in this way—that is, as social accomplishments—the researcher is encouraged to take a critical stance in relation to them.

This is not a minor point but rather underlines the primary concern addressed in this article. Two apparently opposing perspectives on the nature of experience, knowledge and action, are called into question here. To suggest that, in the objective reality of nursing work, the effect of the nurse's therapeutic gaze is fixity, a version of power that is merely constraining is implied. I would accept that knowledge, as it is understood in the day-to-day context of practice, offers members engaged in interaction certain facilities that can be drawn on in order to "fix" meanings. In this sense, background theoretical knowledge deployed by nurses can be viewed as "structures."[3] However, the fixity accounted for by nurses in May's study may only be a residual effect of power. What is still missing from these accounts of practice is how the appearance of such fixity is accomplished.

May's study offers significant and important insights into the discursive abilities of nurses to account for their work. May's critical analysis offers an important, situated reading on how nurses understand their work. However, as both May and Tilley rely on accounts from nurses engaged in constituting practice in the field—either in the absence of observational cross-checks or in an attitude of unwillingness to triangulate observations with accounts—neither researcher can account fully for how these practitioners accomplish their relationship with the field.

The problem of how researchers can relate to the field they are constituting through research is, I would argue, more profitably addressed through an examination of the practice of nursing itself. Reorienting the relationship between the researcher and the field of practice by examining studies of the field of nursing itself, the discussion now turns to investigate studies that have attended in a more direct way to the nurse–patient interaction.

Analyzing Conversations in Nursing Practice

Attending to subtle shifts in conversation, studies conducted by Mortis[32] and Hunt and Montgomery-Robinson[33] demonstrate a promising turn toward the field in order to generate understanding about how practice is accomplished. These researchers have used conversation analysis as a method for analyzing the way in which nursing practice is constituted in language.

Based on the seminal works of Sacks, Schegloff, and Jefferson, conversation analysis has been influential in identifying consistent relationships between particular speech patterns and situated meanings. Additionally, conversation analysis has been demonstrated to have wide applicability within the ethnomethodological tradition.[34-36] Heritage has described the work undertaken by Sacks and his colleagues as "courageous and perceptive."[37(p235)] The important contribution of conversation analysis is, according to Heritage, even more impressive when one considers that the dominant force at the time these researchers began their research project was Chomsky's view that social interaction was a random process and therefore entirely problematic in terms of its possibilities for analyses.

Certain of their belief that human interaction *was* coherent and meaningful in practice, Sacks, Jefferson, and Schegloff's work continued in the face of such opposition. Their view was that the evident coherence and meaningfulness of social interaction could only be explained through the discovery of some form of organization, however hidden it appeared to their contemporaries. As a result of their persistence, Heritage remarks that the analyses of conversations conducted since their early work has produced a "strongly cumulative and interlocking"[37(p234)] body of knowledge.

Arising from this theoretical base, Hunt and Montgomery-Robinson[33] document a study that begins similarly to Boyle's as these authors ask about the problems faced by nurses working in the community. The difference here is that Montgomery-Robinson maintained her gaze on how the problem was constituted and managed *within* the practice setting. She addressed what she took to be a particular problem for community nurses, that is, gaining access to clients in their own homes in the community. In fact, as Hunt and Montgomery-Robinson note, gaining access is not in reality a problem for nurses at all. It is accomplished routinely by health visitors as a part of their daily work. The study demonstrates how the act of accessing clients in their homes is accomplished so evidently unproblematically.

Of particular note is the distinction made by the authors between their study and the results of previous studies concentrating on categorizing communication in nursing practice as a series of behaviors. The advantage Hunt and Montgomery-Robinson claim for conversation analysis is that it "present(s) movement."[33(p152)] Unfortunately, the authors do not speculate on the nature of this movement. These authors have been unable to extend their argument in this direction as they have inadequately conceived of how action can be linked to their understanding of conversation.

Another study using the techniques of conversation analysis was undertaken by Mortis.[32] As a nurse teacher, Mortis was concerned that the rule-based method of teaching students communication skills did not accurately represent the form that communication takes in everyday nursing work. Perceiving that a more "reality-based"[32(p48)] theory was unavailable in the nursing literature, she adopted conversation analysis to investigate some of the underlying characteristics of nursing talk in practice situations. As such, this represents a study that treats the field seriously as a site where nursing practice is constructed.

Mortis' central finding, based on only two recorded interactions between nurses and patients, was that "I talk" by the patient was not "supported" by the nurse.[32(p202)] Mortis claims that the effect of this strategy is that the patient's experience of a problem is disrupted. Eventually, perhaps after several unsuccessful attempts to have the problem acknowledged by the nurse, Mortis claims that "the meaning of events in [the patient's] experienced context is lost."[32(p202)]

Through the mechanism of not supporting "I talk," Mortis detects a discrepancy in power between the participants in the recorded conversations. Mortis describes a number of conversational techniques employed by nurses to transform patients' experiences of hospitalization. Concerned with reflecting her observations of practice against an ideal model for nursing communication, one that advocates attention to the patient's definition of problems, Mortis claims that patient experiences are "reduced to a state of 'no trouble.' "[32(p203)] The transformation of the experience of patienthood, representing the outcome of strategies enacted by nurses, can only be treated by Mortis as a "reduction." Although Mortis' analysis has identified instances of powerful discourse, she offers no further exploration of the conditions that constrain or enable the production of such scenarios.

The significant contribution of a study such as that conducted by Mortis is that it draws attention to the notion of power in the discourse employed by the nurse to accomplish his or her work. The power is neither physical nor obvious; it leaves no visible scars. Instead, Mortis' analysis demonstrates the immense subtlety of power in discourse, the pervasiveness made evident in Foucault's writings on discipline:[38] the "punishment" of nonresponse to a voiced complaint, the "discipline" involved for patients to become complicit with the nurse in the eventual framing of problems as "no trouble."

Identifying Criteria for Good Practice

Mortis' study can be contrasted with one claiming a similar starting point, that is, the nascent state of debate regarding nurse–patient relationships. Morse[18] approaches the "problem" of nurse–patient relationships using what she describes as the "techniques of grounded theory."[18(p456)] Morse assumes at the outset that nurse–patient relationships are unique and are thus in need of explication and definition. As a distinguishing feature of Morse's approach to the field, this assumption would be opposed by Schegloff, who has suggested that "instead of beginning analysis with the seemingly special features of the persons, settings, or occasions actually being examined, investigators might do well to begin with more general ways of organizing talk, one not limited to specialized jobs or settings, and ask how the more general resources are adapted for particular, situated use.[39(p455)]

Morse claims that "there is no theory about the process of the developing [nurse–patient] relationship"[18(p455)] available to nurses, a point that, incidentally, is easily refuted with reference to a thorough review of this literature conducted by May.[40] Refusing the notion that nurses and patients draw on "general resources"[39(p455)] of everyday talk, adapting these for health care encounters, Morse demonstrates a common presentiment about theory in nursing as something that is lacking and that therefore should be produced for the consumption of practitioners. This position can be described as one of filling the gap between what is taken as best practice, informed by existing theoretical formulations, and empirical findings that never quite measure up to the ideals. Taking a rationalist perspective, Morse demonstrates the way in which such a view of theory production is instantiated as essential for the improvement of practice. This position exemplifies the discursive practices used by Melia 10 years ago, which were challenged in the introduction.

Addressing what she characterizes as a "lack," Morse produces a typology of relationships consisting of the clinical, the therapeutic, the connected, and the overinvolved.[18] From this typology, Morse generalizes that "clinical relationships often occur when the patient is being treated for a minor concern,"[18(p458)] yet, with data consisting only of interviews with nurses, such generalizations seem cavalier at best. Morse suggests that the resulting relationship depends on a number of factors, many of them "outside the control of the individual nurse,"[18(p464)] for instance, specialization, multiplicity of caregivers, and time constraints. Rather than illuminate the process of how relationships are negotiated, such studies only provide devices to legitimate further current organizational structures within which such relationships are discursively reproduced.

Morse's concern is to reduce accounts of processes into similar conceptual boxes. This work is facilitated by the speed implicit with the grounded theory approach, whereby analysis is required to occur simultaneously with data collection. This, I would argue, represents a misguided emphasis at "getting close" to practice conducted in the field. Validity of findings cannot be enhanced merely through the speedy production of themes.

The alternative position suggested by Schegloff's[39] remark that participants in health care encounters draw on existing theoretical notions (possibly adapting them for particular use, that is, institutionalizing them) advertises the advantage of setting aside studies that aim at mere gap-filling. Schegloff cautions investigators regarding "the contingencies of professional practice"[39(p455)] in attempting to apply the principles of conversation analysis to practices other than those of everyday conversation. Such a warning is taken up in Hunt and Montgomery-Robinson's work where they suggest that the analyst may find it beneficial to contrast institutionalized talk with mundane talk in order to discover the "specialness"[33(p153)] of professional conversations.

On the face of it, Schegloff's warning is appealing. Certainly the position taken in this paper has been one that would concur with his claim that investigators would do well to "ask how the more general resources (of talk) are adapted for particular, situated use."[39(p455)] However, when this warning is taken up in the way formulated by Hunt and Montgomery-Robinson,[33] a difficulty arises. That difficulty has to do with the privileging of everyday talk over professional talk. How is a distinction between the two to be made? Here, the conception of power as not only constraining but also enabling action and the constitution of subjects for practice must be considered.

Analyzing Conversations for Difference

Conversation analysis techniques have been applied to medical discourse analysis to explicate how power constrains but also enables action in particular circumstances. For instance, West draws on conversation analysis techniques to examine differences between directives given to patients by male and female physicians.[41] Attending to the effects of power in interactions, West's analysis concludes that male physicians tend more often to draw on directives that take the "form of an imperative,"[41(p108)] positioning the physician in a hierarchically superior position to the patient as someone with an inalienable right to direct. Conversely, female physicians were observed by West more often to phrase their directives to patients in a "mitigated" form that "minimized status differences between physician and patient and stressed their connectedness to one another."[41(p108)]

Significantly, West notes that it is not so much the similarities exhibited by physicians from one gender or another that are of interest but rather those instances where female physicians were observed to make their directives more im- perative, just as male physicians were, in some situations, observed to make their imperatives more mitigated. She suggests that here lies the ground, within the "mundane activities of social life [where the resources for] doing gender"[41(p109)] are located. Such a perspective avoids the dualism of male versus female ways of "doing physician." Importantly, such approaches retain difference as an inherent analytic device. Rather than leaving the analysis at the point of noticing general differences between male and female physicians, West leaves open the possibility that, in some circumstances, male physicians draw on what might typically be understood as female conversational techniques to give directives, just as, in other circumstances, female physicians use what might typically be understood as pre- dominantly male techniques to give their instructions to clients. The question that begs to be asked then is, in what circumstances? What are the conditions of possi- bility that underlie such differences in approaches?

To the extent that such questions arise from West's analysis, I would argue that she has (wisely) extended conversation analysis from its typical usages in social inquiries. A comment on conversation analysis by Bjelic and Lynch[42] is apposite here. While acknowledging the important part played by conversation analysis within the wider ethnomethodological project, they note that attending to the ordi- nary and mundane in conversations bears a cost in analytic terms: "conversation analysts may find it more sensible to investigate how doctors interview patients or inform them of diagnostic outcomes than to investigate how they organize *diagno- sis*. What gets lost in the bargain are the uniquely identifying features of the work studied . . . The medical gaze becomes subservient to the interests of initiating and sustaining a line of talk, while the patient's body primarily becomes a site for the selective activation of the turn-taking system of conversation."[42(p76)]

Bjelic and Lynch's comments suggest a profitable way to attend to the influence of power and the social on action in order that the researcher is able to mark shifts and movement within the practice relationship as it is constituted in the field. Al- though conversation analysis offers a way of demonstrating the process of that relationship—that is, how utterances follow on from one another—it cannot nec- essarily explain the "following" as signifying the presence of forms of power. A wider perspective that takes social action as instantiated through language offers such a possibility to the analytic project.

EXPERIENCE AND MOVEMENT: VALIDATING INTERPRETATIONS OF SOCIAL CONSTRUCTIONS

Once the subject of nursing has been de-centred as a certain, objectifiable, and rationally grounded set of practices, an appeal to objectifiable external sources on which to validate findings becomes impossible. For who now will be the "expert panel"? Where can the researcher turn to establish the validity of findings gener- ated within the social constructionist perspective?

Cohen locates this problem within the very process of interpretation and what he describes as our "inclination to generalize."[43(p350)] The process of interpretation necessarily depends on the ethnographer's project of making sense of what is seen and heard, of translating one form of text into another. Cohen cautions, however, against making a "theoretical virtue"[43(p351)] out of the practice necessity.

Drawing attention to what is, at times, a deeply suppressed reflexivity fundamental to interpretive research, Cohen's warning is particularly suited to analytic projects that attend to "difference." For how will difference be conceptualized in nursing practice? There are a number of social theorists whose work illuminates this problem. And here, the discussion returns to consider, more directly, how the relationship between the researcher and the field can be given rigorous treatment in ethnographic studies.

The concepts of *experience* and *movement* are central to this discussion. Experience is understood here to represent expressions of difference. This position is reflected in Gadamer's statement that "experience is initially always experience of negation: something is not what we supposed it to be. In view of the experience that we have of another object, both things change—our knowledge and the object."[28(p354)]

The mark of an event as an experience to be recounted by a member of the group under investigation or by the researcher rests not only in the recognition of something new, but in the object having been recognized in a different way than expected. Here, Gadamer's crucial point about experience arising from *within* its own historicity is underlined. The experience of negation is only possible when the previously held understanding of the object is available for reflection against what is experienced as different from expectations. To reiterate, experience is taken within the context of this article not as an incremental process of accumulating experiences, based on a rationalist version of "better knowledge" as Benner claims.[21] Rather, the perspective adopted here is one in which experience is treated as a totality of continually expanding "horizons"[28(p302)] fully implicated in the ongoing accomplishment of understanding in the day-to-day events of the life-world.

This version of experience sits alongside the concept of movement as a sensual response to experience. Such an understanding of movement used within an analytic project has been developed by Lyotard[4] and recently advanced further by Munro.[44] Lyotard[4] has developed the idea of moves and countermoves in language games from the writings of the later Wittgenstein. Munro[44] situates Lyotard's writings within a wider consideration of social action drawing in notions of power and the embodiment of control technologies. The aim in field studies, I would argue, is to place movement in context so that it bears application for the terms of validity required for a robust theoretical position toward studies of practice. This will now be explored.

The position I am advancing here is that movement, achieved by linguistic and discursive strategies, can form the field to which the researcher can relate. Within this field, interpretations can be tested, questioned, and reflected upon. Ultimately, the interpretations can be revised if, at some later point, due to the nature of experience, the researcher comes to understand this movement in a different way.

The nature of the movement accomplished can be said to locate the researcher's gaze. For example, if the stated aim of the workers at a particular community health clinic is to promote the health of individuals attending the clinic, the researcher's focus will be on the manner in which this action, as a form of movement, is achieved. From which position does the nurse begin? How does she move during the encounter? What is the patient's response to the nurse's moves? How does the patient position himself or herself in relation to the nurse? How does the nurse position himself or herself in relation to the patient? How does this position constrain the patient? What is the patient able to accomplish from his or her position? How is movement expressed by nurses and patients? How is their future conduct affected by this movement?

The aim of interpretations arising from such questions can then be to reorient discussions about practice by addressing the field, not as an unchanging physical setting, aspects of which can be controlled through an appeal to external sources of validity, but rather as a life-world of which and from which members have and generate experiences. The field is everything members make use of to enact practices together; it is made present (though not always visible) through their linguistic expressions and is accounted for in both verbal and behavioral terms as they move themselves and others around in the field.

This movement, to reiterate, can be explored as an effect of the differences marked by social actors based on their experiences of the field, formulated through power relationships and through the accomplishment of hierarchical domination in social encounters. Every attempt should be made in the course of collecting materials from the field to remain as open as possible to the changing life-world on display before the researcher. Openness is necessarily limited by the ever present movement inherent in understanding as described by Gadamer. Strathern[45] has demonstrated how this "fact" can be turned to advantage. "Every inversion we deploy is self-referential . . . but the deployment of *particular*, concrete inversions is not. The particularity creates a context, defined necessarily by the internal referencing itself as 'outside' . . . Any such contextualisation can of course be recaptured as in turn self-referential, in the same way as 'other' can always be collapsed as a version of 'self.' But to regard this last position as a final one is to *hide the movement* through which it was reached."[45(p279)] Here, Strathern denotes a self-conscious approach to fieldwork, an approach that remains aware of the inversions deployed in an effort to preserve difference, to distinguish between self and other. I would argue that it is within this self-conscious and critical approach to the field that the "positions" referred to by Strathern are maintained in analytic "play." Keeping positions provisional, the analyst then excavates the movement conditioning the positions attained. Strathern's comment reflects the complex, systematic approach to the field advocated in this article. By reorienting the approach taken to the field, preserving difference and the domination it implies, a critical analysis can offer valid representations and explanations of organized action that attend to difference and power as consequences of the social enactment of practice.

Approaches to the life-world of practice should be made with a questioning mind, one that constantly problematizes understandings. The results to be aimed for are rich, contextualized materials reflecting social interaction offering the potential for explaining conditions supporting routinized actions across members and locales. Provisional explanations can be offered regarding the conditions under which such changes to routine action might take place. The advantage of having extensive research materials available for future consideration is that explanations can be collapsed and rebuilt in different ways to reflect new understandings of movement that might arise as a result of a constant alertness to difference that enriches experiential horizons.

Any interpretation necessitates the building up of stories emerging from the field. Some stories will do more work at offering explanations of action than others. The ability to return, to work up new stories based on new understandings interpenetrated by structurated experiences, remains the primary advantage to the rich potential of field studies.

·   ·   ·

Concerned with the apparently naive treatment of power and knowledgeable action within many contemporary studies of nursing practice, this article has addressed some central issues to be considered by researchers prior to entering the field in order to study how social action influences the practice of nursing. The nature of field studies as they are presently represented in nursing research was problematized. It was suggested that use of the terms *field studies* and *ethnography* has been abused in many nursing studies. Reasons for this abuse were linked to unexamined perceptions that researchers operate under pressure from practice to construct prescriptions for "good" practice. It was argued that this has had the effect of turning researchers' gaze away from the field of practice, in search of information about populations who at varying times come into contact with nurses. As a result, understanding about practice situated within the field of practice is rare. It was argued that, as practice is constituted within the field, a study concerned with understanding how practice is constituted must necessarily have a much clearer notion of the field than that currently available in the nursing literature.

Reorienting the notion of the field involved examining issues of validity, for, once the social constructionist perspective is taken, previously held notions of validity as an appeal to external sources located in an objective reality cease to apply. Here, the centrality of language as a fundamental structure drawn on to constitute practice was examined. Studies that examine the language of practice were reviewed, and the importance of establishing such studies on adequately conceptualized theories of action was underlined.

The importance of maintaining a value on difference was advanced as a central tenet to reorienting discussion about validity in interpretive research. Taking Lyotard's work on language games as a background for this discussion and applying this work to notions of experience and movement, it was argued that questions raised about the validity of interpretation are more appropriately addressed within the field. That is, having de-centred the subject of nursing as an objective reality, the bases on which judgments are to be made regarding the constitution of practice also come under review. Placing a value on understanding difference not only has implications for the validity of the interpretive project but also on directions for analysis.

REFERENCES

1. Porter S. Nursing research conventions: objectivity or obfuscation? *J Adv Nurs.* 1993;18:137–143.
2. Melia KM. "Tell it as it is"—qualitative methodology and nursing research: understanding the student nurse's world. *J Adv Nurs.* 1982;7:327–335.
3. Giddens A. *The constitution of society.* Cambridge, England: Polity Press; 1984.
4. Lyotard JF; Bennington G, Massumi B, trans. *The postmodern condition: a report on knowledge.* Manchester University Press; 1984. Original work published 1979.
5. Leininger M, ed. *Qualitative Research Methods in Nursing.* Orlando, Fla: Grune & Stratton; 1985.
6. Morse JM, ed. *Qualitative Nursing Research: A Contemporary Dialogue.* Rev ed. Newbury Park, Calif: Sage; 1991.
7. Morse JM, Johnson JL, eds. *The Illness Experience: Dimensions of Suffering.* Newbury Park, Calif: Sage; 1991.
8. Bergum V. Dialogue: on bracketing. In: Morse JM, ed. *Qualitative Nursing Research: A Contemporary Dialogue.* Rev ed. Newbury Park, Calif: Sage; 1991.
9. Lipson JG. The use of self in ethnographic research. In: Morse JM, ed. *Qualitative Nursing Research: A Contemporary Dialogue.* Rev. ed. Newbury Park, Calif: Sage; 1991.
10. Boyle JS. Field research: a collaborative model for practice and research. In: Morse JM, ed. *Qualitative Nursing Research: A Contemporary Dialogue.* Rev. ed. Newbury Park, Calif: Sage; 1991.
11. Chassé MA. The experiences of women having a hysterectomy. In: Morse JM, Johnson JL, eds. *The Illness Experience: Dimensions of Suffering.* Newbury Park, Calif: Sage; 1991.
12. Wilson S. The unrelenting nightmare: husbands' experiences during their wives' chemotherapy. In: Morse JM, Johnson JL, eds. *The Illness Experience: Dimensions of Suffering.* Newbury Park, Calif: Sage; 1991.
13. Aamodt AM. Ethnography and epistemology: generating nursing knowledge. In: Morse JM, ed. *Qualitative Nursing Research: A Contemporary Dialogue.* Rev ed. Newbury Park, Calif: Sage; 1991.
14. Giddens A. *New Rules of Sociological Method: A Positive Critique of Interpretive Sociologies.* London, England: Hutchinson; 1976.
15. Hiraki A. Tradition, rationality, and power in introductory nursing textbooks: a critical hermeneutics study. *ANS.* 1992;14(3):1–12.
16. Purkis ME. Entering the field: intrusions of the social and its exclusion from studies of nursing practice. *Int J Nurs Stud.* 1994;31(3).
17. Garfinkel H. *Studies in Ethnomethodology.* Englewood Cliffs, NJ: Prentice Hall; 1967.
18. Morse JM. Negotiating commitment and involvement in the nurse–patient relationship. *J Adv Nurs.* 1991;16:455–468.
19. Field PA. An ethnography: four public health nurses' perspectives of nursing. *J Adv Nurs.* 1983;8:3–12.

20. Brink PJ. Issues of reliability and validity. In: Morse JM, ed. *Qualitative Nursing Research: A Contemporary Dialogue.* Rev ed. Newbury Park, Calif: Sage; 1991.

21. Benner P. *From Novice to Expert: Excellence and Power in Clinical Nursing Practice.* Menlo Park, Calif: Addison-Wesley; 1984.

22. Wolf ZR. Nursing rituals. *Can J Nurs Res.* 1988;20(3):56–69.

23. Wolf ZR. Learning the professional jargon of nursing during change of shift power. *Holistic Nursing Practice.* 1989;4(1):78–83.

24. Tilley S. *Negotiating Realities: Making Sense of Interaction Between Patients Diagnosed as Neurotic and Nurses in Two Psychiatric Admission Wards.* Edinburgh, Scotland: University of Edinburgh; 1990. PhD thesis.

25. May C. Affective neutrality and involvement: staff nurses' perceptions of appropriate behaviour on general medical and surgical wards. *J Adv Nurs.* 1991;16:552–558.

26. May C. Individual care? Power and subjectivity in therapeutic relationships. *Sociology.* 1992;26(4):589–602.

27. May C. Nursing work, nurses' knowledge, and the subjectification of the patient. *Sociology of Health & Illness.* 1992;14(4):472–487.

28. Gadamer HG; Linge D, trans-ed. *Philosophical Hermeneutics.* Berkeley, Calif: University of California Press; 1976.

29. Foucault M; Porter C, trans. What is enlightenment? In: Rabinow P, ed. *The Foucault Reader.* New York, NY: Pantheon Books; 1984.

30. Munro R. Managing by ambiguity: an archaeology of the social in the absence of management accounting. Paper presented at the 8th Standing Conference on Organizational Symbolism Conference, Copenhagen, July 1991.

31. Foucault M; Sheridan A, trans. *The Birth of the Clinic: An Archaeology of Medical Perception.* London, England: Routledge; 1973. Original work published in 1963.

32. Mortis W. Conversation analysis of nurse–patient talk in a Calgary hospital. Calgary, Alberta, Canada: University of Calgary; 1990. Thesis.

33. Hunt M, Montgomery-Robinson K. Analysis of conversational interactions. *Recent Adv Nurs.* 1987;17:150–168.

34. Schegloff EA, Sacks H. Opening up closings. *Semiotica.* 1973;8:289–327.

35. Sacks H, Schegloff EA, Jefferson G. A simplest systematics for the organization of turn-taking for conversation. *Language.* 1974;50:696–735.

36. Watson G. Introduction. In: Watson G, Seiler RM, eds. *Text in Context: Contributions to Ethnomethodology.* Newbury Park, Calif: Sage; 1992.

37. Heritage J. *Garfinkel and Ethnomethodology.* Cambridge, England: Polity Press; 1984.

38. Foucault M; Sheridan A, trans. *Discipline and Punish: The Birth of the Prison.* London, England: Penguin; 1977. Original work published in 1975.

39. Schegloff EA. On an actual virtual servo-mechanism for guessing bad news: a single case conjecture. *Social Problems.* 1988;35(4):442–457.

40. May C. Research on nurse–patient relationships: problems of theory, problems of practice. *J Adv Nurs.* 1990;15:307–315.

41. West C. Not just "doctors' orders": directive–response sequences in patients' visits to women and men physicians. *Discourse & Society.* 1990;1(1): 85–112.

42. Bjelic D, Lynch M. The work of a (scientific) demonstration: respecifying Newton's and Goethe's theories of prismatic color. In: Watson G, Seiler RM, eds. *Text in Context: Contributions to Ethnomethodology.* Newbury Park, Calif: Sage; 1992.

43. Cohen AP. Post-fieldwork fieldwork. *Journal of Anthropological Research.* 1992;48(4):339–354.

44. Munro R. Just when you thought it was safe to enter the water: multiple control technologies and the making of members' moves. 1993;3:249–271.

45. Strathern M. Out of context: the persuasive fictions of anthropology. *Current Anthropology.* 1987;28(3):251–281.

Fuzzy Logic: Enhancing Possibilities for Nursing Intervention Research

Lynn Rew, EdD, RN, C, FAAN
Associate Professor
Assistant Dean for Student Affairs
School of Nursing
The University of Texas at Austin
Austin, Texas

Paul R. Waller, PhD, RN
Assistant Professor
School of Nursing
The University of Texas at Austin
Austin, Texas

Edward M. Barrow, MS
Professor, Information Systems
Keller Graduate School of Management
Chicago, Illinois

Fuzzy logic as an approach to developing knowledge and decision making in complex situations is offered as a possible way to enhance nursing intervention research. This article introduces the philosophical background of fuzzy logic and provides examples to illustrate possible nursing research applications. Nursing scientists are challenged to examine carefully their decisions in conducting nursing intervention research and to consider the implications these have for clinical practice.

IS NURSING SCIENCE about certainty and predictability? Is it about uncertainty and complexity? Are nursing scientists prepared to face the challenges of developing a human science even if it means letting go of cherished beliefs and methods borrowed from traditional science? Can nursing intervention research include methods based on traditional logic and at the same time entertain the possibilities of systems based on fuzzy logic? Can the developers of nursing informatics embrace fuzzy logic as an algorithm appropriate for approximating the truth about human phenomena?

The authors gratefully acknowledge the assistance of Norvell Northcutt, PhD, Director of Data Services, Austin Community College, Austin, Texas, in the early stages of development of this article.

PURPOSE

This article raises questions concerning the complex phenomena inherent in nursing intervention research. The purpose is to provoke examination and discussion of the types of logic used in conducting nursing intervention research and to issue a challenge to nursing scientists to consider applying rules of scalar or "fuzzy" logic to processes of collecting, analyzing, and interpreting data about nursing interventions. The focus is on the philosophy underlying fuzzy logic, which includes questions about meaning, truth, and logical connections of ideas.[1] The focus is not on the mathematics of data analysis using fuzzy set theory nor is it on a comparison of methods guided by traditional (binary) logic *vis-à-vis* those of fuzzy logic. Finally, the intent of this article is not to dictate what should be a standard for nursing intervention research. Rather, it is a call to imagine and explore what may be possible.

NURSING INTERVENTION RESEARCH

Nursing scientists are currently expanding the body of knowledge about nursing interventions. For example, Grobe[2] is developing a lexicon and taxonomy of nursing interventions through linguistic analyses of nurses' own vocabularies while McCloskey and Bulechek[3] are refining their classification system of interventions based on content analysis of various documented sources. Jennings notes that as the cost of health care increases, nursing has many opportunities to explore the efficacy of nursing interventions and the client outcomes associated with them.[4] She adds a caveat that nurses who embrace such opportunities to study nursing interventions can affirm the wholeness of human clients by preventing these clients from being reduced to mere mechanistic variables. To respond to this warning, nurse scientists must be willing to examine not only the research designs and methods used to answer important questions about nursing interventions, but they must also be willing to probe the philosophical foundations of data collection, analysis, and interpretation.

The majority of nurse clinicians and nurse researchers alike share a common background in nursing practice that is based on scientific methods. Researchers carry the bulk of responsibility for posing and answering questions that are relevant to nursing practice. Furthermore, nursing scientists are obliged to interpret and disseminate their findings in a manner that is meaningful and useful to nurse clinicians. Nursing science is accountable for conducting this work with as much precision and certainty as possible. Yet the subjects of much nursing scientific endeavor—nursing clients and their nurses—are extremely complex, as is the nursing process itself. Therefore, it is imperative that nursing scientists be fully aware of the implications of their choice of design and methods as well as the philosophical assumptions on which their decisions rest.

The empirical philosophy of natural science values the observation of objects and events without regard for the context of those objects and events. The goal is to discover universal laws that can be generalized and that explain the cause and effect of selected situations. Hempel refers to these laws as deductive-nomological explanations that have universal form; that is, statements can be made that when specific conditions are met, certain other events will always, and without exception, occur (cause and effect).[5]

Early developments in nursing science were based on this philosophy of logical positivism, including the belief that a theory is either "true" (given a truth value = 1) or "false" (given a truth value = 0), and that a single scientific method is sufficient to develop a body of knowledge for a discipline.[6] However, as nursing science has evolved, other philosophies of science, such as historicism with its emphasis on the historical context of situations, have influenced the methods of nursing theory development and research.[7] Schumacher and Gortner suggest that nursing science should now consider scientific realism as a philosophy that acknowledges "truth" as a regulative ideal; science is conducted to arrive successively ever closer to an approximation of the truth.[8] They argue that causation remains an important consideration with regard to nursing research because clinicians need to know the consequences of specific events such as interventions.

Methods of nursing research have grown in number and variety, encompassing both quantitative and qualitative designs. Such diversity in designs and methods enable nurse scientists to describe, explain, predict, and understand much about the processes of nursing. Regardless of design and method chosen to answer specific questions about the outcomes of nursing interventions, how well do nursing scientists understand the systems of logic they employ when collecting, analyzing, interpreting, and discussing their findings? The majority of empirical research in nursing is based on traditional logic, an outgrowth of logical positivism. This means that complex, uncertain, and frequently chaotic events such as human attitudes and behaviors are forced into linear models of description, explanation, and prediction. For example, Moriarity notes that family phenomena of special interest to nursing are "complex, multidimensional, and interactive, and as such may be empirically elusive."[9(p12)] An alternative to the characteristic empirical and binary (true/false) approach to the study of human phenomena is to consider the burgeoning branch of "fuzzy logic" with its potential to describe vague and rapidly changing phenomena. Fuzzy logic allows for uncertainty and degrees of truth (ranging from 0 to 1) rather than the simple truth and falsehood of traditional methods.[10]

FUZZY LOGIC AND STATISTICAL INFERENCE

Fuzzy logic is a generic term that refers to knowledge and decision making based on vagueness and uncertainty found in some continuous phenomena. Lofti A. Zadeh, a professor of computer science and electrical engineering at the University of California at Berkeley, is known as the "father of fuzzy logic." Zadeh studied the management of uncertainty, decision analysis, and approximate reasoning. His initial work on fuzzy set theory was published in 1965. Prior to this publication, the only theory that permitted scientists to deal with uncertainty in complex situations was that of statistical inference. Statistical inference, however, was limited to situations in which uncertainty could be attributed to randomness under the laws of large numbers.[11] In recent years, theories of chaos have been developed, and there is now evidence that what was once attributed to random occurrence actually may be part of a higher order, complex pattern that is sometimes stable and sometimes unstable. Chaos has become a method of doing science as well as a theory.[12]

Many of the phenomena of interest to nursing scientists are not based on assumptions of objective and certain truth. Rather, they flow out of vague and complex situations that are rapidly, if not constantly, changing. Davidson and Ray assert that the science of complexity is useful in understanding systems, including the human environment, which tend *not* to exhibit totally predictable behavior.[13] They suggest that using multiple types of inquiry allows nursing scientists to move beyond the limitations of methods and consider what is possible. Within the philosophy of the science of complexity or the science of chaos, fuzzy logic provides another method for viewing reality.

Consider, for example, an astronomer taking photographs of distant objects in space: when photographs are taken from telescopic lenses located on Earth, the resulting images include interferences due to the long distance and extraneous events in the atmosphere between the observer and the observed. However, when scientists send a probe into space to take snapshots of the red spot on Jupiter, then run these images through a computer equipped with fuzzy logic programs, the program enhances the image with other possibilities, and the images become closer approximations of the reality that exists in outer space. The greater detail in the final photograph of Jupiter's red spot results from creating a reality rather than from measuring only the raw data and believing that we can observe reality.

Traditional statistical inference concerns propositions that are either true (1) or false (0) but addresses also the problem of uncertainty: How certain are we that the proposition is true or false? Quantitative values are applied to our belief in the truth of the proposition. Fuzzy set theory deals with propositions that have less precise meanings. If a nurse researcher proposes, "there is a good chance that this group intervention for clients with human immunodeficiency virus (HIV) will work when the amount of client discomfort is quite large," elements of both traditional and fuzzy logic sets are present. The first part of the statement about the good chance is a statement of uncertainty, and the rules of probability will enable the researcher to test the uncertainty. The second part of the statement, "when the amount of client discomfort is quite large," is not a statement of uncertainty, rather it is a statement of imprecision. All numbers that could represent "quite large" are found in the fuzzy set between the values of 1 (completely true) and 0 (completely false), and are reported as decimals.[14]

In traditional scientific methods, analysis is based on the laws of probability, which are in turn derived from mathematical models that represent the occurrence (and/or nonoccurrence) of specific events. As Kerlinger indicated, "Random events, *in the aggregate* [emphasis in the original] occur in lawful ways with monotonous regularity."[15(p117)] The consistency of these "lawful ways" provides the basis for hypothesis testing. The probability of an event occurring is mathematically derived *a priori,* and observations obtained in controlled situations are then compared against that predetermined probability. If the observed data occur more or less frequently than can be attributed to a predetermined level of chance (probability), the null hypothesis of no difference between groups is rejected, and the alternative hypothesis of a "true" difference between groups is accepted, at the stated level of probability.

The same consistency may be applied using alternative lawful ways. Fuzzy logic is not to be confused with false or syllogistic logic. The conventions used in joint and implicative fuzzy logic statements provide the same level of rigor as traditional inference. The difference lies in the treatment of truth as a continuous function instead of a binary (yes/no) function.

The following examples of nursing intervention research illustrate the limitations of using only probability and traditional logic and the possibilities of enhancing our understanding of complex human phenomena by using fuzzy logic. Hypothetical examples were constructed to provide a contrast between traditional and fuzzy logic. These examples minimize distractions that might occur from using real examples that could contain elements extraneous to this comparison.

HYPOTHETICAL NURSING INTERVENTION RESEARCH EXAMPLES

A team of nurse researchers wanted to determine whether sexually abused children who attended a court-mandated, community-based group intervention exhibited lower levels of depression at the end of the 8-week intervention than those children who did not attend the group intervention. The investigator measured the children's levels of depression by using the Child Depression Inventory.[16] Data were collected from 24 school-aged (mean = 10 years) children, 12 randomly assigned to a control group, and 12 assigned to the nursing intervention group. Data were analyzed by a one-way analysis of variance (ANOVA) technique. Results of this analysis were as follows: $F (1,22) = 3.108$, $p = .09$.

The researchers concluded that the outcome of the intervention was not significant; there was no statistically significant difference in the children's levels of depression following the intervention. The null hypothesis, which states that there is no difference between the two groups of children at the conclusion of the intervention, was retained. The null hypothesis is considered to be, *a priori,* a statement of the truth with a truth value of 1. With no significant differences in means between the two groups, at the preset level of $p < .05$, the conclusion was drawn that the relationship between the independent variable (group membership of the children) and the dependent variable (level of depression in the children) was 0.

The final outcome was that the findings were not generalizable and, therefore, would probably not be published and would not inform practice.

In another hypothetical study of a nursing intervention, single (ie, unpartnered) adult clients newly diagnosed with HIV often experience difficulty developing intimate relationships. A hypothetical nursing intervention study was developed to examine the efficacy of a possible means of helping these clients to ease their skill in developing such relationships with new acquaintances. An experimental design was used, randomly sampling clients from a sexually transmitted disease clinic. Clients were subsequently randomized into either a control or a treatment group.

Control-group clients ($n = 24$) participated in ongoing support groups for those newly diagnosed with HIV, conducted by one of the clinic nurses. Treatment-group clients ($n = 24$) participated in an intervention specifically developed to address issues of developing trust and intimacy while dealing with being HIV-positive. These 24 clients were randomly divided into 3 groups of 8 each to facilitate group dynamics. The intervention included lecture/discussion and role-playing sessions conducted by a clinic nurse. Lecture/discussion sessions focused on problem identification, values clarification, and problem-solving processes, and explored new and different ways of expressing intimacy and sexuality while practicing safer sex. Role-playing scenarios involved meeting new people at social gatherings and moving toward greater intimacy in dating relationships.

Clients' satisfaction with their personal intimate relationships and comfort in initiating new relationships were measured at the first meeting of the groups and at a point 2 months later. While there were no statistically significant differences between the groups at the initial measure, by 2 months later there was a significant difference between the treatment and control groups ($t = 3.14$, $df = 22$, $p < .01$) in both the satisfaction and comfort measures. The researchers concluded that the nursing intervention was statistically significant because the analysis of data revealed differences in the groups (control and intervention) at the preset level of confidence ($p < .05$). Furthermore, the researchers published their results and nurse clinicians found the study to be clinically significant. Based on the rigor of the researchers' methods of data collection, analysis, and interpretation, they were convinced that the nursing intervention caused the effects of increased client satisfaction and comfort in initiating relationships. Thus, nursing practice was changed as a consequence of the research.

In both these intervention studies, the researchers did communicate their findings to the nurse clinicians who conducted the control and intervention groups. The clinic nurses working with clients who were positive for HIV were not surprised by the findings and reiterated that the intervention had evolved out of their listening closely to the expressed needs of these clients and responding to what they heard by planning an intervention that addressed these needs directly. The group facilitators of the children's group, however, were very surprised by the findings of the first study. They noted that they would continue to offer their structured group intervention to the sexually abused children because they could observe gradual changes in the children's mood over the 8-week period of the intervention. Their observations of the children in the control group, those who did not receive a structured group experience, convinced them that something more needed to be done to help these children recover from the trauma of their abuse.

What is different about these two intervention studies? The rigor in design and methods is comparable. Both involve complex situations involving content with high emotional valences. Are the differences in outcomes due to the abstractness of the concepts investigated (client satisfaction and comfort vs. depression)? If that were true, we would expect the results of the study of depression in abuse situations to be more significant than those of the study of comfort and satisfaction in new relationships among clients newly diagnosed with HIV. Are the outcomes different because children change more rapidly than adults? Is it true that the intervention in the study of the children was not effective? Do the rules that define the efficacy of an intervention preclude us from accepting the worth of the first study?

STATISTICAL AND CLINICAL SIGNIFICANCE

In considering the usefulness of research on nursing interventions, statistical significance and clinical significance represent two distinctly different ways of interpreting and utilizing research findings. The former type of significance is based on assumptions and approaches using traditional rules of logic. When scientists establish a very rigorous level of accepting the efficacy of an intervention, they attempt to imitate a binary representation of "truth," which produces a statement that is interpreted as either true (truth value = 1) or false (truth value = 0). But what is the value of research that does not meet *a priori* standards of acceptability, standards that are rigorous and demand that a hypothesis is accepted if, and only if, statistical significance is achieved at a confidence level of 95% or 99% with a particular sample of data? Limitations of these approaches include the need for large samples with broad variability, *a priori* choice of an arbitrary significance level, and the independence of hypothesis testing.[17] Moreover, Slakter, Yow-Wu, and Suzuki-Slakter note that "if the sample size is large enough, the null hypothesis of no treatment effect or no relation will always be rejected at any alpha level."[18(p249)] Thus, statistical significance may be meaningless in terms of clinical significance. These approaches, although demonstrated as worthy time and again, are mechanistic and may not be appropriate as the only approaches in developing human sciences.

Clinical significance, on the other hand, takes into consideration such issues as the context of the phenomenon under investigation. Human responses are rarely black and white and, philosophically, nursing practice functions with approaches to human processes that must include many dimensions. The "truth" about these processes is more likely to exist as grey or fuzzy areas somewhere in between the presence and absence of truth. Specifically, in intervention research, proportion of improved subjects and the subjects' own judgments about qualitative differences in their lives as a result of the intervention are worthy of investigation. Answers to nursing inquiry in these areas may not be readily amenable to the binary logic of traditional scientific methods and computer programs. Questions of interest to nursing often cannot be answered by dichotomous alternatives of true or false. Use of fuzzy sets and fuzzy logic may allow us to capture a picture that is closer to the "truth" about human phenomena.

If a fuzzy logic approach had been designed and used in the analysis of the hypothetical examples given above, interpretation of results might lead to the conclusion that the outcome of both interventions are significant; there is clinical significance, and the results are worth disseminating to inform practice. The decision to consider the findings as clinically relevant would not be left to a dichotomous choice to retain or reject a null hypothesis; the results would not yield a certainty of truth or falsity but rather an approximation of the truth, which would be a sharper reflection of the real situation. Similarly, other considerations would be allowed to determine whether a decision to employ a proposed intervention should be introduced into practice. Such considerations would include probable waste of human energy, time, and material resources, all of which contain subjective meanings and values.[17] Above all, the ethical imperative to do no harm is essential to these considerations.

•   •   •

This article was written to provoke readers' interest in the types of logic employed in nursing intervention research methods. We introduced the system of fuzzy logic with a brief explanation of the values of various truth statements that can be made when truth is viewed as probabilistic rather than deterministic and dichotomous. The term *fuzzy* refers to the shades of grey and imprecision that it claims to address. Moreover, although we suggest that a departure from traditional logic be considered when analyzing, interpreting, and disseminating the results of nursing intervention research, we underscore the need to continue to employ the most rigorous of research design, methods, and analysis to answer the questions that need to be studied. We assert that as nurse scientists, we should explore the possibilities of expanding our approaches to developing a science that is fully human and that fully embraces the human condition in all its uncertainty and complexity.

REFERENCES

1. Woodhouse MB. *A Preface to Philosophy*. 4th ed. Belmont, Calif: Wadsworth Publishing; 1990.
2. Grobe SJ. Nursing intervention lexicon and taxonomy study: language and classification methods. *ANS*. 1990;13(2):22–33.
3. McCloskey JC, Bulechek GM. *Nursing Interventions Classification (NIC)*. St. Louis, Mo: Mosby Year Book; 1992.

4. Jennings BM. Patient outcomes research: seizing the opportunity. *ANS.* 1991;14(2):59–72.
5. Hempel CG. *Philosophy of Natural Science.* Englewood Cliffs, NJ: Prentice Hall; 1966.
6. Webster G, Jacox A, Baldwin B. Nursing theory and the ghost of the received view. In: McCloskey JC, Grace HK, eds. *Current Issues in Nursing.* Boston, Mass: Blackwell; 1981.
7. Jacox A, Webster G. Competing theories of science. In: Nicoll LH, ed. *Perspectives on Nursing Theory.* Boston, Mass: Little, Brown; 1986.
8. Schumacher KL, Gortner SR. (Mis)conceptions and reconceptions about traditional science. *ANS.* 1992;14(4):1–11.
9. Moriarity HJ. Key issues in the family research process: strategies for nurse researchers. *ANS.* 1990;12(3):1–14.
10. Stewart I. Mathematical recreations: a partly true story. *Sci Am.* 1993;268(2):110–112.
11. Zadeh , Kacprzyk J. *Fuzzy Logic for the Management of Uncertainty.* New York, NY: Wiley; 1992.
12. Gleick J. *Chaos: Making a New Science.* New York, NY: Penguin; 1990.
13. Davidson AW, Ray MA. Studying the human–environment phenomenon using the science of complexity. *ANS.* 1991;14(2):73–87.
14. Neapolitan RE. A survey of uncertain and approximate inference. In: Zadeh LA, Kacpryzk J, eds. *Fuzzy Logic for the Management of Uncertainty.* New York, NY: Wiley; 1992.
15. Kerlinger FN. *Foundations of Behavioral Research.* New York, NY: Holt, Rinehart & Winston; 1967.
16. Kazdin AE. Childhood depression. In: Mash EJ, Terdal LG, eds. *Behavioral Assessment of Childhood Disorders,* 2nd ed. New York: The Guilford Press.
17. LeFort SM. The statistical versus clinical significance debate. *Image: Journal of Nursing Scholarship.* 1993;25(1):57–61.
18. Slakter MJ, Yow-Wu BW, Suzuki-Slakter NS. *, **, and ***; Statistical nonsense at the .00000 level. *Nurs Res.* 1991;40(4):248–249.

Understanding Human Action through Narrative Expression and Hermeneutic Inquiry

Cynthia Peden Eberhart, PhD, RN
Assistant Professor of Nursing
Sacred Heart University
Fairfield, Connecticut

Barbara B. Pieper, PhD, RN
Associate Professor of Nursing
The Sage Colleges
Troy, New York

As nursing science strives to study human beings within the context of their experiences, this article proposes an alternative, interpretive research approach for the study of human phenomena. A discussion of the relationships between human experience, goal-directed and intentional human action, narrative expression, and hermeneutic inquiry is presented to ground the method in philosophy. The interpretive sequence designed to bring understanding through interpretation of human action fixed in language or narrative text is then outlined. Application of the method is illustrated through two research projects investigating the activity of expert clinical thinking and the activity of current public health nursing practice.

NURSING SCIENCE, concerned with the study of human responses to health and illness within the context of a person's experience, is now challenged to develop alternative paradigms and research methods consistent with an emerging human science movement. In the last decade, there has been an ongoing debate in the nursing and social science literature regarding the limitations of the positivistic paradigm and the traditional research model used by the natural sciences for the study of human beings.[1-6] As a result of this debate, the sciences concerned with the human phenomenon are currently reexamining the philosophies of science with the aim of developing a "human science."

A central concept to the positivistic paradigm used by the natural sciences and to the development of a human science is the notion of causality. Inherent in the traditional positivistic notion of "science" is the assumption of causality, which implies that the universe is ordered and that all events (including human actions/

These studies were supported by research grants from Alpha Omega Chapter, Sigma Theta Tau International, Adelphi University; Sacred Heart University; and Delta Pi Chapter, Sigma Theta Tau International, The Sage Colleges.

41

experiences) are causally determined. In direct contrast to the traditional notion of causality, a "human science" must create an alternative to the causal paradigms given the reality that human beings experience events from a perspective of free choice enabling change and creative expression.[4] The study of human phenomena of concern to the profession of nursing is consistent with an acausal human science paradigm that views human action and experience as intentional and goal directed. Hermeneutic or interpretive methods of inquiry based on the notion of acausal human action offers nursing a research methodology appropriate for the study of human beings within the contexts of their experiences. The purpose of this article is to present a hermeneutic research methodology based on the philosophy of human action created to study two timely topics for the profession of nursing. The methodology designed for the interpretation of human action fixed in narrative text was adapted from the work of Ricoeur[7-13] on narrative, time, and action; Polkinghorne's[4-5] publications on methods of inquiry for the human sciences; and Schon's[6] work on professional knowing in action. The work of Ricoeur, Polkinghorne, and Schon addresses a common philosophical perspective of human action that purports that action, informed by meaning, is intentional and goal directed and occurs within the contexts of human experience. Ricoeur[7-11] and Polkinghorne[5] contend that action can be captured in narrative and interpreted to facilitate an understanding of the activity of human experience. Schon's[6] work links knowing in professional practice to informed human action within situational context. The interpretive sequence based on the philosophical notion of human action was created to study and reveal the meaning of the activity of nursing practice within actual practice situations. A discussion of the relationship between the philosophical concepts of human action, human experience, narrative expression, and hermeneutics is outlined to ground the method in philosophy and provide a background for understanding the interpretive sequence. The hermeneutic approach to inquiry is then discussed within the context of two studies investigating the activity of expert clinical thinking and the activity defining the current practice of public health nursing.

HUMAN ACTION, HUMAN EXPERIENCE, AND THE NATURE OF NARRATIVE EXPRESSION

Human action reflects the realm of the human experience or human existence. Philosophically, the notion of human action has been a topic of historical debate. Polkinghorne[4] contends that human action is one of the subjects that divides the humanities from the physical sciences. The development of a human science paradigm must look toward both the humanities and the sciences as sources of knowledge about human phenomena, and the notion of human action becomes a crossing point for the two perspectives. Although human action is sometimes driven by uncontrolled external forces or accedes to habitual responses, humans have the capacity to deliberate and decide action. This deliberation is acausal and takes place in a realm of meaning. Human action, from the perspective of narrative expression in the human sciences, is viewed as acausal and nondeterministic. The idea of cause in this paradigm is completely changed from physical cause to expressive cause. Human action is seen as more than ordered physical movement. Human science views human action as the result of the human competence to comprehend particular movements as the acts of agents. Human action from this perspective reflects "the physical texture of the embodied agent's meaningful statement, and bodily movement is 'caused' by the meaning to be expressed."[5(p142)] The hermeneutic methodology presented in this article is based on the philosophical premise that human action is both intentional and goal directed.

Ricoeur[12] makes an important connection between narrative (an organizational scheme expressed by language in story form) and action through a discussion of the human being as a speaking subject and acting subject. He points out that human action is rule-governed behavior formed by language and, more specifically, by speech acts in general. Thus, human action is spoken action in that we speak of the semantics of action and designate ourselves as the agents of our actions.

In human science research, narrative represents the primary form by which human experience is made meaningful. Narrative is one of the operations of the realm of meaning.[5,9] The realm of meaning in the philosophical sense is not a thing or a substance but an activity. The goal of studying narrative meaning is to uncover and make explicit the operations that produce its particular meaning, and to consider the implications this meaning has for understanding human experience. Much of the confusion concerning the realm of meaning has been related to an attempt to identify meaning as a substance rather than performance. Polkinghorne[5] describes the realm of meaning by using the metaphor of building a house. He contends that the activity involved in building the house is different from the structure it produces. Thus, the products of the realm of meaning that activity produces include both names of elements and relations among elements. In this view, narrative has a temporal component that portrays the actions of the actor as an active experience. Active experience is explicitly purposive because it is characterized by remembrances and anticipations against a succession of presents. Narrative is the fundamental scheme for linking individual human actions and events into interrelated aspects of an understandable composite. That is, narrative can portray a changing situation in a way that makes meaningful the connections between specific events and actions, thus revealing how and why they occurred over time. Human action in a narrative account is an expression of meaningful existence in that the organization of the action manifests the narrative organization of the human experience.[5,7,9] Action in this sense must be distinguished from other philosophical viewpoints that contend that human action is only physical movement.

Narrative understanding is a type of reasoning that involves the gathering together of events into a plot or organizing theme that relates the significance of events to the theme of the story.[9] In this scheme, the plot configures the events into a whole, and the events are transformed from a mere succession of independent happenings into meaningful happenings that contribute to the whole theme. Polkinghorne[5] contends that the understanding of plot draws on the human ability to understand human activity as actions. The plot can draw on information from the physical sciences, personal beliefs and attitudes, responses to actions, and processes of deliberation in reaching decisions. A plot has the power to articulate and consolidate these complex threads of multiple activities by means of an overlay of subplots.

The connecting concepts used in narrative configuration are based on a definition of human action encompassing the key concepts of goals, motives, and agents. The narrative form organizes individual events through a framework of human purposes and desires, which includes the limits and possibilities posed by the physical, cultural, and personal environments. Action in the narrative scheme is both purposive (intentional) and purposeful (goal related). In narrative, actions occur because of their agents and relate to the intended consequences rather than to antecedent events. Because actions are intentional and goal directed, they portray the experiences of the agent in a way that reflects the meaning of the experience.

Polkinghorne[5] carefully connects the understanding of human action with the temporal order of human existence through Ricoeur's notion of the plot inherent in narrative expression. Ricoeur[9] asserts that central to the notion of a plot is the concept of time. Plot is always controlled by time because human action is pervaded by an awareness of the crucial concepts of time and change. Temporality is a major dimension of human existence. Narrative expression allows for the development of a plot that can explain activities in terms of connections among events. Because narrative is particularly sensitive to the temporal dimension of human existence, it specifically conveys the sequence in which actions and events occur.

Drawing on his belief that the unity of human existence (the will and the body) manifests itself in meaningful human action, Ricoeur[7,9] contends that human action can be interpreted to bring forth a fuller understanding of the human experience. He argues that human action can be captured in text and read to bring forth an understanding of the meaning of action. He asserts that human actions "leave their mark" when the spoken word is converted to the written form. This contributes to the formation of patterns constitutive of human action.

Ricoeur[7] contends that consciousness on the part of the author of action is not always adequate to provide a full understanding. He asserts that interpretation is necessary to disclose the meaning of action (ie, the plot of the narrative), as it is oftentimes masked by its metaphorical dimensions. He states that with simple actions the meaning and the intention overlap. With more complex actions, however, some segments of the text are so remote from the initial simple segments that the intention of the action of the author can only be fully understood through objective interpretation. In this type of objective interpretation, the objective meaning of the action becomes separated from the intentions of the author and produces unintended outcomes. In this view, action is no longer a transaction to which the course of action would still belong, but instead it "constitutes a delineated pattern which has to be interpreted according to its inner connections."[7(p322)] It is important to note here that there can be no prototypic treatment of the relationship between narrative and action as the particularity of each context or situation shapes the actions constructed by the actor. In this view, the sequence of actions are never predictable.

INTERPRETATION AS A STRATEGY TO REVEAL THE MEANING OF HUMAN ACTION INHERENT IN NARRATIVE EXPRESSION

Interpretation of text and/or text analogue is a method of inquiry in the human sciences that strives to understand or to comprehend meaning of the written word. The interpretive method for human science inquiry is derived from the philosophical notion of hermeneutics. Hermeneutics, meaning interpretation, is an ancient Greek word translated as the process of bringing understanding through language.[14] Contemporary hermeneutics is an attempt to make clear, or make sense of, the meaning of a text or text analogue that in one way or another is unclear.[15]

Historically, the act of text interpretation dates back to the ancient Greek culture. The term *hermeneutics* dates back to the 17th century, when it was introduced as a method for biblical and classical literary interpretation to clarify the meaning of text. Dilthey, who maintained that valid representation was a derivative of experienced meaning, introduced the use of hermeneutics as a method of inquiry for the human sciences at the turn of the century. Dilthey credits Schleiermacher with the refinement of hermeneutic technique. Schleiermacher's hermeneutic approach was divided into two parts. The grammatical part of the approach dealt with the meaning of individual words in coexistence with the surrounding text; the psychological approach interpreted the individual and cultural understandings of language.[4] Dilthey and Schleiermacher strived to maintain the objectivity of the empiricist tradition, separating subjective and objective knowledge in a search for the truth.

The subjective versus objective knowledge displayed by the text has been an issue at the core of different philosophical orientations to hermeneutic inquiry in the postpositivist movement. The philosophical hermeneutics of Heidegger and Gadamer reject the notion that objective knowledge can be derived from the text, maintaining that objective knowledge of the author's meaning is not possible. Heidegger and Gadamer were not concerned with the notion of human action as an expression of experience, but with the notion of being as an expression of existence. For Heidegger, interpretation was not a tool for knowledge. Rather, he believed that the very nature of the human realm was interpretive. Heidegger maintained that objective knowledge was not possible, as truth occurs in our engagement of the world. Consistent with Heidegger's critique of objective knowledge and the concept of truth, Gadamer believed that it was not possible to discard one's own cultural context in identifying the author's intentions. Gadamer asserted that the best understanding we could attain is the result of the fusion of our horizon with the text.[4]

Ricoeur asserts that hermeneutics addresses meaningful human action. Ricoeur's hermeneutic project contends that human action can go through a kind of objectification without losing the character of its meaningfulness and, thus, can become the object for a human science.[4] He believes that the investigation of action can lead to an understanding of the realm of human existence. Recognizing both the cultural and unconscious structures of human existence, Ricoeur[7] maintains that the objective meaning of the action is separated from the intention of the author in textual interpretation. This is not to imply that actions of human agents are not both purposeful and purposive, but that many actions of the agent are not clear to the conscious awareness. The notion of the revelatory power of the text allows an objective interpretation capable of reconstructing the inner connections of the complex actions not known to the conscious awareness of the agent.

THE HERMENEUTIC STRATEGY DESIGNED FOR THE INTERPRETATION OF ACTION FIXED IN THE NARRATIVE

The hermeneutic sequence that is outlined below is comprised of two parts that are based on the premise that the action fixed in the narrative manifests the organization of the human experience. The first part of the hermeneutic strategy was designed to reveal the common subplots (names of the elements embedded in the realm of meaning) comprising each plot (the relationship among the elements, representing the activity constitutive of the realm of meaning) noted in the text. This part of the textual interpretation seeks to name and describe the elements common to the activity under investigation. The second part of the interpretive sequence portrays the interrelationship of the subplots and events within situational context to portray the sequence of action known as the plot line and, thus, reveal the activity constitutive of the realm of meaning.

The two-part strategy is presented in an outline comprised of six phases. It is important to note that the abstract process of text interpretation transcends the linearity and concreteness of the sequencing depicted below. The dialogue with the text is for the most part intuited during the reading experience. The sequence of phases that follows is not intended as a formal model of representation but as a flexible guide for textual interpretation.

Phase One

The first phase of the interpretive process concerns using the criteria for sample selection and obtaining the text of the participant's narrative account of the experience through interview. In this phase, the issue of reliability of information arises. Reliability in interpretive research deals with the trustworthiness of the information related in the interviews. Narrative studies do not have formal proofs of reliability.[5] They rely on the details of their procedures for procuring the best possible information, which evokes a sense of trustworthiness for the validity of the information used for study. Some examples of procedures for procuring reliable information include the development of the following:

- criteria for selection of an appropriate sample;
- a structure for capturing the phenomenon for study, including a preliminary research question, additional probes for the interview, and directions for information to be relayed in the interview that are given to the participant prior to the interview;
- pilot studies to test the criteria for selection, questions, and probes for their value and so forth; and
- multiple interviews with participants to clarify information in the text and expand on the original narrative that was collected.

In the two studies investigating the practice of nursing reported below, Schon's[6] conceptualization of *knowing-in-action* and *reflection-in-action* was adapted to collect narrative accounts of nurses' experience. Schon contends that knowing in the practice professions takes the form of intentional, goal-directed action and refers to this kind of knowing as *knowing-in-action*. Knowing-in-action is the ordinary mode of practical knowledge that is expressed as a tacit or unconscious process. He also describes another way of knowing referred to as *reflection-in-action*, in which the tacit knowledge embedded in the practice of knowing-in-action can be made explicit. When practitioners reflect on their actions in practice, talk provides a window into the practical knowledge and reasoning that informed action.[1]

The narrative interview is designed to capture reflection-in-action. Though the interview is unstructured, participants are asked in advance of the interview to reflect on their actions in a specific experience. Additionally, participants are asked to come to the interview prepared to relay the experience in a narrative or "story-like" format by sequencing their actions so that their "story" has a beginning, middle, and end. The role of the researcher during the interview is to seek understanding of the participant's experience through clarification with attention to sequencing of the actions that occurred.

The last activity of Phase 1 of the hermeneutic sequence is the transcription of the audiotaped interviews into a written text. The text is carefully checked against the audiotape to ensure that the language in the text accurately reflects the verbal description of the experience. At this point, the actions reflecting the experience of the participants are considered fixed in the narrative expression of the text. The meaning and intentions of the actions of the participants are considered to be separate, and thus the text is assumed to have revelatory power that permits critical reflection on action apart from the intentions of the participants.

Two examples of the application of Phase 1 of the sequence are cited below in the sections addressing the methodology for obtaining reliable information.

Phase 2

The entire text is read to glean a perspective of the whole. The reading of the whole is focused on intuiting the overarching plot of the actions representing the meaning of the participant's experiences. The temporal sequence and progression of actions, as well as the significance of the actions for the participants, are used as a focus to sense the meaning of the overarching plot.

This reading of the text provides entry into the spiral of interpretation or what is referred to as the *hermeneutic circle*. Dillon[16] describes the reading experience during text interpretation as the ability to be open and engage one's self in the text. The reading experience between reader and text is compared to an encounter between persons: a dialogue that builds shared meaning between them. The overarching meaning of action that sustains the whole text is intuited by listening to all voices in the text, feeling with them, and distilling from them what is considered to be the quintessence of the circle of understanding. At this point, the meaning inherent in the plot is not explicit, but this reading helps to establish an orientation toward the participant's experiences that is reflective of the actions in the narrative.

Phase 3

Following the reading experience of the entire text, each part of the text was reflected upon. The parts of the text are usually represented by each of the individual interviews or experiences of the participant transcribed into narrative form. Each part of the text delineates a sequence of action representing the thoughts of the participant during the experience being discussed. Each individual narrative is read, and the sequence of actions is reconstructed by the researcher in the order in which the actions occurred. The reconstruction of action, supported by the text, is a necessary part of the interpretation because authors do not always relate their stories in an ideal format that reflects the sequence of the actions as they occurred. Reconstructing the temporal sequence of action in each part of the text facilitates an understanding of how the participant understood and experienced the situation.

Phase 4

The reading then continues with the parts of the text (individual narratives) to locate regions of the text that provoke thinking and raise questions. These regions evoke a conversation that strives to understand the implicit meanings of the actions of the participants in light of the events embedded in the text. This understanding directs further conversation with the text, the self, and others (ie, literature, other researchers) to make explicit the meanings represented by the actions in each part of the text. The meanings derived from the parts of the text lead to the development of the subplots of the text. The subplots of the text denote the meaning of the elements that comprise or make up the overall plot.

Phase 5

The now explicit meanings of the parts or subplots of the text are again interpreted in light of each other. Because of the temporal nature of narrative expression, it enables a reconstruction of the plot line or structure (the schematic whole representing the significance of individual actions) of each narrative account of an experience configuring action into a story. The recognition of the meaning of the whole or the plot line unfolds in a dialectic process characterized by the activity of tacking back and forth interactively between the subplots and events in the narrative to give form to the plot. The dialectic between subplots looks for similarities and differences among the actions in light of the events of each narrative to ground an understanding of the whole. This approach reconstructs the temporal order of the subplots and events denoting the actions of the agent(s). The reconstruction of the plot represents the agent's motives and goals (ie, purposive and purposeful action). The understanding of the whole or plot line conveys the relationship of the names of the elements to uncover the activity constitutive of the realm of meaning.

Interpretive ideas and conclusions supported by excerpts from the text in Phases 2 through 5 can be recorded in a journal format so that events and actions can be referenced in light of each other to derive the subplots and then the plot of a narrative. The qualitative analysis computer software program MARTIN developed by Diekelmann, Lam, and Schuster at the School of Nursing, University of Wisconsin/Madison, is also compatible for recording the interpretive analysis (software is available through the School of Nursing, University of Wisconsin/Madison).

Phase 6

The sixth phase of the hermeneutic sequence addresses the issue of validity in interpretive research. The concept of validity for an interpretive study differs from validity defined by methods of the positivistic sciences. Interpretive research strives to place emphasis on the meaning of human existence, not on the use of formal models of representation and their particular type of rigor as a depiction of reality. In interpretive research, the concept of validity means a well-grounded and supportable conclusion. Conclusions of interpretive research are supported by a strong and convincing argument where the researcher presents evidence (excerpts from the text) in support of the conclusions to argue that alternative conclusions are not as likely. The results of interpretive research remain open and subject to change, using scholarly consensus as a test of validity.[5]

To address the issue of validity, the transcribed interviews, as well as the interpretation, should be shared with an interpretive research committee. This approach has been suggested by Diekelmann, Allen, and Tanner[3] and has been found to work well in practice to gain consensus and clarity on the interpretation of the text.

AN INVESTIGATION OF THE ACTIVITY OF EXPERT CLINICAL THINKING IN NURSING

A study by Eberhart[17] portrayed the activity of expert clinical thinking within the context of a nurse's experiences. Specifically, the study addressed the thought processes inherent in the nurse's ability to identify changes in the health status of her clients prior to the appearance of traditional clinical evidence. A review of the empirical and inductive research literature on clinical judgment and intuition revealed a number of perspectives of clinical thinking that were unable to explain the activity of thinking inherent in the nurse's experience of this recognitional ability. The work of Dreyfus and Dreyfus[18] and Schon[6] on judgment and thinking in practice, two pilot studies, and reports of the recognitional ability in the literature led to the development of procedures to procure information for study. The following report will describe the approach used to obtain reliable information for hermeneutic analysis. In addition, an overview of the findings of the study will be presented in light of the two-part hermeneutic analysis based on the notion that the realm of narrative meaning is not a substance but an activity.

THE METHODOLOGY DESIGNED TO OBTAIN RELIABLE INFORMATION FOR ANALYSIS

An investigation of the recognitional ability common to the experience of expert nurses escaped the categories of applied science because the characteristics of this ability remained unintelligible. Thus, there was no context for the application of a specific method to provide direction for inquiry into this problem.

The literature and two pilot studies were used to formulate a methodology to obtain the best possible information for study. A pilot study was conducted to ascertain the problems that would be encountered in a study of tacit knowledge. The first pilot study confirmed that participants were unable to articulate a clear and cogent account of their thought processes, and that the most useful information was communicated in the form of a narrative account of a situation where the nurse experienced the recognitional ability.

The initial pilot study also demonstrated that the ability to relate a clear and cogent account of a situation where the recognitional ability occurred varied from nurse to nurse. Building on these findings, it was evident that another pilot study was necessary to identify one expert nurse who could relate a clear and detailed account of both the situation where the recognitional ability occurred and his or her understanding (in terms of both thought and feelings) of it.

Five expert nurses were selected through peer nomination for inclusion in the second pilot study. Four criteria were noted to be crucial to the selection of participants. The first criterion specified was that the nurse have at least five years of practice experience in critical coronary care nursing. Five years of practice experience in the same specialty area of practice was identified by Benner[2] to be the point where a nurse demonstrates the expert judgment characteristics described by the Dreyfus Model of Skill Acquisition. The specialty area of critical coronary care was also chosen because the recognitional ability has been described frequently in association with thromboembolic events. This association has been identified in accounts of the recognitional ability described in the literature.[2,19–20]

The second criterion used for the selection of participants for the pilot study was a minimum educational level of a baccalaureate degree with a major in nursing. The effects of educational preparation on the abilities to practice nursing are unknown. Thus, a homogeneous educational background at the baccalaureate level was deemed appropriate for inclusion in the study.

The third prerequisite for participation in the study was that all participants should have experienced the recognitional ability within the last year. This criterion was deemed important because of the ability to remember the details of the situation. The last criterion stipulated for participation in the pilot study was that the nurse consistently demonstrate effective problem solving/decision making in nursing practice.

Five participants were nominated, and five expert nurses agreed to participate in the second pilot study. Schon's[6] conceptualization of reflection on knowing-in-action and reflection-in-action were operationalized in this study through audiotaped interviews where the five expert nurses were asked to reflect on their actions in situations where they experienced the recognitional ability. To facilitate this process, each nurse was sent a letter prior to the scheduled interview date with instructions for relating the narrative account of their experiences. These instructions provided structure prior to the interview, which helped the participants to provide a detailed, narrative account of their actions in the situations where they experienced the recognitional ability. Each participant came to the interview prepared to relate at least one situation where she experienced the recognitional ability. The interviews were unstructured, and questions were asked during the interview only for the purpose of clarifying the information that was being related by the participant with attention to the sequence of the actions.

After the five interviews were completed and the transcripts were reviewed, one nurse was clearly able to verbalize her experience during the situation in vivid detail and give a cogent, analytic account of her understanding of her actions during the recognitional ability. The expert nurse was now asked to continue reflection on knowing-in-action over an extended period of time to allow for multiple experiences with the recognitional ability. The audiotaped interviews with the expert nurse were transcribed into a written format. After each interview, the transcript was shared with and reviewed by the nurse. This sharing of information stimulated a dialogue between the nurse and her practice. The dialogue with practice that began to occur, analogous to what Schon[6] called a *reflective conversation* with practice, enabled this nurse consciously to reflect on and reveal more of her actions over the subsequent interviews.

The interviewing process ended after a series of five interviews over a 7-month period of time, when it became clear from reviewing the transcripts that there was no new information about the recognitional ability that the nurse was reporting. The once-unintelligible thought processes (implicit and explicit actions) inherent in the recognitional ability of expert nurses were frozen in a narrative text.

OVERVIEW OF STUDY FINDINGS ILLUSTRATING THE ACTIVITY OF EXPERT CLINICAL THINKING

The text reflecting the narrative expression of action was interpreted by employing the two-part hermeneutic strategy outlined above. The first part of the interpretation emanated from the meaning of the subplots of the text. The interpretation arising from these subplots represented the elements of thought common to the action embodied in the text. Four characteristics of thought common to the nurse's experience of the recognitional ability emerged during the interpretation. Detail of these characteristics illustrated by excerpts from the text are reported elsewhere.[17]

The first characteristic denoted two distinct types of information used by the expert nurse for thinking. The nurse used the theoretical concepts of pathophysiology; physiology; knowledge of scientific principles and nursing and medical research findings; as well as objective, tangible parameters (eg, knowledge of diagnostic and treatment results, medication effects, etc) for thinking. Theoretical concepts provided the nurse with acontextual information necessary to guide practice. The other information used for thinking included unquantifiable, practical, perceptual information (sensory data, maxims,[2] family dynamics, personal likes and dislikes, etc) found only within the context of the unique client situation. This practical, contextual information is the other realm of information that enabled understanding of the whole situation.

The second characteristic describes the process of understanding meaning within situational context. The key characteristic "understanding" describes how the whole picture of the situation is assimilated by comprehending how and why information relates to other information within the context of specific client situations. Understanding the meaning of a patient situation took the form of a dialogue (akin to Aristotle's notion of Phronesis) between acontextual, theoretical information and contextual, practical, perceptual information to recognize constructive as well as destructive possibilities within the client's changing situation.

The third characteristic of expert thinking described the temporal nature of understanding within the changing context of the client's situation. A distinct element of time in terms of past, present, and future informed the nurse's understanding. The implicit meaning of the situation was understood by reference to the past in light of the present situation. However, key to expert clinical thinking is an orientation to the future, informed by attention to the present, and the ability to recollect the past. This characteristic described the nurse's ability to anticipate the possibilities in the situation and put the necessary supports in place to "control" the situation so that the anticipated possibilities were realized.

The final characteristic representative of the nurse's thought processes unfolded the moral, ethical nature of expert thinking in nursing practice. Foundational to the thought processes of the expert nurse was an ethical, moral concern to "do good" for the client. This element of concern pervaded the nurse's thinking as she strived to understand the meaning of the situation, and the same concern informed her future actions once she understood the situation. Specifically, this characteristic describes a process of empathic understanding and advocacy within the ethical, moral realm of thinking. The nurse used a type of empathic understanding to uncover the implicit, personal meaning in a client's situation. This characteristic also describes the concept of advocacy as the translation of the nurse's moral commitment into action to actualize the possibilities for "the good" of the patient.

The second part of the interpretive analysis addresses the connections or relations among elements (or the characteristics of thought) by interpreting the plots in the text reflective of the narrative action within the context of the nurse's experience of the recognitional ability. Although the common characteristics representing the elements of the nurse's thought process are emblematic of the recognitional ability, they portray a static depiction of thinking. A static perspective of the elements of thought cannot illustrate the action-oriented activity of thinking, and thus, the second part of the interpretation was crucial to this study. This study used two narrative accounts of the nurse's experience of the recognitional ability to provide a context for the interpretation of the plot lines. Interpretation of the plot lines illustrated the relations among the events of each narrative and elements of thought (interpreted above) to illustrate the nurse's activity of thinking within the context of her experience of the recognitional ability.

Conclusions from the interpretation of the plot within the context of the two situations from the expert nurse's practice revealed that the activity of thinking inherent in the nurse's experience of the recognitional ability was embodied within the interrelated qualities of understanding and intervention. These qualities were reflective of the nurse's ability to deal effectively with the indeterminate and changing contexts of practice situations.

The text informed us through the interpretation of the nurse's actions reflective of her "intervention" within the context of the two patient situations above that her activity of thinking is a continuous process of understanding. The nurse's understanding is continually informed by a dialectic between the universals (theoretical information) and the particularities (practical, perceptual information) within the context or boundaries of the patient situation. Information is assimilated within the dialectic in the situation for the purpose of comprehending or making sense of the meaning of the situation as a whole. Making sense of or understanding the meaning inherent in each unique situation embodies a temporal component. Understanding meaning within context is dependent on the ability to view the past, in relation to the present, which then molds the direction of future possibilities for thought and action. The actions of the nurse that were interpreted within the context of the patient situations she was engaged in also inform us that her temporal understanding and intervention embraced an interrelated, ethical, moral character concerned with knowing and doing "the good" for the patient. Intervention based on understanding the meaning of the situation embodies the ideal of advocacy. Advocacy in the practice of the expert nurse reflects her professional, moral commitment to learn the meaning of "the good" that informed her "doing of the good" for each patient in her care.

The textual analysis of the plot lines of the two exemplars informed the findings of this study that, although there are common elements representative of expert thinking, there can be no common framework or structure to guide expert thinking in the indeterminate situations encountered in nursing practice. The narrative action in the text informs us that expert clinical thinking in nursing is a practical rationality, reflective of the capacity to understand human existence that is rich and full of meaning and is experienced only within context. No rule-governed or logically organized system of rules (in the empirical sense) to guide thinking can capture the expression of such meaning, as no two situations were alike.

AN INVESTIGATION TO DEFINE THE ACTIVITY OF CONTEMPORARY PUBLIC HEALTH NURSING PRACTICE

Pieper[21] conducted a study to investigate the activity of public health nursing practice as a basis for defining the current state of this nursing specialty. A review of the literature revealed that while the definition and function of this specialty practice remains controversial, there is a paucity of research in the area. Additionally, the study of the experience of the staff public health nurse was absent. An assumption of the study was that the context of practice is constantly shaping the function and definition of public health nursing. The work of Schon[6] was used to conceptualize practice as arena in which the exchange of theory and action come together in the development of tacit or practical knowledge that may reveal the concepts, interventions, roles, and values of the practitioner that develop over time and allow them to function effectively in their work. Though tacit, this knowledge is expressed in skilled action and judgment. The challenge for the study was threefold: (1) to identify practitioners who had developed practical knowledge, (2) to capture tacit knowledge expressed through action, and (3) to reveal the meaning of the activity of practice as a basis for defining the current specialty of public health nursing. Again, as there was no specific method to provide guidance for a study of this nature, an extensive literature review provided the background for methodological direction.

OBTAINING RELIABLE INFORMATION FOR ANALYSIS

Because of the diversity of public health/community health nursing practice, official public health agencies were selected as a beginning point for data collection because of their historic and legal obligations to the community. To maximize the variety of community settings and the variation of information,[22] three agencies representing inner-city, urban-suburban, and rural areas were selected. Potential study participants were identified from the pool of staff public health nurses in the selected agencies. The staff level of practice was selected because these nurses conduct the day-to-day activities of practice. From this participant pool, peer nomination was used, based on developed criteria to identify a nurse whose practice had reached an expert level of practice,[2] thus signaling the use of tacit knowledge. The criteria for peer nomination was developed from the literature and included a minimum of 3 to 5 years of public health nursing practice.[2,23] Being able to make a difference in patient outcome by demonstrating an intuitive grasp of clinical situations and operating from a deep understanding of the total situation were also used as criteria.[2] In addition, a baccalaureate in nursing was required to ensure an educational background in public health nursing.

The most frequently nominated nurses from each agency were contacted by the researcher, and further study participation criteria were explored with them. The nurses had to be able to articulate in rich detail two or three narrative accounts from their practice within the last year that exemplified for them public health nursing practice. While all the nurses felt they could provide rich, detailed stories, this could only be verified by the researcher during the interview itself and by review of the transcripts.

Before the audiotaped interview with the researcher, participants were asked to consider in advance the practice situations they chose to relate. This was done to allow the participant time to select carefully situations that reflected the current practice of public health nursing. Instructions were mailed to the participants to assist them in considering the type of detail to include in their narrative accounts from practice. This included the details of what the context of the event was from the practitioner's point of view, what happened, what the practitioner was thinking at the time, what the concerns were, and what their feelings were during and after an incident.[2,6] Each interview was audiotaped and lasted approximately 2 to 3 hours.

Each nurse was interviewed once, and two to three situations were collected per nurse. A total of eight narratives from practice were collected. Interviews were transcribed into written text and were reviewed by the researcher for the variety of practice problems and nursing roles reported by the participants. Collection of the text stopped at this point because redundancy of information was achieved.[22] The actions of the nurses now captured in written text provided an account of contemporary public health nursing practice that could be reflected on and interpreted to reveal the meaning of practice, and thus the contemporary definition of public health nursing.

OVERVIEW OF STUDY FINDINGS ILLUSTRATING THE ACTIVITY OF CONTEMPORARY PUBLIC HEALTH NURSING PRACTICE

Using the hermeneutic strategy described, each individual narrative was interpreted to reveal the meaning of the subplots of the text. Five characteristics of practice emerged during this phase of interpretation. These characteristics, supported by narratives, represent the boundaries or elements of public health nursing practice. Again, details of the findings of this study are reported elsewhere.[21]

Protecting the vulnerable in communities, as a subplot, portrays the nurses' historic and ongoing work of reaching out and providing care to individuals and families in sickness and in health. The actions of the nurses depict the special skills involved in reaching out to those in need as well as the nurses' knowledge and use of informal community networks to identify patients, obtain information, and shape patient needs and agency purpose to secure care for clients. The narratives reveal risk taking, moral dilemmas, and backup to other services in order to create positive outcomes for clients.

The use of caring practices such as frequent visiting, particularly in the absence of needed resources and services, is another element of practice identified from the narratives. Caring practices are not well discussed in this specialty arena. Yet these nurses move beyond traditional intervention strategies to help patients/families maintain their daily concerns. Also, finding the right level of involvement within each client context is a skill well depicted.

Creating a healing environment was a third element of practice identified in the study. Nurses understood clients' problems in a holistic framework and worked to achieve health using a notion of higher integration, which included reintegration into community life. Frequently, these nurses could achieve patient goals beyond what other practitioners could achieve because they believed in creating a context where patients could heal themselves.

Understanding freedom as an element of practice illustrates the skills public health nurses have developed to understand the context of a person's life to design goals and interventions that make sense for each unique caregiving situation. Nurses use the terms *going with the flow* and *working within reality* to describe their open stance with situations as they allow situations to unfold over time and determine the contextual goals for each client. These narratives transform our static notion of providing resources and portray a relational knowing used to facilitate a client's use of outside help.

Commitment was the last element of practice identified. Many of the narratives were overwhelming stories of violence, drug addiction, or abuse where the outcomes were uncertain, but the nurses recognized the need for long-term involvement. They believed there were possibilities in these very harsh situations even though accomplishing any goal may seem remote to an outsider. The flexibility of the public agency enabled these nurses to visit clients in light of uncertain outcomes, and the text revealed a sense of obligation on the part of the nurse to visit these clients in need.

The second phase of the interpretive analysis moved to understanding the relations or connections among the elements or subplots of practice to make explicit the plot revealing the meaning of the activity of practice. Polkinghorne[5] states that the primary dimension of human activity is time; that is, the sequence in which the elements of action configure in a particular context can be decisive in defining what the activity is. Through reflection on the subplots in relation to the overall plot, it was noted that each of the subplots appeared in all the narratives, but in a slightly different configuration. For example, sometimes caring practices were the goal of care. In another narrative, caring practices were the means to accomplish a different goal. Interpreting the recurrence of all the elements of practice in different sequences in new contexts revealed the meaning of the activity of practice. Public health nurse practice is context dependent and cannot be quantified or identified beyond the essential elements representing the boundaries of practice. Performance is based on situational appreciation in which the means and ends are interactively considered within a situation. The rationality that guides activity is practical—understanding within a context in which the elements of practice are creatively reconfigured anew by the nurse in light of each different situation to solve effectively the problems of his or her patients. The text reveals that there can never be a static, linear definition of practice. Rather, practice can only be identified by its boundaries or elements in which public health nurses use the creative art of their practical rationality to respond to the uniqueness of each client context.

•   •   •

As human disciplines, such as nursing, strive to develop tools that provide a fuller appreciation of human lives, the realm of meaning challenges us to recognize the multiple layers of human experience. Because the realm of human meaning is contextual, and human existence is characterized by multiple realities, human science researchers need to create methodologies appropriate to the study of specific human phenomena. Thus, multiple research methodologies become necessary in the development of a human science paradigm.

One commonality in the development of a human science is the use of linguistic data reflective of the realm of meaning. Narrative is one linguistic form that attends to the temporal dimension of human existence and organizes human experience in a way that gives significance to the events in human lives and form to the actions that are taken in relation to such events. This article has presented a hermeneutic research methodology based on the philosophical relationship between human action and narrative expression and the premise that the realm of human meaning is an activity with a temporal dimension. This hermeneutic methodology provides nursing science with another direction for working with linguistic data to uncover knowledge relative to the meaning of human existence.

REFERENCES

1. Argyris C, Putnam R, Smith D. *Action Science.* San Francisco, Calif: Jossey-Bass; 1985.
2. Benner P. *From Novice to Expert Excellence and Power in Clinical Nursing Practice.* Menlo Park, Calif: Addison-Wesley; 1984.
3. Diekelmann N, Allen D, Tanner C. *The NLN Criteria for Appraisal of Baccalaureate Programs: A Critical Hermeneutic Analysis.* New York, NY: NLN Press; 1989. Publication 15-2253.
4. Polkinghorne D. *Methodology for the Human Sciences.* Albany, NY: State University of New York Press; 1983.
5. Polkinghorne D. *Narrative Knowing and the Human Sciences.* Albany, NY: State University of New York Press; 1988.
6. Schon D. *The Reflective Practitioner.* New York, NY: Basic Books; 1983.
7. Ricoeur P. The model of the text: meaningful action considered as a text. In Dahlmar FR, McCarthy TA, eds. *Understanding and Social Inquiry.* Notre Dame, Ind: The University of Notre Dame Press; 1977.
8. Ricoeur P. The human experience of time and narrative. *Research in Phenomenology.* 1979;9:17–34.

9. Ricoeur P; McLaughlin K, Pellauer D, trans. *Time and Narrative*. Chicago, Ill: University of Chicago Press; 1984; I.

10. Ricoeur P; McLaughlin K, Pellauer D, trans. *Time and Narrative*. Chicago, Ill: University of Chicago Press; 1985; II.

11. Ricoeur P; McLaughlin K, Pellauer D, trans. *Time and Narrative*. Chicago, Ill: University of Chicago Press; 1988; III.

12. Ricoeur P. The human being as the subject matter of philosophy. *Philosophy and Social Criticism*. 1988;14:203–215.

13. Ricoeur P. Narrative identity. *Philosophy Today*. 1991;35(1):73–81.

14. Palmer RE. *Hermeneutics*. Evanston, Ill: Northwestern University Press; 1969.

15. Taylor C. Interpretation and the science of man. *Review of Metaphysics*. 1971;25:1–51.

16. Dillon D. The encounter between reader and text. *Phenomenology - Pedagogy*. 1983;1:93–95.

17. Eberhart CP. *A Portrait of Clinical Thinking in Indeterminate Practice Situations: A Study of Expert Nursing Practice*. Garden City, NY: Adelphi University; 1992. Dissertation.

18. Dreyfus HL, Dreyfus SE. *Mind Over Machine: The Power of Human Intuition and Expertise in the Era of the Computer*. New York, NY: Free Press; 1986.

19. Pyles SH, Stern PN. Discovery of nursing gestalt in critical care nursing: the importance of the gray gorilla syndrome. *Image: The Journal of Nursing Scholarship*. 1983;15:51–57.

20. Smith S. An analysis of the phenomenon of deterioration in the critical ill. *Image: The Journal of Nursing Scholarship*. 1988;20:12–15.

21. Pieper B. Toward a New Definition of Public Health Nursing: An Interpretive Study. Garden City, NY: Adelphi University; 1992. Dissertation.

22. Lincoln VS, Guba EG. *Naturalistic Inquiry*. Newbury Park, Calif: Sage; 1985.

23. Brykczynski K. An interpretive study describing the clinical judgement of nurse practitioners. *Scholarly Inquiry for Nursing Practice*. 1989;3(2):75–104.

Inquiry into Nursing As Textually Mediated Discourse

Julianne Cheek, PhD
Senior Lecturer
Research Fellow, Faculty of Nursing

Trudy Rudge, RN, RPN, BA
Doctoral Candidate
Lecturer, Faculty of Nursing,
University of South Australia
Underdale, South Australia, Australia

Nursing has yet to realize the full potential afforded by the method of inquiry known as discourse analysis. This article outlines the basic tenets of discourse analysis as a method of inquiry into nursing knowledge and practice. It uses a report of a study of the discourse of case notes to illustrate the applicability of this approach to the nursing arena. Finally, the article moves on to discuss the possibilities and limitations of this mode of inquiry for the ongoing generation and critique of nursing knowledge.

DISCOURSE ANALYSIS is an interdisciplinary approach to inquiry that uses the techniques from many disciplines, including cognitive psychology, sociolinguistics, and literary and cultural studies in order to explore the way in which texts both construct, and are constructed by, versions of social reality. It is important to note that because discourse analysis does draw on this variety of perspectives, there have been a number of ways in which the term *discourse analysis* has been used.[1] However, the approach is underpinned by the notion of language as a meaning-constituting system that is both historically and socially situated.

In such a mode of inquiry, discourse as "a system of statements which cohere around common meanings and values . . . [that] are a product of powers and practices, rather than an individual's sets of ideas"[2(p231)] is conceived of not only as a linguistic construction but as a particular way of talking and thinking about reality; "a domain of language use that is unified by common assumptions."[3(p7)] At any point in time, various discourses or discursive frameworks may coexist in a given social context. These discourses may complement or oppose each other.

An important assumption that underpins discourse analysis as a form of inquiry is that language cannot be considered as transparent or value-free. Even the language that we take to be the most natural—that is, the spoken word, or talk—does not "have" universal meaning but is assigned particular meanings by both speakers and listeners according to the situation in which language is being used.[1] Further, texts not only represent and reflect a certain version of reality, they also play a part in the very construction and maintenance of that reality itself. There is a dynamic relationship, or reflexivity, between the text and the context in which the text is produced, which in turn is then reproduced by the text. As we have stated previously, this challenges the notion that texts are neutral and value-free receptacles or conveyors of information.

Hence, the analysis of text and talk that is possible by using discourse analysis is not, and should not be, limited to the micro level of analysis. When it is grounded in critical and postmodern understandings of the world and reality, discourse analysis involves more than merely analyzing the content of texts for the way in which they have been structured in terms of syntax, semantics, and so forth. Rather, discourse analysis is concerned with the way in which texts themselves have been constructed in terms of their social and historical "situatedness." Indeed, Van Dijk concludes that a limitation of some forms of discourse analysis is that they "paid more attention to the intricacies of the structures or strategies of text and talk itself than to the conditioning or conditional structures and processes of the social contexts of their actual use."[4(p7)]

Discourse analysis thus links an analysis of the cognitive elements of belief acquisition with the social structures that express, constitute, and reproduce a textual reality.[4] Thus, as Lupton[5] points out, discourse analysis differs from traditional modes of content analysis, semiotic studies and ethnomethodologies in that it seeks to move the analysis into the realm of the social relations that reflect cultural hegemonic influences. In such an analysis, "text is not a dependent variable, or an illustration of another point, but an example of the data itself."[5(p146)]

INQUIRY INTO NURSING AS TEXTUALLY MEDIATED REALITY

As a form of inquiry, discourse analysis has much to offer analyses of nursing, nursing practice, and nursing knowledge. However, the application of discourse analysis as an approach to inquiry in nursing and the health sciences is relatively undeveloped. There is no doubt that nursing is a discipline that is constituted discursively. As such, discourse analysis can "show how such contextualised discourse may express, describe, enact, legitimate and reproduce more global levels of . . . [nursing] structure and culture."[4(p9)]

Nursing is an act that can be characterized as both text and talk. Discourse analysis is therefore able to deal, from an integrated, theoretical perspective, with these two seemingly different practices as they are embedded within nursing. Discourse analysis can provide valuable insights into how nurses interact with clients in the everyday world of nursing interactions. The fields of communication studies and conversation analysis, which are underpinned by perspectives similar to those of ethnomethodology, have given valuable insights into the structuring of conversations, one of which can be the talk between clients and nurses.[6] Such analysis of the therapeutic encounter can provide insights into not only how the encounter is structured but how such encounters are framed by the belief systems of nursing. Therefore, it is important that such analysis looks at both the content of such conversations *and* the texture of such talk. Discourse analysis provides insights into form and content in that it enables an analysis that makes explicit how such talk both constitutes and reproduces the social act of nursing.[7]

Such an exploration draws on the type of inquiry Smith[8] used to analyze femininity as textually mediated discourse. She argued that the focus of the textual analysis should move from the "organisation of themes and methods of thought to the textual organisation of relations and structures."[8(p162)] Such a refocusing recognizes that there is a dynamic relationship between the nursing text itself and the social relations that shaped the text in the first instance and that contribute to the ongoing interpretation of the text. Thus, "the printed image is interpreted by doctrines of . . . [nursing], and doctrines of . . . [nursing] are inscribed in printed images."[8(pp170–171)] In such a mode of inquiry, meanings as they occur in the text are the product of dominant discourses that permeate those texts. Not only do powerful discursive frameworks provide meaning for the text, they actually frame the text itself in the first place. Meanings are not operating in a social vacuum.

Consequently, the analysis of textual discourse cannot confine itself only to matters of style, subject matter, and manner of communication. Rather, it must embed the textual in the contextual by situating the nursing text in the set of social relations that have shaped that text. To explore the reality of nursing as textually mediated is to view nursing as a complex of relations both vested in texts and mediated by them. The importance of such a conception for methods of inquiry is that "inquiry, therefore, has to begin with the ordinary and unanalysed ways in which we know what we are talking about when we use the concept [nursing] . . . that knowledge is grounded in a complex of actual practices and relations (among them that knowledge itself). These are the original ground from which the instances collected by the concept are constructed. Our method of inquiry explores the complex forming that original ground."[8(p165)]

The discussion now turns to consider an example of the analysis of nursing texts, namely the case notes of two clients, using discourse analysis as a method of inquiry.

CASE NOTES AS TEXTUALLY MEDIATED DISCOURSE

As emphasized in the previous discussion, discourse analysis develops analyses that are capable of interrogating texts generated in many settings. In the research discussed in this article, the authors analyzed the construction of case notes from a rehabilitation setting. The case notes were selected at random from those of patients admitted to the setting. Specifically, the study explored the construction of the case notes of two individuals. For this analysis, we have called the two individuals, whose case notes we have analyzed here, Mr H and Mrs W. Mr H is a 64-year-old man who had suffered a debilitating stroke, and Mrs W is a 79-year-old woman whom her notes describe as "a *fall* who had fractured her femur" (our emphasis). The rehabilitation setting was chosen because of the longer length of stay of individuals in this setting (approximately 4 months for each individual), and because of the myriad inputs from a variety of health professionals in this type of care. Consequently, the amount of documentation developed was extensive in both depth and breadth.

Discourse analysis enabled the webs of documentation developed to be deconstructed and examined in the context of the social relations that determined both the form and the content of the notes. For example, in analyzing the style of communication in the case notes, it was apparent that the discursive frameworks of science and medicine shaped the form of the notes. Both Mrs W and Mr H were represented by chemical notations, blood count results, and other forms of symbols. The language used was objective in tone and depersonalized. The documentation of other health professionals follows the medical form of examination or assessment, plans, prescribed actions, and timelines for evaluation. The use of highly specialized and technical language by the medical staff effectively denies access to the uninitiated, including the individual who is textually constructed in the notes.

The study aimed to develop what Denzin[9] has termed "thick description" in order to allow for "thick interpretation." He suggests that "thick interpretation interprets the interpretations that are present in recorded experience."[9(p159)] It should be noted that from this form of analysis, the intention is not to develop laws or methods of prediction, but instead to map the world of meaning inherent in the textual record of the notes. As Geertz[10] suggests, this allows for the mapping of the terrain as evident from the fine detail of the notes, rather than the mapping of continents of meaning espoused in more global forms of theorizing. Furthermore, such analysis is interpretive rather than predictive in its outcomes. In part, the study drew on the work of Parker and Gardner,[11] who analyzed the text of the progress notes of a single patient. However, it attempted to move on from Parker and Gardner's analysis, in that it was not just an analysis of the text itself but of the text as it is embedded within the contextual structures in which it was produced and which the resultant text plays a part in maintaining.

READING THE CASE NOTES

Both sets of notes began with the documentation of a "rite of admission" into first the acute setting and then the rehabilitation setting. As Foucault[12] has identified, rituals surround admission into institutions such as hospitals. Through such rituals, or examinations, the power relations implicit in the assessment processes are masked from the individual undergoing such assessment. Furthermore, Foucault argued, in this process the individual becomes an object of study, or a case, and this is evidenced by Mrs W's categorization as a "fall."

On analysis of the admission processes in the documentation, evidence of such a rite comprised the report of the ambulance officers who had dealt with both individuals, the computer-generated *pro forma* in the accident and emergency section, and the medical report that verified the condition of the client and enabled the rite of admission to conclude when the legitimacy and "truth" of the individual's condition had been established by both the acceptance of admission into the hospital and the diagnosis by the admitting doctor. In Mrs W's notes, she is represented by the notation - "D: # R) NOF"; in Mr H's notes - "D: R) CVA."

The documentation then assigned each individual an identity number and a specialist team who would assume the responsibility for their care. At this point, each individual's consent to treatment was recorded by their signature and witnessed by the admitting medical officer. It is of interest here that there is no record of information given, or for that matter requested, in the process of obtaining such consent. This was also the first time, in either set of notes, that the voice or presence of the individual undergoing the rite was apparent. The study then followed the development of the web of documentation that was developed around these individuals from the time that they were admitted to the rehabilitation setting to their point of discharge.

The form of each entry was examined, that is, whether it was typed, handwritten, or computer generated. Notice was taken of whether entries were signed or not, how authorship of the various entries was identified (if at all), and how the entries were arranged spatially. This was done to begin to identify differences in spatial arrangements; the authority of form, as evident by the computer-generated, demographic information collected on each patient; the medical profession's disregard for the legal requirements of notation, as evident by the out-of-sequence, glued-in notes, typed from dictaphones used by registrars during ward rounds; or the signalling of particular expertise by designation, as evident by "headings" such as "Medical," "Nursing," and "Speech Pathology" stamped into the notes before entries from each of these groups.

Further, the content of the entries was examined in terms of the ways in which the events of the admissions were reported on: similarities and differences between the various reporting "voices," and the types of language used. In the first description of Mrs W in the nursing notes ("a *fall* who had fractured her femur"), Mrs W is conflated with the accident that has brought about her admission. *She* is the result of an event and has become objectified by such categorization.

The personal experience and knowledge of the patient has little part to play in the objective, scientific style of reporting. The notes are stamped with the epistemic authority of the rational, scientific voice of medicine. The reality that comes to be the individual in the rehabilitation setting is a constructed one, and the text of the case notes both constructs and is in turn constructed by this reality. Thus, the notes record that Mrs W "*claims* she cant [sic] see out of her right eye" (our emphasis). Until it can be verified objectively and in the scientific/medical voice, it is a debatable point as to whether or not Mrs W can or cannot see. Her personal knowing, her reality, is effectively discounted and instead takes on that which is being textually mediated for her. In fact, the personal experience and knowledge of the individual concerned is systematically expunged from the case notes.

Further, such is the dominance of the authoritarian tone of medical discourse that other health professionals mimic the reporting style of the physicians. The nursing entries in the documentation highlight this. Consider the type of language used in Mrs W's notes when she had climbed out of bed to use a commode but had been incontinent on the floor: "Nurse passing her room heard scraping furniture and investigated the noises, *rescued* the patient and *reprimanded* her . . . the client was *reminded* that . . ." (our emphasis). Similar language can be found in Mr H's notes following an incident that results in him falling: "Patient *instructed* to ring bell if he wants anything and not to get out of the bed unaided. Seems *compliant* with order" (signed by a student nurse; our emphasis). It is not that the safety of clients is not important but that there is a conspicuous absence in the nursing documentation of the clients' emotional and personal experience of the reality being imposed on them. The tone of the nursing entries suggests that each individual must accept the reality that has been constructed for him or her and that not to do so is unjustified. The power of one form of discourse to shape and constrain the other is very evident in that nurses conform to supposedly objective, scientific dogma in both the form and the content of their documentation. In so doing, nurses eliminate the personal, subjective experience of both the client and themselves from the notes.

Rodgers[13] notes that dogma, "the unquestioning adherence to authority and tradition"[13(p177)] works against innovation, curiosity, and new ways of knowing and viewing the world. In conforming to scientific and legalistic dogma as to the appropriate matter and style for nursing notes, the voice of the nurse is effectively silenced. The nurses did not report the day as they experienced it but rather used the language of other, more powerful discourses.[11,14] The text is thus interpreted by doctrines of nursing, and doctrines of nursing in turn are enshrined in the text itself. Consequently "rather than normative organisation being expressed in the textually mediated discourse, normative organisation is its accomplishment."[8(p176)]

Pearson and Baker's[15] study of Phaneuf's Nursing Audit, which is a tool for assessing the quality of nursing documentation, bears out these assertions. They write the following with respect to the nursing documentation that they examined: "nursing judgements are not valued by either the nurse[s] who make them or their peers. If the indications of this study are valid, this must also apply to the tasks that they carry out . . . most of what nurses write is data which are valued by medical, paramedical and administrative staff. They [nurses] are not capturing their own effectiveness in their documentation."[15(p47)]

The following entry in the case notes highlights the truth of Pearson and Baker's assertions. The speech therapist working with Mr H recorded in the notes that "*ward staff* have described his wife's considerable emotional difficulties, and it is clear that a certain lack of rapport currently exists between them" (our emphasis). Yet the nursing ward staff do not document this information and concern but instead share this information informally, leaving it to the other health professionals to report in the notes. Hence, they fail to capture their own effectiveness in the textual record, and important information held by nursing staff is recorded incidentally via a speech therapist. Instead, nurses continue to report the more trivial aspects of their caring role, such as "Mr H watched TV till 2400 hrs" in the quest to "objectify" their reporting.

Although it has not been possible to report on this study in its entirety, the illustrations given highlight the potential afforded by discourse analysis to explicate aspects of nursing practice in both its textual and wider contextual spheres. There is a place for scientific/medical discourse in the health arena and the client's case notes; however, the issue is that it should not be used to exclude and silence other equally valid discourses.

LIMITATIONS AND POSSIBILITIES OF DISCOURSE ANALYSIS

Having discussed the potential and applicability of this mode of inquiry for the explication of aspects of nursing practice, we would be remiss in not pausing to consider some of the limitations of this approach. Discourse analysis has developed from a variety of perspectives, all of which have left their own imprint on its form and content. Although this is one of the strengths of discourse analysis, it can also be one of its limitations. Most notably, if the various origins of discourse analysis in their turn become suppressed or concealed, the resultant analyses can be flawed by an inadequate examination of the very context of discourse analysis itself.

Furthermore, if discourse analysis remains focused only on micro levels of analysis, the resultant analyses will not confront the political and social realities that frame the discourse. Similarly, if exploration of power and power relations is not included in the examination of communications that occur in institutional settings, the effect of the hierarchical power relations on such communications remains unconsidered in the subsequent analysis.[1,7] In reaction to these sorts of concerns, contemporary developments in discourse analysis are fostering an interdisciplinary debate that will strengthen and add vigor to its theoretical framework. Hence, as discourse analysis continues to move into an interdisciplinary framework, the importance of the social and power relations that structure and are embedded in text and talk is being brought to the fore. Even those areas that previously focused on the micro levels of analysis are seeking to enter into debate with, and incorporate insights from, those forms of analysis that focus on the macro levels of analysis.[7] Although these links between the macro and micro perspectives are important in order that discourse analysis can provide rigorous forms of analysis, these links do not as yet present a coherent perspective. This, Van Dijk[1] considers, is the project of discourse analysis in the 1990s.

These current developments in discourse analysis present unique possibilities for inquiry into nursing. To provide a rigorous investigation of text and talk as it relates to nursing, both text and context require explicit and systematic analysis. Hiraki,[16] in her critical hermeneutic study of textbooks, has begun this project with an analysis of the beginning texts used in undergraduate education programs.

A discourse analysis that cogently links the social and textual construction of reality is one that allows the acknowledgment of ideological representations embedded in such texts. At the same time, it allows an understanding of the power that textual reality has to present "factual" reality in such a way as "to captivate a reader in its content, [*and simultaneously*] . . . achieve constitutive innocence."[17(p2)] It is not just that the textbooks *represent* nursing as a process that is technical in its intent, but that these practices are *constituted* by the taken-for-granted nature of the authority embedded in both the content *and* form of such texts. A textbook has certain connotations assigned to it by society. As such, these texts have the weight (and some are very weighty indeed) of the audience's interpretation of the text's passive voice as the very foundation of a work that will "let the facts speak for themselves."[17(p7)] Hence, it is important not to conceive of the audience of such nursing textbooks as passive recipients of the material presented by the text. The audience of such textbooks is alert to the authoritative voice of this form of communication and is being prepared to accept the reality within such texts as a guide for practice and discourse.

While textbooks are an obvious source of ideological hegemony in nursing, other forms of documentation textually mediate nursing and its practices. In a similar vein to the text of textbooks, nursing documentation is permeated with practices of factual and objective reporting. Analysis of medical case notes indicates that both the form of the documentation and the tone of the content remain influenced by the voice of medical science. Why is this so? Discourse analysis shows that in documenting nursing care in these notes, nurses continue to mediate the social reality of nursing through a form of documentation that expunges the personal experience of the patient and the effectiveness of nursing care. Such objective documentary reality closes out the presentation of the social reality of nursing care and the social reality of the patient. The outcome of this is that the voice of both the patient and the nurse are silenced in the notes. This allows the domination of medical science to be reproduced in the very area in which the nursing voice could, and should, be heard.

•   •   •

Through discourse analysis, textually constructed reality is robbed of its "innocence" as a "passive conveyor" or "receptacle of knowledge." Instead, such textual constructions of reality are able to be exposed as conditioning of, and conditional on, social structures.

As an innovative mode of inquiry, discourse analysis offers researchers a way in which to explore the textually mediated reality of nursing. If nurses are to understand the production of nursing knowledge, and its impact on the everyday reality of nursing practice, researchers cannot ignore the significance of this form of analysis for such understanding.

Furthermore, textual analysis can make explicit how the social and textual realities of nursing are not separate. With discourse analysis, it is possible to proceed from the analysis of nursing practice, to the texts that mediate it, to the knowledge that is represented in the context and texts of such practices or vice versa.

Such research will not gloss over the complexities of such interactions, but provide valuable insights into the relationships between power, knowledge, and nursing practice. The insights provided by the analysis of the discourse of medical case notes is indicative of this.

As ideological analysis is central to this process, it is our belief that discourse analysis allows for the development of counter-ideological standpoints that, through critique of the dominant discourses of nursing, may potentially open up alternative configurations for both the textual and social reality that is nursing.

REFERENCES

1. Van Dijk TA. The future of the field: discourse analysis in the 1990's. *Text.* 1990;10(1/2):133–156.
2. Hollway W. Heterosexual sex: power and desire for the other. In: Cartledge S, Ryann J, eds. *Sex and Love: New Thoughts on Old Contradictions.* London, England: Women's Press; 1983.
3. Abercrombie N, Hill S, Turner B. *Dictionary of Sociology.* 2nd ed. London, England: Penguin; 1988.
4. Van Dijk TA. Discourse & society: a new journal for a new research process. *Discourse and Society.* 1990;1(1):5–16.
5. Lupton D. Discourse analysis: a new methodology for understanding the ideologies of health and illness. *Aust J Public Health.* 1992;16(2):145–150.
6. Fisher SA. Discourse of the social: medical talk/power talk/oppositional talk? *Discourse and Society.* 1991;2(2):157–182.
7. Fairclough N. Discourse and text: linguistic and intertextual analysis within discourse analysis. *Discourse and Society.* 1992;3(2):193–217.
8. Smith D. *Texts, Facts and Femininity.* London, England: Routledge; 1990.
9. Denzin NK. *The Research Act.* Chicago, Ill: Aldine; 1989.
10. Geertz C. *The Interpretation of Cultures: Selected Essays.* New York, NY: Basic Books; 1973.
11. Parker J, Gardner G. The silence and the silencing of the nurse's voice: a reading of patient progress notes. *Aust J Adv Nurs.* 1992;9(2):3–9.
12. Foucault M. *Discipline and Punish.* London, England: Tavistock; 1977.
13. Rodgers BL. Deconstructing the dogma in nursing knowledge and practice. *Image.* 1991;23(3):177–181.
14. Cheek J, Rudge T. Deconstructing the discourse of case notes. Presented at The Australian Sociological Association Conference; December 1992; Adelaide, Australia.
15. Pearson A, Baker B. A comparison of quality care using Phaneuf's nursing audit. *Aust Clin Rev.* 1992;12:41–48.
16. Hiraki A. Tradition, rationality, and power in introductory nursing textbooks: a critical hermeneutics study. *ANS.* 1992;14(3):1–12.
17. Green BS. *Knowing the Poor.* London, England: Routledge & Kegan Paul; 1983.

A Heideggerian Response to Blumer's Symbolic Interactionism

Daphne Stannard, RN, MS, CCRN
Doctoral Student
School of Nursing
University of California, San Francisco
San Francisco, California

At first blush, Chicago school symbolic interactionism (SI) closely resembles Heidegger's hermeneutic phenomenology. Both perspectives were influenced by Edmund Husserl, and both seek to understand human beings in their lived experiences. Additionally, both perspectives have similar methodologic considerations. This article elucidates Blumer's three major premises of SI, examines them from a Heideggerian perspective, and discusses the methodologic implications of both perspectives.

SYMBOLIC INTERACTIONISM (SI), as a theoretical perspective, has a wide following and has been extensively applied to research conducted in the fields of sociology, nursing, and psychology, to name only a few. Confusion can result, however, when SI is referred to in general terms, as there are three recognized schools of thought within this perspective: the (1) Chicago, (2) Iowa, and (3) Minnesota schools. This article examines the Chicago school, as represented by Herbert Blumer, who acceded to the intellectual leadership of the school after the father of SI, George Herbert Mead, died in 1931.[1]

Phenomenology is another broad, theoretical perspective encompassing several different schools of thought, all referred to in general terms as phenomenological perspectives. Edmund Husserl, who is considered to be the father of phenomenology, is known for his work in transcendental phenomenology.[2] Jean-Paul Sartre is thought of as an existential phenomenologist, and Martin Heidegger, a student of Husserl's, created his own branch known as *hermeneutic phenomenology.*

At first blush, Chicago school SI, under the leadership of Blumer, resembles Heidegger's hermeneutic phenomenology. Both perspectives were strongly influenced by Husserl, and both seek to understand human beings in their lived experiences. In addition, they have similar methodologic considerations. There are some crucial differences, however, that merit attention. The purpose of this article is to elucidate Blumer's three major premises of SI, to examine them from a Heideggerian perspective, and to discuss the methodological implications for both theoretical perspectives.

THE THREE PREMISES OF SI

Blumer[3] claims that SI rests on three premises. The first premise is that human beings act toward objects on the basis of the meanings that the objects have for them. According to Blumer, a human being is an organism that not only responds to the action of another without interpreting that action (nonsymbolic interaction) but also makes indications to others and interprets their indications.

Central to this ability is the notion that human beings have selves—that is, that they can be objects of their own actions. Whenever a human being is interpreting another's indications, he or she is recognizing what it is like to be that person. Blumer is quick to point out, however, that human beings only know what they know from first-hand experience. We form our objects of ourselves through a process of role taking.[3]

Blumer defines objects as anything that can be indicated or pointed to and can be classified into three categories: (1) physical objects, such as books or chairs; (2) social objects, such as friends or family members; and (3) abstract objects, such as moral principles or ideas. Objects are the product of interpretation of action (symbolic interaction). Furthermore, the worlds that exist for human beings are composed of objects. Thus, to understand a human being's world, it is necessary to identify the objects in that person's world.[3]

SI attends to, and focuses on, the meanings that human beings create and place on objects during acts of interpretation (the source of meanings will be further explored with the second premise). It is important to note, however, that this perspective acknowledges the import of meanings on behavior, whereas behaviorism, for example, either pushes the meaning aside as unimportant or regards meaning as a neutral force between the factors responsible for human behavior and the behavior itself.

According to Blumer, human beings engage in action and must be seen in terms of action. Action always takes place in a particular situation. Whatever the acting unit—be it an individual or a family—all action is formed by interpreting that specific situation. As Shibutani[4] noted, "Transactions are not mere expressions of cultural patterns; they are constructed step by step as the participants align and realign their respective contributions in a reciprocating manner."[(p158)] In this way, human beings are self-interpreting.[3]

Blumer's second premise is that the meaning of objects is derived from, or arises out of, the social interaction that one has with other human beings.[3] Blumer and Heidegger differ greatly regarding the source of meanings. Blumer's position is that of an idealist: human beings need to "see" and experience the world in order for the world to exist. The twist that Blumer adds to the conventional idealist position is that because human beings are self-interpreting, not only does one need to perceive that world, but one must also interpret it before reality is constructed.

The idealist position is similar with respect to meanings. As Blumer[3] notes,"Symbolic interactionism sees meanings as social products, as creations that are formed in and through the defining activities of people as they interact."[(p5)] The meaning of an object for a human being is related to the interpretation of how other human beings act toward the human being with regard to the object.[3] As Shibutani[4] noted, many meanings have conventional norms, thereby decreasing the amount of actual interpretation needed between two human beings from similar cultural backgrounds.

Blumer distinguishes between two types of interaction: (1) nonsymbolic and (2) symbolic interaction. Nonsymbolic interaction occurs when one responds directly to the action of another without interpreting that action. Blumer characterizes this kind of interaction as a reflexive kind of response. Symbolic interaction involves the interpretation of the action. The characteristic mode of interaction, according to Blumer, is on the symbolic level, as human beings seek to understand the meaning of each other's action.[3]

The third and final premise of Blumer's perspective is that these meanings are handled in, and modified through, an interpretive process used by the human being in dealing with the objects he or she encounters.[3] Blumer suggests that the process of interpretation has two steps: first, the human being interacts or communicates with herself or himself; second, because of the self-communication, the human being selects, suspends, and regroups meanings in light of the situation. Blumer writes, "This process is in play continuously during one's waking life . . . Indeed, for the human being to be conscious or aware of anything is equivalent to his indicating the thing to himself."[3(p13)]

A HEIDEGGERIAN RESPONSE TO THE THREE PREMISES

Hermeneutic phenomenology is primarily a philosophy and secondarily a research methodology. Heidegger believed that asking the same epistemological questions as his mentor, Husserl, would lead him to the same pitfalls. He therefore sought to reframe the questions in ontological terms. His definition of a human being refers to what it is to be a human being. As Heidegger states, "When we designate this entity with the term Dasein, we are expressing not its 'what' . . . but its Being."[5(p67)] *Dasein,* in colloquial German, means everyday human existence, and so Heidegger uses the term to refer to human beings.[6] For the purposes of this article, *human being* will be used in place of *Dasein.*

The ontological source for the understanding of being is in our shared background practices. These practices have in them an interpretation of what it is to be a person, a culture, and a society. Human beings are special kinds of beings in that their way of being embodies an understanding of what it is to be. Human beings, when socialized and brought up in a culture, make interpretations of the interpretation in the background practices. Heidegger[5] calls this self-interpreting way of being *existence.* Additionally, human beings take a stand on their self-interpreting way of being—on existence—through their involvement with things and people.[6]

Understanding is part of our ontological structure; it is always already before us in the familiarity of our shared background practices.[7] Interpretation is a derivative mode of understanding, as understanding is the basis for all interpretation.[6,8] The shared background is what makes possible shared and individual understandings and interpretations of our world.[7] As Dreyfus[6] explains, "If it was not for the clearing opened up by the understanding of being in language, tradition, and other human practices, we could never encounter beings as beings at all."[(p39)] Thus, understanding makes it possible to uncover things in our world; it discloses the world.[7]

Heidegger would claim that Blumer has already fallen into the Cartesian trap by forcing human beings to be objects of their own action in order to understand another human being's world. In Heidegger's perspective, understanding and interpretation are both prior to the subject–object distinction because they are part of a human being's ontological structure.[8] Heidegger would agree with Blumer that human beings are self-interpreting, but Heidegger would argue that his notion of self-interpretation is ontological in nature, not merely representation or a mental process. Our ontology is more basic than mental states and intentionality.[6] Thus, from a Heideggerian perspective, Blumer's notions of self, interpretation, and role taking are too mentalistic and intentionalistic.

Heidegger is considered to be a hermeneutic realist, in that he believes the world exists without human beings; however, human beings are needed to make the world intelligible and meaningful. Heidegger's position differs from the traditional metaphysical realism against which Blumer[3] rallies. Meaning is dependent on human beings but is understood in context. Human beings grasp the meanings directly from the situation, in a mode of being that Heidegger calls *ready-to-hand.*[9]

Human beings spend much of their lives in this mode transparently coping with equipment that is functioning smoothly. It is our everyday coping practices on the basis of which everything is intelligible and understood. For that reason, Heidegger[5] maintains that this mode, which is taken for granted and passed over, provides the ontological foundation for intelligibility and understanding. Because human beings are absorbed in practical activity, there is no "I."[6]

In the *unready-to-hand* mode of being, a disturbance or breakdown occurs, causing the "I" to show up. Heidegger leaves a place for traditional intentionality in this mode.[6] With a disturbance, aspects of equipment or practical activity often become noticed.[7] Additionally, the meaning of objects in relation to a structural whole of interrelated meanings is briefly lit up, surfacing from the background.[8] Thus, researchers often focus on this mode of being. However, Benner and Wrubel[9] warn that reading back from a mode of breakdown to the ready-to-hand mode may not provide an accurate interpretive account.

The final mode of being is called *present-at-hand.* Activities that characterize this stance include theoretical reflection and conventional, natural scientific activity. This mode is founded on the other two modes of being, but they get covered over when everyday, practical activity stops. Explanation of how things work occurs at this level as determinate properties can be examined.[6] It is in this mode that investigations in the Cartesian tradition of inquiry take place.[7] Heidegger[5] refers to the present-at-hand as a "deficient mode of concern."[(p103)]

Explanation and understanding of reality and meanings, therefore, require all three modes of being. What is extraordinary about Heidegger's position is that understanding is needed for explanation, thereby turning the traditional rationalist argument on its head. In other words, explanation cannot occur without background understanding. Heidegger's critique of Blumer, then, is that Blumer's idealist perspective regarding the source of meanings often smacks of individualism and capricious choice.

Heidegger would criticize Blumer on the importance of symbolic interaction, pointing out that much of our dealings with other human beings occurs in the ready-to-hand mode. For Heidegger, interpretation only surfaces with a disturbance in the unready-to-hand mode.[6] Blumer's emphasis on action is in general agreement with a Heideggerian perspective. However, Heidegger would maintain that to overcome the deficits of behaviorism, Blumer overcompensated and became too mentalistic. To avoid the same trap, Heidegger accepts intentional directness as essential to human activity but denies that intentionality is mental. Heidegger uses the term *comportment* to refer to our directed activity, precisely because it has no mentalistic overtones.[6] Finally, Heidegger would agree with Blumer that human beings need to be studied in their actions: Heidegger writes, "One is what one does."[5(p283)]

METHODOLOGIES: IMPLICATIONS FOR RESEARCH

Although there are some important differences between the two perspectives, the gap narrows when examining the methodological considerations of SI and hermeneutic phenomenology. Both Blumer and Heidegger agree that studying self-interpreting human beings requires a different approach than that used in the natural sciences.

The method of inquiry for the natural sciences is that of scientific explanation and prediction—that is, detached observation, quantification, and experimentation. This is the present-at-hand mode of being.[5] To understand human beings, one must study them when they are engaged in practical activity, because the ready-to-hand mode is primordial, nonmental, and the closest a social scientist can get to the background practices. Heidegger writes, "We must . . . choose such a way of access and such a kind of interpretation that this entity can show itself in itself . . . in its average everydayness."[5(pp37–38)] Blumer would agree with Heidegger that the present-at-hand mode does not get at understanding. He writes, "No theorizing, however ingenious, and no observance of scientific protocol, however meticulous, are substitutes for developing a familiarity with what is actually going on in the sphere of life under study."[3(p39)]

The access both are describing is phenomenology, which guides the social scientist away from theoretical abstractions to the reality of the lived experience.[10]

Although Blumer never explicitly calls his methodology *phenomenology*, he believes that social scientists must "return to the empirical social world."[3(p34)] At another point, he notes, "Respect the nature of the empirical world and organize a methodological stance to reflect this respect. This is what I think symbolic interactionism strives to do."[3(p60)]

Hermeneutic phenomenology goes one step beyond "the things themselves."[5(p50)] Hermeneutics means interpretation, thus the methodology that Heidegger is calling for is interpretation of the phenomena. The reason any interpretation is needed at all is that there is no direct way to access the background practices. One can get close to the background practices through participant observation of human beings in the ready-to-hand mode, but even this method has limitations. Human beings have no language for clearings and the way things show up; the background practices, therefore, can sound like a belief system and human being as an entity with determinate properties.[6] This structural cover-up of the phenomenon is one "which must first of all be wrested from the objects of phenomenology."[5(p61)] Blumer sounds very close to Heidegger at this point when he says that "the metaphor I like to use is that of lifting the veils that obscure or hide what is going on . . . The veils are lifted by getting close to the area and by digging deep into it through careful study."[3(p39)]

Even though the philosophical underpinnings differ in these two perspectives, the methodologies proposed are similar. Both Blumer and Heidegger call for inductive study of the phenomena in question and for study of the phenomena in as naturalistic a setting as possible. An aspect Heidegger developed that has no SI analogue is the hermeneutic circle of understanding. Briefly, we are always already in a hermeneutic circle of understanding because we are self-interpreting. Simply put, the establishment of a point of view, a perspective, is the forward arc, and evaluation forms the reverse arc.[11]

When considering the unit of analysis, some distinctions between SI and hermeneutic phenomenology emerge. Blumer's perspective is based on the notion that the whole is founded on the parts, which is to say that one cannot understand a family or group without first studying the individual. SI, therefore, is best suited to study the individual as the unit of analysis or the family as context.[12-13] Heidegger's perspective, on the other hand, is based on the notion that what counts as a part depends on the whole. In other words, Heidegger believes that one cannot understand the individual without first understanding the family or group.

•   •   •

In the past, there has been confusion surrounding these two perspectives. Without careful analysis, they appear to be making the same points using different language. In fact, however, the language used in any theoretical perspective is one of the more important pieces, as the terminology shapes how one will view the area under study. To that end, the validity of either perspective is determined by the researcher's taken-for-granted preunderstanding as well as the formal and informal lines of inquiry.

REFERENCES

1. Burr WR, Hill R, Nye FI, Reiss IL, eds. *Contemporary Theories About the Family: General Theories/Theoretical Orientations.* New York, NY: Free Press; 1979; 2.
2. Turner JH. *The Structure of Sociological Theory.* 5th ed. Belmont, Calif: Wadsworth; 1991.
3. Blumer H. *Symbolic Interactionism: Perspective and Method.* Englewood Cliffs, NJ: Prentice Hall; 1967.
4. Shibutani T. Herbert Blumer's contributions to twentieth-century sociology. In: Johnson J, Faberman HA, Fine GA, eds. *The Cutting Edge: Advanced Interactionist Theory.* Greenwich, Conn: JAI Press; 1992.
5. Heidegger M. *Being and Time.* New York, NY: Harper & Row; 1962.
6. Dreyfus HL. *Being-in-the-World: A Commentary on Heidegger's Being and Time, Division 1.* Cambridge, Mass: MIT Press; 1991.
7. Plager KA. *Hermeneutic phenomenology: a methodology for family health and health promotion study.* 1991. Unpublished manuscript.
8. Palmer RE. *Hermeneutics: Interpretation Theory in Schleiermacher, Dilthey, Heidegger and Gadamer.* Evanston, Ill: Northwestern University; 1969.
9. Benner P, Wrubel J. *The Primacy of Caring: Stress and Coping in Health and Illness.* Menlo Park, Calif: Addison-Wesley; 1989.
10. Field P. A phenomenological look at giving an injection. *J Adv Nurs.* 1981;6:291–296.
11. Packer MJ, Addison RB. *Entering the Circle: Hermeneutic Investigation in Psychology.* Albany, NY: State University of New York Press; 1989.
12. Schvaneveldt JD. The interactional framework in the study of the family. In: Nye FI, Bernardo F, eds. *Emerging Conceptual Frameworks in Family Analysis.* New York, NY: Praeger; 1981.
13. Uphold CR, Strickland OL. Issues related to the unit of analysis in family nursing research. *West J Nurs Res.* 1989;11(4):405–417.

Through a Feminist Lens: A Model to Guide Nursing Research

Sheila M. Bunting, RN, PhD
College of Nursing
University of Tennessee, Memphis
Memphis, Tennessee

Jacquelyn C. Campbell, RN, PhD, FAAN
Anna D. Wolf Endowed Professor
Johns Hopkins University School of Nursing
Baltimore, Maryland

The purpose of this article is to consider and compare the characteristics of nursing and feminist research, including the beliefs about knowledge, preferred methods of inquiry, purposes, and relationships with research participants. It is proposed that, as a practice profession developed primarily by women, nursing used survival strategies that continue to affect practice and research. It is suggested that feminist theory and methodologies could contribute approaches to research that could expand nursing's vision. A model is offered for examining the epistemology and methodological frameworks underlying feminist and nursing research studies.

DURING THE PAST decades, the development of nursing theory and research has accelerated, and nursing scholarship has come into its own. Because nursing is a profession with a high membership of women and one that sees itself as advocating for women and children as well as men, the relationship between feminism and nursing has been questioned and explored.[1-4] The value of feminist methodology to illuminate nursing research has been suggested by MacPherson[5] and by Duffy,[6] among others. This article seeks to bring together and to carry forward some of the ideas offered by these feminist nurses. The purpose of this article is to examine the characteristics and purposes of nursing research and the principles and characteristics of feminist research to find areas of common epistemology that can direct methodology for a feminist nursing research.

AMBIGUITIES IN NURSING RESEARCH

Polit and Hungler[7] in their discussion of why research in nursing is necessary and important made the comment that nursing is a poorly understood phenomenon. Given the self-questioning and debates of nursing scholars[8-10] about the identity and nature of nursing's primary focus, this statement would seem to be justified; there is much that is not known about nursing. Scholars who attempt to analyze nursing often come from and focus on different experiences of this very complex entity, each giving a valid but partial perspective of the whole. Questions to be pondered are these: What is an appropriate perspective or stance from which to study the phenomena of interest to nursing? What lens (or lenses) will help us to be able to see and communicate the elements of our research discipline more clearly? The authors believe that examination of tenets of feminist perspective will assist and inform the inquiry. We will begin with questions about the research methodologies used in nursing research.

A MODEL FOR ANALYZING RESEARCH METHODOLOGY

Harding,[11] a feminist philosopher of science, addressed the confusion she heard when feminists and others talked about methods in their research. Her discussion dealt with the concerns of whether or not some approaches to research were always or never aligned with feminist principles. Similar concerns have been posed by nursing scholars about the appropriateness of applying objective versus humanist methods to nursing science.[12–13] Harding[11] took the stance that it is the purpose of the inquiry, the explanatory hypotheses, and the relationship between researcher and informer or "subject," rather than the methods used to gather information, that distinguish feminist from nonfeminist research. The authors believe that the same criteria applied to nursing research would yield interesting questions and illuminate some of the methods' controversy.

Method versus Methodology versus Epistemology

Harding defined *method* as "a technique for (or way of proceeding in) gathering evidence."[11(p3)] She argued that all such techniques can be subsumed under observing; listening to or questioning informants; or examining records (including pictures and diagrams) such as historical documents, texts, and medical records. Each of these procedural methods can be used in differing ways to produce new views and alternative explanations of phenomena, but Harding believed that the methods themselves are not bound to a philosophical stance. If this is true, it is not the data-gathering technique but the reasons why it was chosen that bring the question into the political arena. *Methodology* is defined by Harding as "a theory and analysis of how research does or should proceed."[11(p3)] The "shoulds" or methodologies of research are based on the epistemology of the researcher. An *epistemology* is a theory of knowledge. Epistemology guides methodology because epistemology concerns the questions of what can be known and who can be a knower. The world view or ontology of the researcher (which includes beliefs about the nature of the world) is the foundation for his or her epistemology. Firestone clarified the relationship between the two concepts as these concern research: "Higher order theoretical principles about the nature of the world (ontology) and how one knows it (epistemology) govern the conduct of research."[14(p106)]

Choices of the authorities one appeals to in legitimating knowledge are also influenced by one's experience of the world. These authorities may be respected sources, such as God, or the Bible, or *The New York Times,* or they may be process oriented as in logic, common sense, past experience, or statistical probability. Time-honored practices ("we've always done it that way") as well as policies and laws may serve as criteria against which ideas may be judged. Based on these categories listed by Harding,[11] the authors have proposed a framework to begin to understand and analyze the methodology of research. Questions to the researcher would include the following:

- *Epistemology:* What are the researcher's beliefs regarding the nature of knowledge? Included in this question are the following: What can be known? Who can know? How can one know it? What knowledge is valued? These questions are indicated in the assumptions (written and tacit) on which the study is based.
- *Methodology:* How should the investigator go about conducting the research; that is, what procedures are acceptable, given the ontology and epistemology of the researcher?
- *Purpose:* What is the research trying to achieve?
- *Focus:* On what group of persons does the study focus?
- *Benefit:* What group(s) will benefit from the research?
- *Relationship of researcher to investigator:* What is the nature of the relationship of the researcher to the investigator? (This question could include similarities and differences in class, race, gender, sexual orientation, etc, as well as the research relationship).

APPLYING THE MODEL TO NURSING RESEARCH

The questions encompassed in the model will be seen to be interrelated and overlapping. The concepts are not easily separated and considered in exclusion of one another because of their inherent interrelationships. Nonetheless, they are a beginning.

Nursing's Rich and Paradoxical Epistemology

In nursing research, as in all instances of inquiry, the knowledge and previous experience of the researcher will greatly influence his or her findings. One's vision is conditioned by what one has seen before as well as one's position relative to the subject of inquiry—one's perspective.

Nursing views the world from a range of perspectives influenced by the many and diverse roots from which it has developed as an activity, an occupation, a profession, and an ideology. The rich history of nursing includes the influences of midwives and other healers, the military, the religious and secular orders, medical dominance, and the powerful social reform movements in Europe and the United States.[1,15–16] Despite the diversity in its heritage, many scholars urge the discipline to come to some agreement on a paradigm for nursing in the conduct of research.

Paradigm Debates

The significance of paradigm content for nursing research, practice, and education is recognized. For those who believe there is one "right" paradigm for nursing, its use in constructing, implementing, and handing down basic principles to future nurses is seen as essential in shaping the discipline and profession. Because of the crucial role played by the dominant paradigm in the creation, application, and legitimation of nursing knowledge, the selection of that paradigm has been seriously discussed and debated in the community of nursing scholars. Paradigms influential in nursing research in the past were those of the positivist or realist, and the less naive and radical postpositivist positions, which were based on the assumption of one reality "out there" that can be examined. A contrast to the realist paradigm has been the naturalist or constructivist paradigm. This paradigm is premised on multiple realities that are socially constructed and interpreted by individuals within the context and cultures of their lives.[17] The methods used for research conducted from each of the paradigms tend to be different. Interpretive and interactive (or qualitative) data gathering and analysis have been more commonly employed in studies in the naturalist paradigm, whereas objective, quantitative measurements have been implemented in the postpositivist paradigm. The so-called scientific method has been considered more rigorous and therefore more acceptable and believable by practitioners of traditional research. Nurses, however, have managed to make good use of both quantitative and qualitative paradigms. A helpful quote from Ackerman,[18] quoted in Wilson[19] about ways of knowing, sheds light on the duality of qualitative/quantitative ways of knowing: "The Engaged style of knowing demands effective human contact between the individual and the object of his/her attention. The Analytic style gives the individual precision tools with which to manipulate the environment."[18(p855)]

Methodology for a Paradoxical Epistemology

Nurses, in their practice, have learned to use both the engaged and analytic styles of knowing referred to by Ackerman.[18] In the realm of clinical instruction, most nurses have learned and taught all of Carper's[20] patterns of knowing to students and other nurses during their nursing careers. New members are taught to assess the client's signs and symptoms, using the most precise measurements possible, *and* to listen with the "third ear" of interpretation and synthesis. Nursing's epistemology is not monolithic, but as varied and paradoxical as its origins. Nurses have learned to use many types of knowledge and many tools to accomplish their goals. The inconsistencies described above raise a question. How can nursing accommodate these differences in the discipline's methodology? An analysis of the purpose of nursing research may lead to an answer.

The Purpose of Nursing Research

To continue the analysis according to the questions derived from Harding's[11] discussion, the model will now be used to examine the purpose of nursing research as a general activity. Though nurse scientists have engaged in basic research to build a body of nursing knowledge, the primary purpose of all nursing research is (at least tacitly, indirectly, and/or eventually) directed at improved practice.

Diers[21] listed distinguishing properties of research problems in nursing. Problems must, according to Diers, "involve a difference that matters" in client care, and "a research problem is a nursing research problem when nurses have access to and control over the phenomenon being studied."[21(pp14–15)] Diers'[21] criteria for nursing research may be construed as political, meaning that they are influenced by differences in power and a desire to change the balance of that power. The second criterion definitely limits nursing research problems to areas where nurses have power and control over the study. How does nursing obtain and nurture this power, and how is it used to promote the good of clients and the profession? In this article, it is maintained that the power necessary for action comes as a result of the recognition by others, other professions, and nursing clients. This recognition involves the services that nursing has to offer—the recognition that nursing care can make a difference in the health and quality of life of individuals and groups.

In a sort of "credo," Styles[22] wrote what she believed about the nature and purpose of nursing. These characteristics are applied here to the nature and purpose of nursing research. Her comments about nursing defined it as a force for social good with humanitarian concerns for human responses to health and environment. Styles made the observation that nursing, in order to make its contribution, depends on

- the expertise of its practitioners;
- the recognition and support of the public;
- an enabling political, economic, and legal climate; and
- the ability of the profession to maintain unity within diversity.

Reviewing the purposes attributed to nursing research by Diers and Styles, and applying the above model, some conclusions may be drawn about the goals of nursing research. First, it is clear that nursing research as an activity has the primary purpose of creating and validating knowledge for practice that is for the good of nursing clients.[23] The *secondary* purpose of nursing research is to improve the (political) position of the profession. This comes across clearly in the literature; nurses cannot do much good for society unless they can prove that their service makes a cost-effective difference in outcomes. As Styles[22] shrewdly observed, nursing's ability to contribute depends on, among other variables, the recognition and support of the public and an enabling political, economic, and legal climate. Nursing will have to create and nurture these supports. If nursing's history and the history of the development of other professional disciplines may be used as a guide, others cannot be depended on to provide these favorable conditions.

Feminists historically have been engaged in moving society toward change and have incorporated their beliefs and strategies into their research. Characteristics of feminist research are reviewed here for help in formulating ways to promote nursing's position.

CHARACTERISTICS OF FEMINIST RESEARCH

Feminist research has been described in many different ways. Responding to the question in the proposed model, "What group will benefit from the research," the authors appreciate Harding's simple statement that the bottom line and a basic tenet of feminist research is that it is *for* women. It can also be for men, for all human beings, and/or for particular groups of human beings, but it must have some benefit for women. Duffy and Hedin[23] have elaborated on this notion by describing the following additional characteristics of research from the feminist perspective:

1. *A feminist consciousness rooted in an attitude of equality,* thereby replacing hierarchies with horizontal relationships. This is a partial answer to the question, "What is the nature of the relationship of the researcher to the investigator?" As MacPherson[5] describes this characteristic, feminist research has participants as partners in the research process, the identification of questions, the conduct of the research, and the dispersion of the resulting knowledge. It is noted here that these horizontal relationships would characterize the research team as well as the relationships with participants.
2. *The aims of including women* (although not all research on women is feminist) *and studying phenomena of practical concern to women.* This is responsive to the question, "On what group of persons does the study focus?"
3. *"Conscious partiality"* in which the biases of the researcher are "acknowledged, brought into the open and dealt with."[23(p531)] Proceeding with a reflexive approach, the researchers examine their own values, assumptions, individual attributes, and motivations.[24]

Reinharz,[25] in an extremely useful review of feminist research methods, has also identified 10 "themes" of feminist research. A number of these themes are particularly useful to add to the above list:

4. *Feminism is a theme, not a research method.*
5. *Feminists use a multiplicity of research methods.*
6. *Feminist research aims to create social change.*
7. *Feminist research strives to represent human diversity.*

In the last (#7) criterion listed above, it would be important explicitly to include ethnicity, culture, gender, sexual orientation, and class. Reinharz[25(p240)] also notes that feminist research "involves an ongoing criticism of nonfeminist scholarship," a theme that could be stated slightly differently:

8. *Feminist research critiques prior scholarship (nonfeminist and feminist) especially for androcentric and ethnocentric bias.*

As a final theme, keeping in mind the basic tenet of research being for women, the authors would add the following:

9. *Feminist research portrays women's strengths.* As Chinn and Wheeler so beautifully state this characteristic, "A feminist perspective does not seek to romanticize or idealize these women, but rather, to develop insights that allow us to appreciate their struggles, understand their limitations and see their joys and their pains as similar to ours."[3(p76–77)] This tenet of feminist research speaks to the question in the proposed model to guide research, "What is the research trying to achieve?"

Keeping in mind MacPherson's[5] partnership model in terms of research dispersion and publication as well as its conduct, a research report in a popular women's magazine is as important as an article in the most prestigious academic journal. Thus, much of feminist research is published in popular press book form. However, feminism, like nursing, has political and prestige issues. In academia, where the value of knowledge is often determined, feminism or women's studies are frequently marginalized and the knowledge gained considered less legitimate. Research reports that are accessible in language and format to a diverse audience of women are often given the label of being unscholarly by academia. Such reports would then not count toward promotion and tenure or be considered by funding agencies as the basis for further funding. Although most feminist scholars overtly resist these pressures, they often devise a modification of the methods preferred by the discipline within which they were trained. In this way, they increase the chances that their research will be accepted within their discipline.

Reinharz also stated in her discussion on the acceptance by most feminist scholars of a multiplicity of research methods that "because feminists value inclusiveness more than orthodoxy, we allow room for creativity in all aspects of the research process."[25(p244)] This would be a useful lesson to apply in nursing in the search for uniquely nursing research methods.[26–27] Reinharz[25] described experimental research that can be classified as feminist because of the aims of the research and its influence in creating social change that has been beneficial to women. Jayaratne[28] also discussed the power of statistics from experimental and/or survey research in creating policy more friendly to women. Such changes in policy generally would not be made without "hard data" to support them.[29]

In nursing, there is more and more emphasis on the need for "clinical trials" to establish the efficacy of nursing interventions. This demand has been from the public, through Congress, as well as from the profession and funding agencies. Practitioners also want to know which nursing interventions work, and often experimental research is the only known basis on which to make those determinations in a way that can be broadly applied. The literature, both feminist and nursing, has many useful critiques of the limitations of experimental and/or statistics-based research. The challenge, for both nursing and feminism, is to find creative ways of integrating experimental research and shaping its use within acceptable paradigms and methodologies. Reinharz stated, "combining the strengths of experimental method with the strengths of other methods is probably the best way to avoid its weakness while utilizing its power."[25(p108)]

APPLYING THE MODEL TO FEMINIST RESEARCH

From the themes described above, it is apparent that the purpose of feminist research is to create social change that will benefit women. Feminist research assumes that *all* women are legitimate knowers and that those experiencing particular complexities are the most knowledgeable about that exigency. For instance, feminist scholars are far more likely to respect the interpretation of events by women themselves, groups such as battered women or women of a particular ethnic group, rather than to rely totally on "expert" interpretation of data from these women. Another part of the epistemology of feminist research is the value placed on critique. As stated above, most feminist scholars support a multiplicity of methods, although within feminism there has been a similar debate to the debate within nursing about the relative value of quantitative versus qualitative approaches to research. The differentiation of method from methodology and the necessity of interdisciplinary perspectives have been very helpful to feminism in that discussion. As a result of that discourse, most scholars in women's studies now recognize that it is how the research is conducted (avoiding exploitation, initiating partnerships, etc) that is more important than the type of data generated. Thus, there can be, need to be, and are, feminist approaches to cellular biology as well as feminist approaches to psychology. Whatever the nature of the data collected, feminist research insists on analysis of those data within the context of real women's lives and demands that analyses be done in such a way that women and/or other oppressed groups are empowered rather than portrayed in ways that reinforce stereotypes.

At the same time, feminist critique has highlighted the reality that induction-based methods also can be exploitative, be hierarchical, and/or fail to expose existing oppression.[30–31] Research participants often are enmeshed in their own experiences and unable to see the larger picture. As Gorelick[31] points out, hidden determinants of people's conditions can often be discovered through the research process, especially using such methods as action research or focus-group discussions. Other methods of discovery need to be used in conjunction with women's stories, such as analysis of the larger, historical and social structure within which a more immediate, personal context occurs. Barry's[32] analysis of prostitution and the Dobashes'[33] classic work on wife beating are examples of such approaches. Fine[34] admonishes feminists to "critically interpret" women's voices, not just record and group them—that this is part of the reflexive stance.

PARALLELS BETWEEN NURSING AND FEMINISM

Nursing faces the question of the audience for the product of its research. Whereas the primary purpose of nursing research is the generation of knowledge for the improvement of nursing practice, a secondary purpose is to improve the (political) position of the profession. This is done by documenting and publicizing nursing's accomplishments to the consumer and to the funding and policy-making hierarchies (patriarchy). The need for this legitimation comes across clearly in the literature; nursing's power to promote change depends on its ability to demonstrate that its services are valuable and make a cost-effective difference in outcomes. Much of the progress in gaining power to practice has been earned historically by this route.[35] Nurse scientists must therefore play by the rules of those in power, meet their criteria, and publish in their journals.

Though many nursing scholars[12-13] have raised concerns that much of the quantitative research engaged in by nurses is inconsistent with the philosophy and humanistic focus of nursing, nurses continue to use methods and meet standards set by other disciplines. This is an effort to gain recognition from the larger community and to use research results to create social change in a system where it is the more traditional research that is considered a legitimate basis for change. In spite of, and perhaps because of, the power differentials within the system, nursing has learned how to be strong, organized, and powerful.

Feminists too have found themselves divided in their purposes. According to historian Kelly, feminists are torn between joining male-dominated movements for peace and freedom and forming their own separatist coalitions: "The tension between the need for separation and the will to create social change runs deep in the women's movement and in each of our lives as do the related tensions between the claims of class, race, and sex."[36(p55)]

It is clear that the parallels between nursing research and feminist research are striking: the concern for social good, the concern for attention to ethnic diversity and ethnocentrism in scholarship (though relatively recent), and the (sometimes unstated) issues of prestige and politics of the disciplines. (See Table 1.) For the most part, the ontology and epistemology that underpin feminism and nursing are congruent. The beginnings of a feminist–nursing research method exist, have already been applied in many studies,[37-40] and can be further developed and refined in the future. Nursing does not need to "borrow" feminist research methods; these are already multiple and open to variation.

Potential Contributions from Feminist Research

Though their priorities differ, nursing shares a vision with feminism in that the ultimate goal for research and other political activities is a change in the larger social system.[41-42] Feminist historian Kelly[36] pointed out that feminists can see the world not only as it exists but the way that it could be, an optimistic vision that keeps them hoping and working toward a better, more humane reality. This idealism and optimism of feminism could make a contribution to the multiple paradigms of nursing and nursing research.

Other contributions that feminist research principles can make to nursing include the social and political awareness that has become an increasingly influen-

Table 1. Comparison of nursing research and feminist research

	Nursing research	**Feminist research**
Epistemology	Engaged & analytical Nurses are legitimate creators of knowledge	Engaged & analytical Women are legitimate creators of knowledge
Methodology	Client-centered research	Action research
Purpose	Primary: Create & validate nursing knowledge as the basis for practice for the good of clients Secondary: Improve political position of profession	Primary: Improve women's lives Secondary: Change social system for good of all humans
Focus population	Nursing clients or patients	Women
Benefit	Clients/patients Researcher Nursing	Women Researcher Feminism/women's studies
Relationship between investigator and participant/subject	Hierarchical (although, less so from constructivist paradigm)	Women/Researcher Feminism/Women's Studies Partnership

tial part of the reality of nursing as a profession and a discipline. As to the value placed on the self-respect, self-determination, and humanity of both nurse and participant articulated by Styles,[22] these issues need to be explicated in nursing research rather than assumed or taken for granted. Duffy and Hedin[23] recommend a high level of reflexivity on the part of the nurse researcher, a conscious scrutiny of his or her premises, values, and biases. This has been an important ingredient in the research of the second wave of feminists (1966–the present). Using a reflexive stance, the researcher can acknowledge biases, allowing these and their influence on the study to be questioned. This would be an important contribution to nursing research, which is often conducted as though class, racial, and other biases were not relevant to research. Unexamined biases regarding class, race, gender, sexual orientation, and other characteristics can be insidious in their corruption and contamination of nursing research and practice.

Contributions Nursing Can Make to Feminism

A contribution that nursing can make to feminism is its historical expertise on holism and health of persons and groups. The patriarchal society in which we live is a part of nursing's reality as a professional discipline. Through many creative strategies, nursing has learned to make contributions to the larger society. Nurses have gained credibility by "seeing" the world through the patriarchal lens and conducting practice and research in a way that provides results that are valued within that reality. The alternative to this coexistence is to separate from the larger community and to work only with those who see the world through a similar lens to our own. This alternative may be a viable one for some feminist philosophers;[43–44] it is not a possibility for nurses. Given the agreed-upon humanitarian mission of nursing, such an approach would be a contradiction in terms.

CONCLUSION

A lens alters the slant of light to change the focus and, therefore, the impression of the observer. Just as there are many nursing lenses, there are many feminist lenses. These are influenced by the differing values, classes, races, educations, sexual orientations, ethnicities, ages, national origins, and life experiences of the feminists. Hall and Stevens state that one can only speak of "feminisms" that share three basic principles: (1) a valuing of women and their experiences, ideas, and needs; (2) a recognition of the existence of conditions that oppress women; and (3) a desire to change these conditions through criticisms and political action.[24(p17)]

Nursing, with its rich and diverse background, has used many strategies to survive successfully as a predominantly female practice discipline. It can also use its abilities to view the world from many perspectives to improve its science.

Nursing practice and nursing research have demonstrated a valuing of the experiences, ideas, and needs of clients, including women, throughout their history in their attention to ethics of research[45] and to the design of studies that tap and validate the personal interpretation of informants.[46–48] A recognition of and a focused desire to change the conditions of oppression that exist for nurses and their clients have been slow in coming to the rank and file of nurses. Some of us, as nurses, have operated as though we could accomplish our practice and research in a biosphere safely insulated from the contamination of the political climate, ignoring the politics of race, class, and economics. However, these forces and other interests have influenced the actions and reactions of the larger world as well as our own perspectives and motivations as nurses. We now recognize that we do not operate in a vacuum, and we are being presented with the opportunities to become sensitive to political aspects of our world.[49] We also have the obligation and the challenge to be aware of and address the social, class, ethnic, racial, and other biases that have resulted in blind spots in our research.[28,50]

•   •   •

Feminist research has a long history of raising consciousness of biases. Hall and Stevens[24] point out that eliminating bias is not only impossible but inappropriate. Therefore, researchers must scrutinize their own values, assumptions, and motivations to determine how these factors influence all research from the conceptual framework through the literature review, design, selection of instruments, data collection, sampling, and interpretation of findings. Integrating these characteristics of feminist research into nursing research methodologies will serve us well, enhancing our vision as we respond to the challenges to diversify our lenses and take up our power in shaping health in our world community.

REFERENCES

1. Bunting SM, Campbell JC. Feminism and nursing historical perspectives. *Adv Nurs Sci.* 1990;12:11–24.
2. Campbell JC, Bunting SM. Voices and paradigms: perspectives on critical and feminist theory in nursing. *Adv Nurs Sci.* 1991;13(3):1–15.
3. Chinn PL, Wheeler CE. Feminism and nursing: can nursing afford to remain aloof from the women's movement? *Nurs Outlook.* 1985;33:74–77.
4. Vance C, Talbott S, McBride A, Mason D. An uneasy alliance: nursing and the women's movement. *Nurs Outlook.* 1985;33:281–285.
5. MacPherson KI. The missing piece: women as partners in feminist research. *Response.* 1988;11(4):19–20.
6. Duffy ME. A critique of research: a feminist perspective. *Health Care for Women International.* 1985;6:341–352.
7. Polit DF, Hungler BP. *Essentials of Nursing Research.* 2nd ed. Philadelphia, Pa: Lippincott; 1989.
8. Brodie JN. A response to Dr. J. Fawcett's paper: "The metaparadigm of nursing: present status and future refinements." *Image.* 1984;16(3):87–89.
9. Fawcett J. The metaparadigm of nursing: present status and future refinements. *Image.* 1984;16(3):84–87.
10. Newman MA, Sime AM, Corcoran-Perry SA. The focus of the discipline of nursing. *Adv Nurs Sci.* 1991;14(1):1–6.
11. Harding S. Is there a feminist method? In: Harding S, ed. *Feminism and Methodology.* Bloomington, Ind: Indiana University Press; 1987.
12. Moccia P. A critique of compromise: beyond the methods debate. *Adv Nurs Sci.* 1988;10(4):1–9.
13. Munhall PL. Nursing philosophy and nursing research: in apposition or opposition? *Nurs Res.* 1982;31:176–177, 181.
14. Firestone WA. Accommodation, toward a paradigm-praxis dialectic. In: Guba EG, ed. *The Paradigm Dialog.* Newbury Park, Calif: Sage; 1990.
15. Dock LL, Stewart IM. *Short History of Nursing.* 3rd ed. New York, NY: Putnam; 1920.
16. Armeny S. Organized nurses, women philanthropists and the intellectual bases for cooperation among women, 1898–1920. In: Lagemann EC, ed. *Nursing History: New Perspectives, New Possibilities.* New York, NY: Teachers College Press; 1983.
17. Lincoln YS. The making of a constructivist, a remembrance of transformations past. In: Guba EG, ed. *The Paradigm Dialog.* Newbury Park, Calif: Sage; 1990.
18. Ackerman JS. Two styles: a challenge to higher education. *Daedalus.* Summer 1969:855–868.
19. Wilson HS. *Research in Nursing.* 2nd ed. Menlo Park, Calif: Addison-Wesley; 1989.
20. Carper BA. Fundamental patterns of knowing in nursing. *Adv Nurs Sci.* 1978;1(1):13–23.
21. Diers D. *Research in Nursing Practice.* Philadelphia, Pa: Lippincott; 1979.

22. Styles MM. *On nursing: toward a new endowment.* St. Louis, Mo: Mosby; 1982.
23. Duffy M, Hedin BA. New directions for nursing research. In: Woods NF, Catanzaro M, eds. *Nursing Research: Theory and Practice.* St. Louis, Mo: Mosby; 1988.
24. Hall JM, Stevens PE. Rigor in feminist research. *Adv Nurs Sci.* 1991;13(3):16–29.
25. Reinharz S. *Feminist Methods in Social Research.* New York, NY: Oxford University Press; 1992.
26. Russell CK, Gregory DM, Phillips LR. Critical juncture: liminality and the development of innovative inquiry methods for nursing. Presented at the Third Annual Critical and Feminist Perspectives in Nursing Conference; March 20–22, 1992; Toledo, Ohio.
27. Thorne SE. Methodological orthodoxy in qualitative nursing research: analysis of the issues. *Qualitative Health Research.* 1991;1(2):178–199.
28. Jayaratne TE. The value of quantitative methodology for feminist research. In: Bowles G, Klein RD, eds. *Theories of Women's Studies.* Boston, Mass: Routledge & Kegan Paul; 1983.
29. Campbell JC, Alford P. The dark consequences of marital rape. *Am J Nurs.* 1989;89:946–949.
30. Cannon LW, Higgenbotham E, Leung MLA. Race and class bias in qualitative research on women. *Gender & Society.* 1988;2(4):449–462.
31. Gorelick S. Contradictions of feminist methodology. *Gender & Society.* 1991;5(4):459–477.
32. Barry K. *Female Sexual Slavery.* Englewood Cliffs, NJ: Prentice Hall; 1979.
33. Dobash R, Dobash R. *Beating of Wives.* New York, NY: Free Press; 1979.
34. Fine M. *Disruptive Voices: The Possibilities of Feminist Research.* Ann Arbor, Mich: University of Michigan Press; 1992.
35. Gortner SR. The history and philosophy of nursing science and research. *Adv Nurs Sci.* 1983;5(2):1–8.
36. Kelly J. *Women, History, and Theory.* Chicago, Ill: The University of Chicago Press; 1984.
37. Campbell JC. Misogyny and homicide of women. *Adv Nurs Sci.* 1981;3(2):67–85.
38. Dickson GL. A feminist poststructuralist analysis of the knowledge of menopause. *Adv Nurs Sci.* 1990;12(3):15–31.
39. Duffy ME. Primary prevention behaviors: the female-headed, single-parent family. *Res Nurs Health.* 1986;9:115–122.
40. Miller S. Understanding fractured identities: feminist postmodern nursing research on career re-entry for new mothers. Presented at the Third Annual Critical and Feminist Perspectives in Nursing Conference; March 20–22, 1992; Toledo, Ohio.
41. Moccia P. Re-claiming our communities. *Nurs Outlook.* 1990;38(2):73–76.
42. Kendall J. Fighting back: promoting emancipatory nursing actions. *Adv Nurs Sci.* 1992;15(2):1–15.
43. Hoagland SL. *Lesbian Ethics.* Palo Alto, Calif: Institute of Lesbian Studies; 1988.
44. Johnson S. *Wildfire: Igniting the She/volution.* Albuquerque, NM: Wildfire Books; 1989.
45. Gortner S. The role of research in ethical inquiry. In: *Proceedings from a National Forum in Nursing.* Chicago, Ill: The Kellogg National Center for Nursing Excellence and the Rush-Presbyterian-St. Luke's Medical Center; March 4–5, 1982.
46. Chenitz WC, Swanson JM. *From Practice to Grounded Theory.* Menlo Park, Calif: Addison-Wesley; 1986.
47. Morse JM. *Qualitative Nursing Research.* Newbury Park, Calif: Sage; 1991.
48. Parse RR, Coyn BA, Smith MJ. *Nursing Research Qualitative Methods.* Bowie, Md: Brady; 1985.
49. Snyder M. Changing agenda: implications for health care policy and research. Keynote paper presented at the 17th Annual Research Conference of the Midwest Nursing Research Society; 1993; Cleveland, Ohio.
50. Porter C. The relationship between sampling methods and fragmentary understanding. Presented at the 17th Annual Research Conference of the Midwest Nursing Research Society; 1993; Cleveland, Ohio.

"Connected Knowing": Feminist Group Research

Marianne Scharbo-DeHaan, CNM, PhD
Assistant Professor, Nurse Midwifery
Nell Hodgson Woodruff School of Nursing
Emory University
Atlanta, Georgia

The tenets of feminist research were incorporated into a group research project that explored the experiences and meanings of being menopausal to a group of midlife women. Nine women including the researcher met for 1 night a week for 6 weeks to discuss their experiences of menopause. It has been suggested that talking to women, in groups, about experiences such as menstruation and menopause is one way to transcend the silence that historically has cloaked these experiences. The texts resulting from the audiotaped group sessions constituted the data for the study. Heideggerian hermeneutics was the interpretive method. Group research with a feminist orientation is described in full. The theme reported here, "connected knowing," captured the process of knowledge creation based on experience and the empowerment of the coparticipants as "experts" that occurred because of the group methodology. Two constitutive patterns, "menopause as an age" and "the biology of it all," not reported here, reflect both the developmental and biological aspects of the phenomenon. The findings confirm that women in groups can challenge medical discourse and generate knowledge that does not dismiss experience.

Groups provide an opportunity for women to see themselves collectively engaged in oral exchanges from which female narratives are found.

—Carolyn Heilbrun[1]

ALTHOUGH MENOPAUSE is a universal and definitive landmark of aging, women of different cultures experience the menopause transition in different ways.[2] While we do not deny the existence of and underlying biological reality in which women age, lose fertility, and cease to menstruate, menopause is also a social construct. Societies transform the physiological event of menopause into a cultural one: women experience menopause in varied contextual settings and assign different meanings to the process.[2] The values and meanings derived from women's interpretations placed on this event are socially constructed. Menopause cannot be understood apart from the larger social system, nor can it be understood as an isolated event in a woman's life. The meanings of menopause to a group of women were the focus of this study.

This project was funded in part by Sigma Theta Tau, Alpha Epsilon Chapter.

88

Historically, menopause has been studied primarily through quantitative research methods. In addition, much of the research has been done within the biomedical framework. The assumptions within that framework are based on the concept that menopause is a biological event characterized by a cluster of symptoms caused by a deficiency of female hormones. Menopause is viewed as an endocrinopathy that needs to be treated by hormonal replacement therapy.[3] Recently, nursing researchers have begun to examine this life event from a different framework. Dickson used a poststructuralist theoretical framework to analyze medical writings and interviews with menopausal women.[2] These provided insightful descriptions of the biomedical and sociocultural influences on women's menopausal experiences. Dickson illustrated points of conjuncture between scientific and medical discourses and the everyday discourse of midlife women. Her recommendation was that nurses should "focus on research and practice based on women's experience rather than to accept uncritically the medical knowledge of menopause" and that "free, open discussions with women could lead to questioning of assumptions behind the scientific and medical discourses and the resulting expectations of menopause."[2(p29)]

The dilemma I saw was this: How can women transcend the silence around this experience; how can they question those assumptions and validate the knowledge that is based on their experiences? In the 1960s and 1970s, women formed thousands of grassroots groups to provide a way to exchange thoughts, experiences, and feelings. Called consciousness-raising groups, these were, in fact, a form of social-action research. According to Fay, what occurred was "in an environment of trust, openness, and support in which one's own perceptions and feelings were made properly conscious to oneself, women could think through their experiences in terms of a radically new vocabulary which expresses a fundamentally different conceptualization of the world . . . coming to a radical new conceptualization is hardly ever a process that occurs simply by reading some theoretical work."[4(p232)]

Heilbrun, too, suggested that the collective articulation of one's experience in a group historically has produced a radically new mode of understanding. She asserted that women must turn to one another for stories so that reality can be rearticulated from their experiences. She identified the need for women to see themselves collectively and establish female narratives. As long as women are isolated from each other and not sharing accounts of their lives and experiences, they will not be part of any narrative of their own.[1] This was the rationale for conducting this research in a group atmosphere. The empowerment of women to claim their experiences was an integral part of this method. The findings of this study confirm that women in groups can challenge medical discourse and generate knowledge that does not dismiss experience. These findings emerged in two constitutive patterns that are not reported here: "menopause as an age" and "the biology of it all" and their seven relational themes. The theme "connected knowing," which is the focus of the present article, captured the creation of knowledge, based on experience, that occurred in the group. The acknowledgment of ourselves as the "experts" concerning this phenomenon was an empowering experience as articulated in the findings.

My interest in menopause was both personal, because I am a woman experiencing menopause, and professional, because women's health is the focus of my practice. My own subjective experience served as a starting point for this research, and in the tradition of feminist inquiry, my experiences were part of the research process. I am attempting to remain visible in this manuscript with the use of active voice. I am a Euro-American, heterosexual, middle-class nurse academic with assumptions that reflect emotional and cognitive experiences that I have had; these assumptions were explicated in the theoretical context of this study, to the group and to my research team members. However, I am also aware that I have assumptions that are so deeply embedded that it is difficult for me to understand and articulate all the ways that they have affected my view of menopause. An assumption evidenced in my feminist perspective is that what we have expressed in this group interaction may reflect historical and social forces beyond the boundaries of the encounter. Furthermore, I also assumed that the forces of the dominant culture that reflect ageism, sexism, and racism may have been internalized unconsciously by myself and the participants and reflected in our dialogue.

JUSTIFICATION

The justification, both for the subject and the method of this study, was provided by feminist scholarship. Menopause, seen by the medical community as failed production or a deficient state, is, on the contrary, according to some women, one more in the succession of empowering rites of passage in a woman's life.[5] It has been suggested that talking to women about their experiences with regard to their bodies and bodily functions such as menstruation and menopause is one way to transcend the denigration and silence that historically has cloaked these experiences.[6] Denial of the psychosexual development that accompanies women's rites of passage, such as menarche or menopause, precludes the acceptance of oneself and the accomplishments that follow from such acceptance.[5] In addition, experiential knowledge from other women can provide an alternative to the official interpretation of this event. If an experience is not made public, it may be disregarded or discounted if it is not congruent with what has been deemed normal by the medical community. In this experience, which is experienced only by women, women are the authorities. Yet many women are unable to discern levels of reality other than those given in the official interpretation of society and, in this case, of the biomedical community.

HERMENEUTIC PHENOMENOLOGY

Hermeneutic phenomenology provided the philosophical underpinning for this study. This approach evolved from an innovative development of the phenomenology of Edmund Husserl by his student Martin Heidegger.[7] Heideggerian phenomenology is a philosophical belief system that holds that our foundational mode of existing as persons is in interpretation and understanding.[8] The aim of phenomenology is to render everyday lived experience intelligible, as this is where meaning resides. Yet precisely because our lived experience is "everyday," much of its meaning remains hidden.[9] Dreyfus asserted that we take so much of what is commonplace for granted that we often fail to notice it and that to see what surrounds us requires phenomenological study.[10]

Hermeneutics is a systematic approach to interpretation that is useful for studying the descriptions and interpretation of people's experience as rendered in written or spoken text. The purpose is to disclose meanings that may be concealed within the language and the culture itself. Van Manen suggested that those meanings can be found in anecdotes and stories.[11] Anecdotes and stories are the poetic narratives that humanize and lay bare the covered meanings; they tell something particular while really addressing the general.[11] Heidegger asserted that this narrative mode of talking and telling stories, in which human beings do much of their everyday living, gives the most primordial and direct access to human phenomena.[8] Understanding and interpretation are foundational modes of a human's being according to Heideggerian hermeneutics, and there is a need for interpretation when one is explicating experience.[12]

FEMINIST RESEARCH

Uncovering meaning is the basis of phenomenology. Hermeneutical interpretation explicates meanings from written texts. Feminist research goes beyond interpretation to the acknowledgement that texts are produced within a social, political, and cultural context. The context requires explication and examination for full understanding of the phenomenon. In addition, feminist research is conducted in an environment that preserves and values women's experiences in context: it recognizes the existence of ideologic, structural, and interpersonal conditions that oppress women, and maintains a reciprocal rather than hierarchical relationship between the researcher and the participants. Feminist research can be conceptualized as research for women rather than research on women.[13–16]

In addition, feminist research is oriented toward empowering women, offering new visions for their experiences, as well as unmasking the oppression and domination in their lives.[14,17] It endeavors not only to describe and interpret phenomena of women's lives but also to raise consciousness and bring about changes in the interest of women. The goals are "both scientific and political," according to Hall and Stevens.[15(p17)] This approach is not only compatible with the philosophical underpinnings of the study, but the focus on the social, political, and cultural context is an integral part of critical hermeneutics.

RESEARCH PROCESS

The purpose of this study was to explore the experiences and meanings of menopause in a group of midlife women who were experiencing this phenomenon. Nine women, including the researcher, met 1 night a week for 6 weeks to talk about the experience of menopause. Texts transcribed from audio recordings of the sessions constituted the data for the study. The data were interpreted according to the hermeneutical method described by Diekelmann, Allen, and Tanner.[18] The coparticipants validated thematic relationships in the common meanings elicited from the text. In the tradition of feminist research, the inquiry was conducted for the purpose of finding answers to the questions women have. It acknowledged women as experts on their own lives and experiences.[15] As an interpretive researcher, I acknowledge that I was involved in this research process. This was made explicit to the group, and it is within such a framework that this research was conducted.

SELECTION OF PARTICIPANTS

The coparticipants were myself and 8 women recruited from the community in a large Southeastern city. Notices about this study were posted in bookstores, laundry/dry-cleaning establishments, the YWCA, supermarkets, a women's center, two universities, a feminist women's health center, and two churches. Participants were not recruited from health facilities or physician's offices in order to avoid recruiting women who were having medical problems. I attempted to maximize diversity with regard to race, socioeconomic status, and sexual orientation by posting notices in supermarkets in racially mixed neighborhoods, by posting notices in a bookstore known to be frequented by lesbian women, and by posting notices in bookstores featuring mostly African-American books.

Criteria for inclusion in the group included being 45 to 55 years old and experiencing one or more of the following physical indications of menopause: night sweats, hot flashes, menstrual irregularities, and absence of menses for 2 to 12 months. Additional criteria included a willingness to attend the discussion group 1 night a week for an hour and a half for 6 weeks and a desire to talk about the experience of menopause.

Fifteen women responded by phone to the notices. Twelve women returned their consent forms. I chose 8 forms randomly from the 12.

DEMOGRAPHICS OF THE GROUP

Demographics were recorded by each member at the last of the 6 nights, on a form with no identifying marks so that I would not be aware of the demographic characteristics of any one of the participants. Each coparticipant contributed a pseudonym that she agreed could be used for any quotes in the findings. Despite my attempts to maximize diversity by posting notices throughout the city, the group was composed of 7 Euro-American women and 1 African-American woman. Five participants reported household income between $20,000 and $40,000 yearly, and 3 participants reported household income over $40,000. The ages of the participants ranged from 47 to 54 years; 6 participants were married, 1 was single/never married, and 1 was divorced. All were college graduates with three participants reporting some graduate education. No one identified herself as a lesbian, but I have not assumed that this sample was heterosexual since information on sexual orientation was not requested.

THE SETTING

Setting is particularly important in qualitative research, and this setting was chosen purposefully because it is a women's organization. The group met in a private meeting room at a newly remodeled YWCA in an intown neighborhood of a large city in the Southeast. The room was large, carpeted, and newly painted in a pastel shade. Chairs were arranged around two long tables. The tables were necessary because of the tape recorder, although I would have preferred a circle with soft comfortable chairs; a circular arrangement would have had a more open feeling to it. The group met early in the evening in the middle of the week during the spring of 1992. I had anticipated that the sessions would last 1½ hours, but after the first session the group decided to extend the time so that each session lasted about 2 hours. There was free parking at the center. I provided refreshments each night, either soft drinks, juice, or ice tea, and usually either pretzels or crackers. In retrospect, we could have shared this feeding function to follow feminist tradition better.

THE INTERPRETIVE PROCESS

Two hundred seventy-one pages of transcribed texts of the group discussions constituted the data for the study. Tenets of feminist research were incorporated into the hermeneutical method described by Diekelmann, Allen, and Tanner.[18] The method is outlined step by step so that the decision trail for the study is clear; however, neither the process nor the method are linear. The process is dynamic and evolving and can never be truly captured in a fixed way.

1. Immediately after every session, I checked the tapes for clarity and took them to a transcriptionist who transcribed the raw data verbatim.
2. When the transcribed texts were available, I listened to the tapes as I read the transcriptions, making notes on the transcriptions about occurrences such as laughter, silences, and sections that needed clarification.
3. I put the tapes and the text aside to contemplate the essence of the session, then I listened and read the text a second time. In this reading, I listened for the stories told during that session. This aspect of the analysis—getting the story using direct quotes from the text—is the first of three levels of analysis in this method.
4. At the next group session, and every session thereafter, the group read this first-level interpretation and corroborated the story. The dialogue and dis-

cussion that ensued became part of the text for that session. This inclusion of the coparticipants in the research and analysis process is basic to feminist research. This was also helpful in the documentation of the effects of these discussions on the coparticipants and me. By engaging the participants in the research, I dealt explicitly with the dilemma of allowing my own theoretical or conceptual leanings to assume a privileged position. As evidenced in the text, the group was very involved in the discussion of the themes and looked forward to hearing the stories every week.

5. Peer debriefing for credibility was attained in multiple ways during this research process. The entire set of transcriptions, 271 pages total, were read by two interpretive nurse researchers who constituted my research team. My research team was involved in discussions of this project from its inception 12 months prior to data collection. We met on a regular basis prior to the initiation of the group to discuss my assumptions and the design of this project. During the actual data-gathering phase, I shared the transcriptions and my first-level interpretation with these colleagues. In further independent analysis, each research team member's interpretation was compared with mine for similarities and differences. Any discrepancies in the interpretations were clarified by referring back to the text and to the coparticipants. They are both white, middle-class women; one identified herself as heterosexual, and one identified herself as lesbian. In addition, one of these women identified herself as menopausal.

6. I reread the transcriptions frequently to make sure that I was clear about the stories. After the final group session, I studied all the texts to see if common or contradictory meanings were present. I then identified themes from the entire text (6 group meetings). This was the second step of analysis. Themes say something particular while addressing the general.[11]

7. I then identified constitutive patterns. Constitutive patterns are present in all texts and express the relationships among themes. Constitutive patterns are the highest level of hermeneutical analysis.

8. I sought validation of themes and the constitutive patterns from my coparticipants in a follow-up session that was held at a group member's home about a month later. I referred all themes back to the original descriptions throughout the analysis process to check for discrepancies and for validation. I assumed that if the interpretations offered were based on shared cultural meanings, they would be recognized by those who share that experience. The themes and constitutive patterns were recognized by the participants and by my research team.

9. As I engaged in the interpretive writing and the dialogue with the literature, the coparticipants met again over coffee and dessert, and we discussed the feminist interpretation and the findings related to the theme "connected knowing." Expert consensual validation, a criterion for trustworthiness in qualitative research, was provided by the coparticipants. Plans were made to

meet again in 2 months. At this meeting, we shared coffee and dessert, and everyone caught up on all the news. There were lots of farewell hugs and good wishes. It felt to me like it was a goodbye with old friends. The group met one more time at a potluck supper for a final verification of the findings. Several coparticipants have offered to read this manuscript, and all participants received a spiral-bound copy of the findings of the study. In interpretive research, the final verification comes from the reader of the manuscript. I have tried to include sufficient excerpts from the text for readers themselves to validate the findings.

GROUP RESEARCH

Because this research took place in a group setting, I was cognizant of group dynamics and group process. The interaction of the members and strategies for group work and termination were identified and addressed within the group and among the research team. However, the influence of the group and group process on the findings was so integral and pervasive that "connected knowing" emerged as an essential theme in the overall interpretation. My assumption going into this project was that this was a voluntary group whose members shared a common experience and presumably wanted to talk about this experience. I assumed that I would be a coparticipant in the group, but also that I would be responsible for providing an atmosphere in which women could tell their stories in a safe place and be heard. I was also aware that, despite efforts to conduct a feminist inquiry without power imbalances, I still had the power that goes along with calling the group together. There was not a time throughout the process that I was not paying attention to that aspect of power. This power issue was addressed by the research team during peer debriefing and with the group members. I attempted to deal with the paradox of power in feminist research as honestly and explicitly as I could rather than to deny the power that I had as the researcher.

FINDINGS AND INTERPRETATION

In the tradition of feminist and critical scholarship, "suspicion" is a feature that provides for a way to uncover ideologies that may be an oppressive feature of any experience.[17] With that in mind, I approached this text from a feminist perspective, with the intention of explicating any hidden meanings that may have been unnoticed by the participants, including myself, and that may serve to sustain the oppression of women in this culture.

The theme "connected knowing" emerged as a result of the group method, and, although it may not be considered an essential theme to the phenomenon of menopause, it was a theme that emerged in every session and reflected the group research process. I am also aware that the mere desire on my part to give some form, and therefore meaning, to others' experiences is forbiddingly arrogant; thus, I have attempted to stay close to the text. As Flax stated, "there is no uniquely privileged standpoint outside the text from which a speaker could claim to understand the whole objectively."[19(p37)] I am aware that what I have provided here is one of many possible interpretations and one plausible story. My perspective on the interpretive process is that of a feminist, and, although the theme "connected knowing" was reflective of the method, my interpretation reflected my feminist perspective.

"CONNECTED KNOWING"

The nature of this group was such that in my observation of the sessions, it appeared that we were good friends who were sitting around having conversations and sharing stories and anecdotes about our experiences concerning menopause. While giving language to the experience may not express the full meaning of menopause, it provided one possible way to elicit the meanings of this phenomenon. We identified the theme titled "connected knowing" from our conversations very early in the study. My use of the term "connected knowing" was guided by the work of Belenky, Clinchy, Goldberger, and Tarule.[20] The conversations in the group were unstructured and informal. The ease with which we conversed, along with the sense of immediate trust, reminded me of a characteristic of connected knowers. "It was almost instant," one member articulated, when referring to the connection that occurred in the group. Another agreed that sometimes "to find that kind of connection takes years and years."

While Belenky and associates' work was not meant to have a developmental basis, it would seem that women of ages 45 to 55, with a multitude of life experiences, would have developed skill in connected knowing.[20] We began this group with an attitude of trust, as put into words at the first meeting by Toni as we shared with each other the reasons that we had volunteered for this project:

I think the opportunity to talk about it is wonderful in an open group where it's private and nobody is really going to be hard about it or judging. I think knowing that somebody else is experiencing the same thing that you're experiencing takes the terror out of it. It takes the discomfort out of a lot of things, just knowing what's going on. I just think it's a wonderful opportunity to hear and share what everybody else has to say. You know, I tried to bring this subject up with my sisters but it's not something that you easily share like that.

Claire added this:

Well, I think for me it was a wonderful opportunity to express some thoughts and some things that were going on, you know, with me that I've been hesitant to talk about, even with close friends or . . . something about being in a group with people that, you know, they don't know that much about you, but yet you have a subject that's pulling you together. And I think that's something that I've felt. You know, there may be some things that I'd be willing to bring up in here that I wouldn't just say to a very close friend.

The group members assumed that other members had something to say that came from their own experiences and would be beneficial to hear. Belenky et al.[20]

stated that connected knowers develop procedures for gaining access to other people's knowledge, and at the heart of these procedures is the capacity for empathy. Because knowledge comes from experience, the way to understand another person's ideas is to share experiences via language. What was reiterated over and over again was that these women wanted to "hear" what other women are experiencing. The following is according to Jessica:

And I'm here because I wanted to know . . . to hear from women who were experiencing and had gone through it, what it's like. I've had a few weird little things happen, but I'm not sure. The other stuff, I would like to talk to other women about to see if they've had anything like that. I was really glad to find out this group was going to form because I have been looking for a menopause group ever since I had the idea that I was entering menopause. And I just wanted to talk to other women, you know, about it, and it really astounded me that this important event in a woman's life, there don't seem to be women talking together about it or at least women's groups that I know of talking together about it.

The physical rhythms of reproduction, the shifts of puberty and menopause, of pregnancy and lactation, seemed to be times when shared stories provide significant ways of understanding each other's and the women's own experiences. Some in the group described how when they were having babies they would seek out their "peer" groups and that learning from each other when children were small was just so "reassuring." Even in the world of printed facts and mass media, the exchange of information about these experiences in conversations seems to create another experience. Even those of us who rely on "hard scientific data" for other things can relate to the power of conversations. Una was the participant who first described the difference:

So I'm interested on the one hand, you know, what the good rigorous research says, but on the other hand at least as much, probably more, I'm interested in what individual women's lives reveal about their own turning points and so . . . I think that anytime someone says something as opposed to reading it has a vitality to it, a realness to it, and when you read about something like menopause it's pretty scary anyway. And you read it . . . it really doesn't help. But when you talk to other women and they share it with you, that's all the difference in the world.

Another participant said, "I'm interested in learning more, I mean, you know, you read it in textbooks and things like that but when it happens to you, you want more information." The unique aspect that is different when talking about experiences rather than reading about experiences is that "reading is so solitary, yes and you don't get feedback. You don't discuss it. This is so intimate."

Levesque-Lopman[6] asserted that while women cannot assume that any woman could speak for "all women," it is important to be concerned with why and how women's descriptions of individual lived experiences differ profoundly from men's descriptions of women's experiences. When the majority of writing on menopause has been done by men and usually from the medical perspective, it is not surprising that women cannot find themselves in the literature. The Western male tradition of defining knowledge only in an objective form has rejected the kind of knowledge that only women have and want about this kind of experience. This was described by Molly:

Well I find reading about it I can't find myself. I'm looking for information and this is not giving me anything. I have a sense of every one of us here has their own unique constellation of symptoms . . . and that feature makes this really like reading good fiction . . . you relate to what resonates for you. This has echoes for me, whereas the literature kind of generalizes. It's linked to the common denominator which none of us are.

Being "linked to the common denominator which none of us are" is an abstract notion of what typically happens, but none of us is "typical." This may be because the common denominator has not been a woman or defined by a woman. The other possibility is that the description of the common denominator was provided by a male expert. Either of these explanations may account for the incongruity between women's experiences and the scientific literature.

Code offered insight into and explanations of the powerful influence of experts and their knowledge on women's lives. She acknowledged the power of institutionalized knowledge that derives out of continued endorsement of some version of the "unity of science/unity of knowledge project."[21(p176)] She argued that the "intransigence of the institutionalized structures of power/knowledge that define what it is to be a woman are stubbornly deaf to criticism and block women's access to the authority they require to take responsibility for their circumstances."[21(p177)] She asserted that "many women live self-fulfilling prophecies, adhering to the options constructed by 'experts' who allegedly know them better than they could hope to know themselves."[21(p177)] It is ironic, Code continued, that "everyone can be an expert about women . . . about what they are and what they can be or do . . . except women themselves, whose self-presentation is often discredited by people who claim to know better in the name of higher expertise."[21(p177)]

For the women in the group, the scientific literature did not provide information that was useful; it did not "resonate." McKeever[22] stated that the type of knowledge women want is shared, embodied experiences. However, this embodied, contextual information that women desire is not readily available because menopause has not been a common, comfortable topic of conversation among women. This may be because menopause is an "age," and age is not a comfortable topic in an ageist culture or because of the stigmatization of women's biological rhythms. This type of knowledge is not easily conveyed in the written word. On the other hand, if what is depicted in the literature as "normative" does not "resonate," then a woman's experiential reality has been discounted. Rather than questioning the "expert literature," women remain silent, and the ideology behind the stigma is not uncovered. How, then, can we know our bodily experiences without the power of medical distortion? Hartman and Messer-Davidow[23] asserted that women construct their selves as agents of knowledge by piecing together stories in narratives that have explanatory power. As women make their narratives known, they apprehend themselves as agents of knowledge.

Authority in connected knowing does not rest on power or certification but on commonality of experience. Members in a group engage in collaborative explorations, with each individual stretching her own vision in order to share another's vision. Through mutual stretching and sharing, the group achieves a vision richer than any individual could achieve alone.[20] Toward the end of the sessions, as the group was talking about what it has meant to them to be in the group, Claire said the following in talking about another member, Jessica:

I wonder if each of us has found somebody in here that you sort of related to, like, well, you're kind of feeling the same way as I am. And in referring to another group member, I feel like she articulates a lot of things that I've felt and that we have a lot of similar concerns, and I think that with a group like this, because it's so different, that there's somebody to kind of say, oh, I understand that about you because I've felt that. And it makes for a real connection and makes me a lot calmer.

A sense of authority arises primarily through identification with the power of the group and its agreed-upon ways for knowing. For women, this often means a turning away and denial of external authority. Women need to jump outside the frames and systems that authorities provide and create their own frames. This is what Belenky and colleagues called "constructed knowledge."[20] A similar notion was articulated by Molly: "And I always knew that it [menopause] was more than biology. And yet you don't get the richness of it, and everything else that's going on, in the written word."

The research encounter and the reflexivity that was part of this method was also an integral part of the connected knowing of the group members. The idea that their voices were being heard, and their experiences were being paid attention to was an empowering experience, as noted by Claire:

Listened to and being heard. And having it echoed back. It's really nice. Like we're part of some whole new work. This is not a coffee klatch session. This is important work for us individually and as a group.

The words of women in groups historically have been trivialized: women gossip, they talk too much, and seldom tell the truth. Even the "coffee klatch" or any of women's ways of getting together in groups have been discounted, as has the knowledge that is generated in them. The false-consciousness that women assume and that society supports prevents them from contradicting this dismissal of their talk. Women gathering in groups has a long tradition in our culture and cross-culturally, as in church groups, sewing circles, and clubs. Groups have been used to mitigate some of the loneliness and desolation that women have experienced as a result of being excluded from the public sphere. Women use groups to become close to other women and to share forms of knowledge about experiences that facilitate understanding of their own experiences.

It was important to me as a feminist researcher to be explicit about my assumptions but also to share my experiences. The self-disclosure encouraged reciprocity, which then resulted in greater mutual understanding of this experience. My participation and presence in this group was visible. At the end, as we talked about what was meaningful about this group, Una said, "I think the fact that you share. You're a part of the same crisis or whatever . . . not crisis, but stage." Another member added that the group is being "listened to. We're being listened to." The group had asked me to share the "facts" about hormonal replacement therapy, which I did at the final session. It was a very brief dialogue because by that time the group had uncovered most of the knowledge they wanted, and I was not seen as the "expert."

I have explicated the theme "connected knowing" which illustrated the process of knowledge generation in a group of menopausal women. The unfolding of this knowledge seemed to result from the feeling of the experience together. A knowledge of menopause resulted that included the experiential knowledge of the experts—the women themselves. In order to act as responsible cognitive agents, some women have found that moving away from conceptualizations of pure knowledge that dismiss experience is necessary.[21] Emotional processes are crucial components of an experience such as menopause. Members cried and laughed together.

The connection that was generated because of the group experience provided the environment for saying what we, the experts, knew about or became aware of menopause. What we knew emerged in the constitutive patterns "menopause as an age" and "the biology of it all" and their seven relational themes,[24] not reported here.

•   •   •

The need for revisionist scholarship in women's health has been identified in the literature.[25] Research for and with women, not on women, and based on experience can generate knowledge that is not a reproduction of the biomedical research. In reflexive research, the knowers are situated in the society they study, and women and others appear not as objects of professional knowers but as the knowers themselves. Thus, the theorizers become subjects of study, and the subjects of study become potential theorizers.[26] Feminist nurse researchers share their class positions as producers of knowledge with the males they have criticized. As feminist scholars, we must "continuously correct in ourselves what we have criticized in others."[26(p260)]

Group research offers a method to access women's experiential, contextual accounts of experiences that are uniquely female. It offers possibilities for moving beyond the dominant perspective on women's health, which is based on a disease/nondisease model. Group knowledge can offer insight into the ways that the nonneutral labels, such as pregnancy and menopause as disease states, reduce the autonomy of women and increase the status of the physician-as-expert. A group has the potential to shatter the self-reflecting world and at the same time project its own image into history.[27]

What was present in the group was not a single voice but a continuing dialogue about experiences and possibilities. Nurses in women's health practice need to hear these kinds of dialogues. Our strategies for health promotion and intervention can only be effective if based on women's subjective experience. Interpretation of texts offers a portal to the world of subjective experience. Subjective experiences and women's voices need to be taken into account in health research.

REFERENCES

1. Heilbrun C. *Writing a Woman's Life*. New York, NY: Ballantine Books; 1988.
2. Dickson G. A feminist poststructuralist analysis of the knowledge of menopause. *ANS*. 1990;12(3):15–31.
3. Mishell D, ed. *Menopause: Physiology and Pharmacology*. Chicago, Ill: Year Book; 1987.
4. Fay B. How people change themselves: the relationship between critical theory and praxis. In: Ball T, ed. *Political Theory and Praxis*. Minneapolis, Minn: University of Minnesota Press; 1975.
5. Randall M. Praise for women of the 14th moon. In: Taylor D, Sumrall A, eds. *Women of the 14th Moon: Writings on Menopause*. Freedom, Calif: The Crossing Press; 1991.
6. Levesque-Lopman L. *Claiming Reality: Phenomenology and Women's Experience*. Totowa, NJ: Rowman & Littlefield; 1988.
7. Palmer R. *Hermeneutics: Interpretation Theory in Schleiermacher, Dilthey, Heidegger and Gadamer*. Evanston, Ill: Northwestern University Press; 1969.
8. Heidegger M; Macquarrie J, Robinson E, trans. *Being and Time*. New York, NY: Harper & Row; 1962.
9. Rather M. Nursing as a way of thinking: Heideggerian hermeneutical analysis of the lived experience of the returning RN. *Res Nurs Health*. 1992;15:47–55.
10. Dreyfus H. *Being-in-the-World: A Commentary on Heidegger's Being in Time*. Cambridge, Mass: The MIT Press; 1991.
11. Van Manen M. *Researching Lived Experience*. New York, NY: The State University of New York; 1990.
12. Packer M. Hermeneutic inquiry in the study of human conduct. *Am Psychol*. 1985;40(10):1,081–1,093.
13. Anderson J. Reflexivity in fieldwork: toward a feminist epistemology. *Image*. 1991;23(2):115–118.
14. Campbell J, Bunting S. Voices and paradigms: perspectives on critical and feminist theory in nursing. *ANS*. 1991;13(3):1–15.
15. Hall J, Stevens P. Rigor in feminist research. *ANS*. 1991;(3):16–29.
16. Parker B, McFarlane J. Feminist theory and nursing: an empowerment model for research. *ANS*. 1991;(3):59–67.
17. Thompson J. Hermeneutic inquiry. In: Moody LE, ed. *Advancing Nursing Science through Research*. Newbury Park, Calif: Sage Publications; 1990.
18. Diekelmann N, Allen D, Tanner C. *The NLN Criteria for Appraisal of Basic Programs: A Critical Hermeneutic Analysis*. New York: National League for Nursing; 1989. NLN Publication #15-2253.
19. Flax J. *Thinking Fragments: Psychoanalysis, Feminism, and Postmodernism in the Contemporary West*. Berkeley, Calif: University of California Press; 1990.

20. Belenky M, Clinchy B, Goldberger N, Tarule J. *Women's Ways of Knowing.* New York, NY: Basic Books; 1986.

21. Code L. *What Can She Know? Feminist Theory and the Construction of Knowledge.* Ithaca, NY: Cornell Press; 1991.

22. McKeever L. *Menopause: An Uncertain Passage. An Interpretive Study.* San Francisco, Calif: University of California, San Francisco; 1988. Dissertation.

23. Hartman J, Messer-Davidow E, eds. *(En)-Gendering Knowledge.* Knoxville, Tenn: University of Tennessee Press; 1991.

24. Scharbo-DeHaan M. *The Experience of Menopause: A Feminist Interpretive Study.* Atlanta, Ga: Georgia State University, Atlanta; 1993. Dissertation.

25. Woods N. Future directions for women's health research. *NAACOG's Women's Health Nursing Scan.* 1992;6(5):1–2.

26. Addelson K, Potter E. Making knowledge. In: Hartman J, Messer-Davidow E, eds. *(En)-Gendering Knowledge.* Knoxville, Tenn: University of Tennessee Press; 1991.

27. Lather P. *Getting Smart: Feminist Research and Pedagogy within the Postmodern.* New York, NY: Routledge; 1991.

Ricoeurean Hermeneutics: Its Application in Developing a Contextual Understanding of Human Experience

Mary Tantillo, PhD, RN, CS
Clinical Senior Instructor
Department of Psychiatry
Strong Memorial Hospital
University of Rochester
Rochester, New York

The purpose of this article is to show the value of using a Ricoeurean hermeneutic approach to accessing the meanings of human experience and developing a contextual understanding of this experience. The article begins with a definition and discussion of contextual understanding and proceeds with a review of Ricoeurean hermeneutic philosophy, with its emphasis on discourse, the paradigm of the text, and the theory of interpretation. An example of a Ricoeurean hermeneutic, methodological approach developed specifically to interpret the meanings of the bulimic woman's experience of relationships is reviewed. This methodological approach is based on the Ricoeurean interpretive dialectics of (a) explanation–understanding, (b) guessing–validation, (c) explanation–comprehension, and (d) distanciation–appropriation, and is guided by certain structural and semantic contexts of the text. The article concludes with examples of the exegesis of the text and a discussion regarding the fruitfulness of a Ricoeurean hermeneutic approach to developing a contextual understanding of human experience.

IN THE PURSUIT of research paradigms that offer access to and development of an understanding of the meaning of human experience, nursing scholars have begun to consider the viability of hermeneutic inquiry.[1-4] In embracing a hermeneutic approach to understanding human experience, we are called to move beyond theoretical understandings of this experience that emerge from a traditional, deductive, and empirical mode of scientific inquiry. Instead, we are asked to consider a comprehension of human experience that is based on the interpretation of lived meanings and actions that are seen as *context-bound* interactive forces.[4-9] This kind of understanding is called *contextual understanding* and can be accessed through a hermeneutic methodological approach.

Unfortunately, there is very little discussion in the nursing literature regarding contextual understanding of human experience or regarding a hermeneutic approach that would reveal this kind of understanding. This article proposes that Ricoeurean hermeneutic philosophy offers an ideal methodological approach to understanding human experience. A Ricoeurean hermeneutic methodological approach emphasizes the understanding of contextual meanings that are revealed by written discourse or a text. The contextual understanding of human experience is developed through an interpretation of a text that is also guided by several contexts. These include the particular questions posed to the text that are based on the interpreter's own context of history, culture, language, and tradition; the structural context of the text; and the semantic context of the text.[4,10–12]

This article will show how Ricoeurean hermeneutics, with its epistemological and ontological aims, is able to reveal a contextual understanding of human experience that can enrich and enhance our present theoretical knowledge about this experience. The article will begin with a description of contextual understanding and will proceed with a review of the main concepts and premises underlying Ricoeurean hermeneutics. This review will show how Ricoeurean hermeneutic philosophy informs a methodological approach to developing a contextual understanding of human experience. Finally, there will be a discussion regarding how a Ricoeurean hermeneutic approach was used specifically in a previous study to develop a contextual understanding of the bulimic woman's experience of relationships.[4] Examples of the interpretive work done in revealing a contextual understanding of this experience are provided.

CONTEXTUAL UNDERSTANDING

In this article, contextual understanding is conceptualized to be the fabric of understanding woven from the meanings of experience as they are lived by an individual in the local, immediate situation of everyday life.[4] The particular meanings constituting contextual understanding can be likened to interactive, experiential forces, where a singular experiential meaning is understood by reference to whatever it is part of, so that meaning in a singular sense and in a wholistic sense are interrelated and can be fully and accurately described. Also, contextual understanding is made up of subjective and intersubjective meanings. The latter are constitutive of the social matrix in which human beings find themselves and act. These meanings embody a certain self-definition, a vision of the agent and society. They are expressed in the language and descriptions constitutive of institutions and practices in everyday life[6] and account for the cultural and historical influences on the meanings of experience. Since meaning that constitutes contextual understanding is assumed to be dynamic and able to come to life through discourse, it can be explicated and made coherent through interpretation. Ricoeurean hermeneutics offers a way of accessing meanings that constitute contextual understanding of human experience.

RICOEUREAN HERMENEUTICS

Ricoeur proposes that hermeneutics is the appropriate philosophical and methodological position for the human sciences. He views interpretation worthy of being called "hermeneutics" if it is part of self-understanding *and* of the understanding of being. Ricoeurean hermeneutics is a reflective philosophy with both epistemological and ontological aims, based on the assumption that humans are unable to know themselves *directly* or *introspectively*. Instead, only by way of a "series of detours does he learn regarding the fullness and complexity of his own being and of his relationship to Being."[13(p7)] For Ricoeur, language is the means to understand humanity's situations and possibilities. It is through its emphasis on language, "the primary condition of all human experience,"[14(p374)] that Ricoeurean hermeneutics reveals a way of understanding the meaning of human experience and the context of this experience.

Ricoeurean hermeneutics is based on the assumption that meaningful experience can be brought to language. However, Ricoeur[12,15] also believes that the subjective and conscious meanings of experience can be clouded, contradictory, distorted, and metaphorical, requiring deciphering and interpretation. Ricoeurean hermeneutics offers an interpretive approach to access contextual meanings of human experience "by bring[ing] to light an underlying coherence or sense of these meanings."[6(p3)] Additionally, Ricoeur believes that language is more than the expression of prelinguistic experience. Language can shape and refashion this experience, revealing different ways of seeing and being in the world. Sentences convey messages from the speaker or writer about something that is not merely language itself.[5] Language possesses its own power and reality while it simultaneously references the world in which we live. While language is commonly thought of as a tool for expression of experience, it is also a context in which we stand and out of which our experiences of time and human action are created. Ricoeurean hermeneutics emphasizes that through exegesis, the interpretation of written discourse, we are able to develop a contextual understanding of the meaning of human experience.[10,12,14,16-21]

Finally, the critical role of context can be seen throughout Ricoeur's entire hermeneutic project. Context is critical in that all interpretation places the interpreter in the middle of the meanings of experience as disclosed by written discourse or a text. Since there is no definite start or end point in understanding human experience, one suddenly arrives in midconversation with the text, in regard to the multiple meanings related to experience.[9] Ricoeur's hermeneutic framework emphasizes that words have meaning only in the nexus of sentences, and sentences are uttered only in particular contexts. Polysemy, the multiple meaning of words, depends on a contextual action that filters out some of the surplus meaning. Interpretation is required to grasp this filtering effect and to develop contextual understanding of the meanings of experience.[11] Ricoeur states that "the simplest message conveyed by the means of natural language has to be interpreted because all the words are polysemic and take their actual meaning from the connections with a given context and a given audience, against the background of a given situation."[22(p125)] The often unclear and metaphorical nature of meanings, along with the circular character of relating parts and whole of meanings in a text, require a hermeneutic approach that examines the various contexts contributing to a contextual understanding of experience. Ricoeur's hermeneutic philosophy supports an examination of the following contexts, which facilitate an explication of the meanings of experience: (a) the interpreter's prejudices and particular questions posed to the text, based on the interpreter's own context of history, culture, language, and tradition; (b) the structural context of the text as a closed system of linguistic signs; and (c) the text as discourse, in terms of its semantic sense and its textual reference to the extralinguistic world.[10,17–18]

Ricoeurean hermeneutics provides a way to understand the opacity or contradiction surrounding the meanings of experience through exegesis of a text—in this article, a transformed, subjective account of a bulimic woman's experience of relationships. This exegesis unfolds the multiple layers of meanings present and moves the understanding of experience away from a solely conscious, subjective account of the person (author) and toward the meanings of experience revealed by the autonomous text. Therefore, the purpose of interpretation is not to understand the mental intention of the author lying behind the text, but to understand the meanings spoken by the text, the world of meaning regarding experience that the text projects in front of itself.[10] This world of meaning constitutes the contextual understanding of experience and reveals a new mode of seeing or being in the world. In Ricoeur's hermeneutics, new modes of seeing and being in the world are relevant to the interpreter's own self-understanding and to the understanding of human experience. In the dialectical interaction with the text, a "fusion of horizons" between the expectations and questions of the interpreter and the meanings of the text occurs. Interpretation becomes a mediation or construction "between each interpreter's own language and the language of the text." [5(p226)] What the text reveals may be different based on our changing horizons and the different questions we learn to ask.[23]

RICOEUREAN HERMENEUTIC CONTEXTS AND CONCEPTS

Before proceeding to an application of Ricoeurean hermeneutics in developing a methodological approach to understanding the meaning of the bulimic woman's experience of relationships, it is important to review briefly a number of basic concepts. An understanding of these concepts clarifies the ways in which certain linguistic structural and semantic contexts are examined and deciphered in the explication of the meaning of experience via exegesis. Also, the importance of both explanation and understanding in Ricoeurean hermeneutics is highlighted through an understanding of these concepts. A number of concepts are discussed within the context of Ricoeur's theory of discourse, paradigm of the text, and theory of interpretation.

RICOEUR'S THEORY OF DISCOURSE

Since Ricoeur views written discourse as the focus of hermeneutics, it is essential to understand the distinction he makes between language as *langue* and language as *discourse*. In reading and reflecting on the meaning of a text, both conceptualizations of language are considered. *Langue* is the culturally determined system of signs, the general code or sets of codes, on the basis of which a speaker produces a particular message or speech event (discourse). Language as langue involves finite sets of discrete entities including phonemes; morphemes and words, referred to as *lexical units;* and phrases, referred to as *syntactical units.* Most importantly, no entity in the structure of this closed system of units has a meaning of its own. Rather, linguistic entities exhibit only formal properties and differences in comparison to other linguistic entities. They have neither substantive qualities of their own nor reference to the real world.[10,24] Langue is critical in the structural analysis of the text. In a structural model, language is not a mediation between mind and things, but constitutes a world of its own, a self-sufficient system of relationships. Recognizing langue as a code for particular speech events helps set the stage for envisioning codes that may exist in an overall text. Ricoeur emphasizes that the codes of the text in a local and in a general sense help establish the inner logic operative within the text and serve to provide the explanatory, objective attitude needed in the work of interpretation.[10,24–25]

Ricoeur also views language as discourse, composed of particular, intentional, contingent, and temporal speech acts. Yet discourse is not merely "transitory and vanishing"; it also involves the synthetic construction of the sentence itself, distinct from an analytic combination of the discrete, structural entities composing the sentence. Discourse may be identified and reidentified through the identification of its propositional content—what the predicate states about the subject in a given sentence. The propositional content, the interplay between subject and predicate, becomes the "object" of the speech act. The propositional content of the sentence is examined in the semantic analysis of the text in an effort to explicate the meaning of experience expressed in written discourse. The meaning, or what Ricoeur calls the "sense" of language, comes from an integrating and semantic approach to the text, exemplifying the importance of understanding in hermeneutic work. During this work, the interpreter focuses semantically on how the sentence itself, apart from the original speaker and dialogic situation, means something.[10]

Furthermore, Ricoeur divides the objective component of discourse, the meaning as propositional content, into "sense" and "reference." The sense is the "what" of discourse, whereas the reference is the "about what" of discourse. This distinction is drawn from Frege's work.[26] The sense correlates with the propositional content within the sentence, while the reference relates language to the world. When a speaker refers to something at a certain time, this is a speech event, but this event receives its structure from the meaning as sense. The dialectic between sense and reference speaks to the relation between language and being in the world. Ricoeur's notion of our ability to bring experience to language is the ontological condition of reference, and this condition is reflected in language.[10,17] For Ricoeur, both the semantic sense of the text and the reference of the text to the world are important in the interpretation of the meaning of experience.

THE PARADIGM OF THE TEXT

Ricoeur views writing as the full manifestation of discourse. He also believes that a text, as written discourse, involves characteristics different from spoken discourse.[18] These characteristics are encapsulated in the concept of "distanciation," which refers to the distance created by written discourse. This distance allows the interpreter to read the text semantically as a work of meaning that is disconnected from the author's subjective, mental intention. In contrast to an immediate dialogical situation, the subjective intention of the speaker (author) and the discourse's meaning in written discourse do not overlap each other. It is the meaning as propositional content of the speech event that is inscribed in writing, not the event as event—the fleeting, psychological intent of the author. Hence, the "text's career escapes the finite horizon lived by its author. What the text means now matters more than what the author meant when he wrote it."[10(p30)]

With the liberation of the text spatially and temporally from the original dialogical situation or original authorial meaning, as well as from the original audience, written discourse evidences a dialectic of meaning and event. It is universal and contigent, an archive preserving tradition for communities and cultures, and a document open to future exegesis. The text opens itself to an unlimited series of readings, all situated in different socio-cultural conditions, "decontextualizing" itself in a way that it can be "recontextualized" in a new situation, rendering an indefinite number of interpretations.[10,18–27]

The semantic autonomy of the text allows it to have revelatory power of its own, extending its reference beyond the boundaries of the original dialogical situation. The text is able to project a world of meaning regarding human experience that is "nonsituational." This world of meaning refers to "being in the world," often only alluded to via metaphoric and symbolic expressions.[10] The interpreter is able to enlarge his or her own horizon of existence and understand the experience of others by examining the world of meaning revealed by the text.

THEORY OF INTERPRETATION

A Ricoeurean hermeneutic approach requires the interpreter to engage in multiple readings of the text. One reads for a sense of the whole of the text and for the meanings of the parts in relation to the whole. Initial readings provide a naive understanding of the text, whereas later readings offer a critical and informed contextual understanding of the text. Reading involves a number of interpretive dialectics that help the interpreter appropriate the meaning of the text and experience its revelatory power to project a new world or "mode of being" in the world. These interpretive dialectics include explanation–understanding, guessing–validation, explanation–comprehension, and distanciation–appropriation. In using a dialectic approach to interpreting the text, both explanation and understanding are required to mediate a fully informed, contextual, and in-depth understanding of the text. In a Ricoeurean hermeneutic approach to interpretation, explanation is the "unfolding of the range of propositions and meanings" in the text. Explanation informs understanding, which is the comprehension or "grasping of the whole chain of partial meanings in one act of synthesis."[10(p72)] In Ricoeurean hermeneutics, structural analysis constitutes the explanatory approach to the text, and semantic analysis constitutes the understanding of and ultimate appropriation of the meaning of the text.

A RICOEUREAN HERMENEUTIC METHODOLOGICAL APPROACH

The development and use of a Ricoeurean hermeneutic approach to access meanings constitutive of a contextual understanding of human experience will be illustrated through discussion of a doctoral dissertation investigating the meaning of the bulimic woman's experience of relationships.[4] Before describing the methodological approach used in the explication of the meaning of the bulimic woman's experience of relationships, it is necessary to provide briefly a context regarding the background and significance of the study phenomenon to nursing, author selection, and the nature of the text used in this study.

Background and Significance of the Study Phenomenon to Nursing

Literature review, present theoretical knowledge, and clinical practice with bulimic women all suggested the need for an interpretive approach to understanding the bulimic woman's experience of relationships.[4] There was no research that substantiated that the theoretical knowledge developed thus far provided an accurate and full understanding of the bulimic woman's experience of relationships. Also, certain deficiencies were noted when critically evaluating theory and research relevant to this phenomenon, including the following:

- the deduction of the bulimic woman's experience of relationships from theory developed from investigations about men's or nonbulimic women's experiences;
- methodological constraints in trying to access the meaning of experience of relationships with quantitative measures;
- the predominance of only the empirical, deductive approach to studying the bulimic woman's experience of relationships and building/supporting theory; and
- the general limitations in theoretical knowledge that emerge from a traditional, scientific mode of inquiry, including its disengagement from the life world, meanings, and the experience of relationships that are part of the human realm.[4-5]

In the search for alternative research paradigms that could access meaning and provide a contextual understanding of the bulimic woman's experience of relationships, Ricoeur's hermeneutic philosophy was discovered. A Ricoeurean hermeneutic approach would allow the interpreter to access the meanings of the bulimic woman's experience of relationships through an exegesis of a text. In this study, the interpreter assumed that the text would bring experience to language and that exegesis could provide a contextual understanding of the bulimic woman's experience of relationships that would enhance and enrich our present theoretical notions of this experience. Since nurses are situated in others' moment-to-moment experiencing and the meanings lived in this experiencing,[7] a Ricoeurean hermeneutic study revealing a contextual understanding of the bulimic woman's experience of relationships furthers nursing's attempts to understand human beings and human phenomena in dynamic, holistic, and experience-near ways. Hermeneutic inquiry can help nursing "move beyond knowing to really understanding"[8(p6)] and provide an additional voice in the discourse about the bulimic woman's experience of relationships.

Author Selection

In this particular hermeneutic inquiry, one 22-year-old, bulimic woman was selected as the author of the text. The details related to method of author selection are discussed in Tantillo.[4] The particular author was deemed as medically stable and as meeting the *DSM-III-R* criteria for bulimia nervosa.[28] All dialogues with the author occurred in a natural setting of her choice and were audiotaped and transcribed verbatim to create a text. The author was asked to describe her experience of relationships with significant others in her everyday life. These people included her parents, sister, spouse, best friend, and the researcher. The researcher only asked questions to clarify the meaning of certain words, issues, or themes as they emerged. General questions included the following:

- What makes this relationship or particular experience meaningful to you?
- What do you value most and least in this relationship?
- What needs do you feel the other person does/does not meet for you in this relationship?
- Does your use of food relate at all to your experience of relationship with this person?[4]

Nature of the Text

In this Ricoeurean hermeneutic inquiry, the text was assumed to be a transformed, subjective account of the bulimic woman's experience of relationships. In transcribing the seven tape-recorded dialogues, the researcher was able to "fix" spoken discourse in a text and preserve the meaning of the speech event. The 394-page text was assumed to be autonomous and independent from the author, making experience public and bringing it to language. The text was more than the author's intention and had the power to disclose a world of meaning regarding the bulimic woman's experience of relationships. Since written discourse is accessible to interpretation, it was able to reveal a contextual understanding of this experience while simultaneously enlarging the interpreter's own self-understanding in this endeavor.

METHODOLOGICAL APPROACH

After spending many months reading and reflecting on Ricoeur's hermeneutic philosophy and engaging in the initial reading of and reflection on the text in this inquiry, the interpreter (researcher) was able to develop a methodological approach to access the meanings of the bulimic woman's experience of relationships. The interpretive dialectics of understanding–explanation, guessing–validation, explanation–comprehension, and distanciation–appropriation guided the exegesis of the text. Although these interpretive processes will be presented below in a sequential and linear fashion, the actual work of interpretation involves a dialectical interaction, an alternating engagement and disengagement with the text. The interpreter initially approaches the text with certain questions regarding the study phenomenon and identifies new questions that emerge from the multiple readings of the text. Initial questions emerge from the context of the interpreter's tradition or historical, sociocultural context, and later questions evolve from the interaction with other traditions represented by the meanings projected by the text. The questions that the interpreter asked of the text in this study included the following:

- What is the sense and reference of the bulimic woman's experience of relationships as disclosed by the text?
- What are the signifying linguistic units of the bulimic woman's experience of relationships as revealed by the text?
- What is the relationship between the constitutive partial meanings of the experience of relationships and the meaning of the experience as a whole as disclosed by the text?
- Are there any symbols or metaphors revealed by the text?
- What is the significance of these symbols or metaphors?
- Do any of these symbols or metaphors specifically relate the experience of relationships to food or to the experience of hunger and eating?
- What is the holistic, contextual understanding or "world" of meaning constitutive of the bulimic woman's experience of relationships as it is disclosed in front of the text?

There is a continuous, to-and-fro movement between the parts and whole of the text as one works to explicate the meaning of the study phenomenon. This dialectical activity constitutes the process of understanding called the *hermeneutic circle,* in which one progresses toward a depth of understanding of the text.[5] The interpretive dialectics employed in this study were used to examine, illuminate, and mediate between the structural and semantic contexts revealed by the text in order to arrive at an informed, critical, and contextual understanding of the bulimic woman's experience of relationships.

APPLICATION OF A RICOEUREAN HERMENEUTIC APPROACH

In reading and reflecting on Ricoeur's hermeneutic philosophy, it is clear that any methodological approach needs to be developed within the context of the particular study phenomenon. Although the specific methodological approach used in this study may not be appropriate for another study, it does provide the reader with examples of how one interacts with the text in explicating the meaning of human experience. What follows is a brief discussion of how the interpreter worked with the text in moving from an initial, naive understanding of the bulimic woman's experience of relationships to a critical, contextual understanding and appropriation of the meaning of this experience. Textual examples of the interpretive work are provided. Details regarding the exegesis and findings are in Tantillo.[4]

Initial, Naive Understanding: The Dialectic of Guessing–Validation

The interpretive dialectic of explanation–understanding was first noted in the text in the movement from initial, naive understanding to explanation because the interpreter used both subjective and objective approaches to the text. Initial understanding is a naive grasping of the meanings of the text as a whole. It involved a dialectical movement of reading and reflection on the relationship between part and whole of the text. Initial understanding aimed at an explication of the reference pole of the meaning of the text—how language relates to extralinguistic reality. In this text, the meanings referred to the bulimic woman's experience of relationships with others in the world. In the initial readings, as with all other readings, the interpreter acknowledges the distanciation created by written discourse and the semantic autonomy of the text.

The first act of understanding involves the dialectic of guessing–validation. The initial understanding of the text took the form of a guess because the mental intention of the author and the verbal meaning of the text no longer coincide, leaving the text open to various constructions of meaning. The interpreter forms guesses about the architecture of the text, significance of part and whole of the text and their relationship, literary genre of the text, and potential horizons of meaning (including metaphoric and symbolic expressions) of the text. These guesses are validated with a logic of probability, via the use of criteria such as coherence, comprehensiveness, contextuality, thoroughness, and applicability.

The first reading of the text revealed that it was a narrative because it was able to disclose the "temporal character of human experience" and "creatively imitate or represent human action."[19(p81)] In this inquiry, the narrative was a "telling" of the lived experience of relationships with significant others in the everyday life of the bulimic woman. The recounting of the bulimic woman's experiences of action and temporality were narrated within the context of her experience of relationships with others. The significant others are viewed as characters, and the bulimic woman, the narrator. The narrative is constructed from various topics and subtopics. The bulimic woman's experience of relationships with each of the significant others was viewed as a topic, whereas subtopics referred to what the text specifically stated about the experience with a significant other. For example, one topic was "the experience of relationship with spouse," and subtopics included "features common to the experience of relationship over time," "changes in the experience of relationship before and after disclosing the secret of bulimia to husband," and "an association between the bulimic woman's relationship with food and the experience of relationship with husband." Topics and subtopics were read within the context of the text as a whole work, a narrative referring to the bulimic woman's overall experience of relationships.

The excerpts below reveal the "secret life" the bulimic woman lived before disclosing her secret of bulimia to her husband. This secret life involved feelings of vulnerability, fears of rejection, and terror regarding telling her secret in the relationship with him. These and similar excerpts helped validate the existence of the subtopic "changes in the experience of relationship before and after disclosing the secret of bulimia to husband."

And I really did hide it! I made a lot of excuses to use a bathroom after I ate. And I know that he suspected something was up, but I wasn't going to tell him then. I guess I just wasn't ready.[4(p88)]

It was a big risk when I told him. I remember . . . I was terrified of telling him, and I just felt . . . if he doesn't reject me now then . . . it will probably be easier after this. I was terrified . . . he was the first person I told, and so I had no idea. . . . I was terrified of being vulnerable! For a year and a half I was keeping this secret. And I felt like I was in control and it was my coping mechanism. Just exposing that—I just felt very vulnerable . . . [but] I felt so out of control with my life.[4(p89)]

Finally, the initial reading of the text revealed that there were features common to the bulimic woman's overall experience of relationships. Although all the excerpts representing the partial meanings that validated this holistic understanding of the experience of relationships will not be addressed here, the initial understanding is completed with a return to the "whole" of the text.[4]

From Explanation to Comprehension

The second main dialectic movement within the dialectic of explanation–understanding is the movement from explanation to comprehension. This second kind of understanding is informed by explanation and culminates in the act of appropriation, the critical and contextual understanding of the text and the world it reveals.[10] In the movement toward a critical and contextual understanding of the text, explanation involves the structural analysis of the text. With the semantic autonomy of the text, there is a suspension of the ostensive reference of the text to the immediate world. During this part of the exegesis, the interpreter views the text as a worldless entity, a closed system of signs, analogous to discourse seen as langue. The beauty of structural analysis as explanation entails its belonging to the same field, semiotics, versus the natural sciences.

Structural analysis, through its consideration of constitutive linguistic units within the whole, helps set limits to polysemic meaning while it also allows for symbolism in the text.[25] Structural analysis assists in the explication of the "sense" component of the sense/reference dialectic of meaning. The meaning achieved is not existential or philosophical in nature but is an inner logic or unified structure of the narrative revealed by the configuration of constitutive linguistic units identified in the text. These units can be viewed as codes that help explain the narrative. Multiple critical readings of the text in this inquiry revealed action, language, and temporal codes. (See Tantillo[4] for detailed discussion of all codes.) Examples of the action and language codes are listed in Table 1. These codes were constituted by interrelated phrases and sentences including units of action, units signifying the one doing the action (the actor), units signifying tentative language, units signifying extremist or dichotomous language, and units signifying temporal experience.

The excerpt below is an example of the interrelated phrases that constituted the action code, "living a secret life":

... I was bulimic when I first met my husband, and *I hid it from him for about two years* ... So, in a way, I felt like *I was living in a secret life* .... I really *did hide it!* I made a lot of excuses to use a bathroom, after I ate ... but *I wasn't going to tell him* then. I guess

Table 1. Codes of the text

Actor codes	Action codes	Temporal codes	Other language codes
Spouse	Telling about it	Chronological time	Tentative language
Mother	Living a secret life	Internally experienced/personal time	Extremist/dichotomous language
Father	Being out of control with the eating		
Sister	I was angry		
Best friend	Holding in emotion		
Researcher	Acting perfect		
	See me as a total person		
	Getting the validation		
	Getting the support		
	Being abandoned		
	Feeling guilty		
	Under mom's control		
	Involved on the sidelines		
	Everything exploded into her world		

I just wasn't ready to tell him . . . . but I also felt alone because the other thing she'd [mother] say is, "You *can't talk to anybody else.*" It was one of those things where you *can't talk to anybody else outside the family about family problems. . . .* I felt like the burden was on my shoulders. I felt very alone. . . . One of the things she did was tell me everything that was going on at the bank. . . . Then she would *swear me to secrecy. I just felt like it wasn't supposed to be talked about.* So, I mean the whole rifle incident [father's suicidal gesture] put a barrier in our relationship. . . . *I grew up thinking that anything that happened in the house was a secret. . . . There's a little pocket that holds all those secrets—supposedly of the family. . . . And I was in such a mentality that you keep everything inside* that I never even thought of asking him or bringing it up. . . . *I was just more aware of that* [father's alcoholism] *than other secrets. . . . Keeping secrets was always there. . . . It's a lifestyle. It's a whole lifestyle.*[4(p126)]

Analysis of the codes in the text revealed that there were particular relationships among the codes, as well as distinctions among them. The codes created "boundary situations" in which the interpreter could develop an understanding of the text that would not be based solely on an intuitive grasping of the intention of the text. The boundary situations and structural law of the narrative in this study revealed that the text was a network of actor, action, "other" language, and temporal codes. This system of codes spoke to a phenomenology of relationships within the culture of the bulimic woman's family and social network.

Comprehension

Whereas structural analysis involves distanciation from the discourse of the text and objectification of the text, the process of comprehension involves a dialectic of engagement with and disengagement from the text. Disengagement involves the critical reflection on plurivocal meanings of each of the codes of the text, whereas engagement involves interaction with the text that allows the interpreter to reflect on the context of the discourse. This latter, reflective process leads to the appropriation of the most probable meaning of the text, an event in which the present reader experiences a "grasping together" of the parts and whole of the text. What is "made one's own" in the process of appropriation is not something mental and behind the text but the "project" of a world.[10] The interpreter does not project his or her own self-understanding or *a priori* notions onto the text, but instead the text offers the interpreter a world of meaning and a new way of being that enlarges the interpreter's own self-understanding and the understanding of the study phenomenon.

In the movement from explanation to understanding, the interpreter engages in a semantic analysis of the text that reveals the extralinguistic meaning of the narrative. The text is read as discourse, constitutive of sentences that bear reference and meaning. The interpreter focuses on the reference of the text, understanding the meaning of the bulimic woman's experience of relationships versus explaining the linguistic structure of the narrative. This semantic analysis is based on a contextual theory of meaning that assists in the critical reflection on the polysemy of words.[4,10–24] Semantic analysis is used to explicate the most probable meanings of the codes rendered by the structural analysis of the text and uses the context of the sentence and surrounding discourse, as well as certain nonlinguistic, contextual factors, to achieve this task.

An example of the semantic analysis of the action code, "see me as a total person"[4(pp166)] helps reveal the kind of work done in this phase of textual interpretation. Although the entire analysis of this code is not discussed here, the analysis of the word *see* in the code will be reviewed. Semantic analysis of this word allows the reader to understand that similar to the entire code, the word *see* means more than what is indicated in an initial, acontextual, literal interpretation. Semantic analysis of the above code revealed that the bulimic woman did not experience mother as "seeing her as a total person." The bulimic woman did not experience mother as someone who could truly and fully "see" her in a holistic sense. This leads one to ask, "What is really meant by the word *see* in the discourse of the text?" This question is answered by turning to the discourse surrounding the statement "see me as a total person" in the text. The word *see* provides us with a good example of the polysemy of ordinary language. Without the context of the narrative, *see* can mean approximately 20 different things. However, when reading the statement within the context of the narrative, it is clear that *see* means more than to "passively perceive with the eye."[29(p1,056)] This meaning indicates a viewing of the person in a physical or empirical context, as *perception* means awareness directly through the senses. The closest dictionary definition to what *see* means in the text is "to understand or comprehend the real character or nature of."[29(p1,056)] Yet this meaning still falls short without the use of the context of the discourse in the text.

The interpretation of the statement "see me as total person" revealed that it meant a kind of comprehension or "grasping together" of the whole person (bulimic woman). This "grasping together" was an active, not passive, process. In a sense, it paralleled what we have defined comprehension to be in the interpretation of the text. To *see* meant to understand the bulimic woman in a critical, informed way. The text revealed that to *see* is a dialectical process, wherein the bulimic woman desires others not only to synthesize the wholeness and complexity of her person and acknowledge her similarities to others, but also to discern, to be acutely aware of her differences from others. To "see me as a total person" meant to look beyond the sum of the parts or the sum of her performances to the bulimic woman as a unique and whole human being. To see in this sense meant to view her actively in a way that involved the eyes, the brain, and the heart. A holistic "viewing" of the bulimic woman is one in which the other can "see" in a "thinking–feeling–doing" way. It is this ability to see that the bulimic woman did not experience in the relationship with her mother. The bulimic woman wished that her mother could "see her as a total person," aside from her accomplishments, as a human being who is also an actor or doer. What was lacking in the experience of relationship with the mother was the bulimic woman's sense that the mother could "see" her pathos, as well as her performance. The following passage reveals the meaning of the word *see* in the context of the statement "see me as a total person" and in the context of the discourse surrounding the statement. This passage speaks to the experience of relationship with the mother and the bulimic woman's feeling that the mother cannot see her in the way described above:

I need somebody that *cares about me as a person, aside from my accomplishments.* And I need somebody that *loves me for me* . . . somebody *to see me as a total person aside from my accomplishments* . . . . my family acceptance came when you did something the right way. When you achieved something, there was acceptance. If you did something . . . negative, there wasn't acceptance. If you did something that was against what my mom thought, it wasn't accepted . . . . it *reflected on me as a person totally.* It wasn't just my behavior. . . . I was her [mother's] showpiece. . . . I always had to be dressed perfectly and *act perfectly,* when I went to meet her co-workers . . . the white gloves and the tan new shoes and the white lace socks. . . . I used to twirl the baton . . . for about nine years very competitively . . . And it was basically all for her . . . there were times that I wanted to quit, and she would tell me . . . "How can you do this to me?" . . . I just felt like a showpiece, her showpiece" . . . I was torn. . . . *She wouldn't like ask me about how I felt* about it . . . She would care so much if I got first place, and she wouldn't ask me, "Are you having fun out there?" . . . That stuff wasn't important . . . *I was sad she didn't recognize that.* . . . When I was 18, I had an abortion, and my mom found out about it . . . the first thing she said was, "I can't believe you did this to me! What are people going to think?" *She didn't ask me if I was alright* . . . *I mean, I really didn't feel acknowledged* . . . I felt very sad, very frustrated, very angry with her. . . . [After my mom found out I had sex at age 16] those whole six months were almost like a "living hell" . . . the silent treatment . . . *basically, almost everything that I was doing as a person, got turned off* . . . When I was in high school and college, and now, I realize that *I wanted her to love me for me and not what I do. And I still don't feel like I get that from her* . . . *her love is still based on what I do* . . . as I got older, her saying, *"I love you,"* seemed to be more connected with me being the perfect daughter . . . I would like the *respect for myself as a person and my feelings* . . . And I just think that's missing . . . *respect for me as a person* . . . [4](pp167–168,170–171)

Appropriation

A semantic analysis of the text allows the interpreter to move toward a critical, contextual, and holistic understanding of the study phenomenon. In the present study, this type of understanding involved the comprehension of the reference of the text and the appropriation of the "world" of meaning of the bulimic woman's experience of relationships. The text is able to refer to an extralinguistic reality because of its semantic autonomy. The interpreter can "imaginatively actualize the potential non-ostensive references of the text in a new situation, that of the reader."[10](p81) In doing so, a new, ostensive reference is created through the act of reading and interacting with the text. In appropriating the meaning of the text, the interpreter attempts to grasp the "world propositions" opened up by the reference of the narrative. Appropriation is complete when the interpreter contextually understands the human experience that the narrative brought to language, the world of human action and the temporality it unfolds in the face of this experience.[19] This contextual understanding represents a "grasping together" of the parts and whole of the text that reveals a mode of "being in the world" in front of itself.

In this study, the appropriation of the text revealed a certain contextual understanding of human action and time as they interacted and formed the "flux" of the world of the bulimic woman's experience of relationships. The text revealed that over time, the bulimic woman knowingly and unknowingly created a way of "being in the world" that was characterized by paradoxes, explosions, and times of loss or terror. This mode of being emerged from and contributed to particular experiences of relationships in the everyday life of the bulimic woman and was one in which she was paradoxically "not being" in order "to be" in relationships with others. Finally, the appropriation of the text revealed that the entire narrative was an "extended" ontological metaphor for human existence. The world of the bulimic woman's experience of relationships was seen as a metaphorical reference about our "being in the world," the paradox, explosions, and times of loss and terror we all experience in relationships with others. The appropriation or contextual understanding of the bulimic woman's experience of relationships was informed by the previous initial readings and the structural and semantic analyses of the text.

•   •   •

In embracing a dynamic and evolving view of man and reality, it is essential that nursing scholars examine and consider methods of inquiry that can reveal the meanings of human experience. These meanings both emerge from and shape the linguistic, social, cultural, and historical contexts of this experience. Contextual understanding of everyday life experiences provides an additional voice in the discourse about human experience. Theoretical understandings of human experience that emerge from a traditional, deductive, and empirical mode of scientific inquiry attempt to order and make coherent the unfolding of experience in everyday life. However, they require an abstraction of the human realm in respect to formal properties. Formalization provides theoretical statements regarding human experience that may be poor in content compared to the fullness of human experience that they are presumed to explain.[5] Conversely, contextual understanding emerges from linguistic data and reveals patterns, contexts of interactive meanings, and the relationship between parts and whole in human experience. Contextual understanding can provide a rich portrait of human experience and can complement the theoretical knowledge regarding this experience.

Both the discussion regarding Ricoeurean hermeneutics and the excerpts above underscore the importance of examining a person's discourse in trying to understand contextually the meanings of everyday life experiences. A Ricoeurean hermeneutic methodological approach emphasizes the interpretation of written discourse and is based on a contextual theory of meaning that helps the interpreter examine critically the overall nature of discourse used to describe human experience as well as the particular words, phrases, and sentences used to describe this experience.

Textual exegesis can reveal the ways in which the contextual meanings of the experiences of time and action are created and recreated from the language we possess. The distanciation and semantic autonomy that characterize written discourse allow the interpreter to develop a contextual understanding of human experience that is no longer tied to the author of the text, the original audience, and the dialogic situation. The contemporary nurse researcher is able to appropriate the meanings of the text and develop a contextual understanding of human experience that is beyond the limited horizon of the author's own existential situation.[30] This appropriation reveals new modes of seeing and being in the world that contribute to the nurse researcher's understanding of others' experiences and enlarges his or her own self-understanding.

REFERENCES

1. Alexander L. *Explication of the Meaning of Clinical Judgment in Nursing Practice Using Ricoeurean Hermeneutics.* Garden City, NY: Adelphi University; 1991. Dissertation.
2. Allen D. Nursing research and social control: alternative models of science that emphasize understanding and emancipation. *Image.* 1985;17(2):59–65.
3. Reeder F. *Nursing Research, Holism and Philosophy of Science: Points of Congruence between M.E. Rogers and E. Husserl.* Ann Arbor, Mich: Microfilm International, University of Colorado; 1984. Dissertation.
4. Tantillo M. *An Interpretive Study of the Bulimic Woman's Experience of Relationships.* Garden City, NY: Adelphi University; 1992. Dissertation.
5. Polkinghorne D. *Methodology for the Human Sciences: Systems of Inquiry.* Albany, NY: State University of New York Press; 1983.
6. Taylor C. Interpretation and the sciences of man. *The Review of Metaphysics.* 1971;25(1):3–51.
7. Munhall PL, Oiler CJ. Philosophical foundations of qualitative research. In: Munhall PL, Oiler CJ, eds. *Nursing Research: A Qualitative Perspective.* Norwalk, Conn: Appleton-Century-Crofts; 1986.
8. Meleis AI. *Theoretical Nursing: Development and Progress.* Philadelphia, Pa: Lippincott; 1987.
9. Ricoeur P. Phenomenology and hermeneutics. In: Thompson JB, trans-ed. *Hermeneutics and the Human Sciences.* London, England: Cambridge University Press; 1981.
10. Ricoeur P. *Interpretation Theory: Discourse and the Surplus of Meaning.* Fort Worth, Tex: The Texan Christian University Press; 1976.
11. Ricoeur P; Thompson JB, trans-ed. *Hermeneutics and the Human Sciences.* London, England: Cambridge University Press; 1981.
12. Ricoeur P. The model of the text: meaningful action considered as a text. In: Thompson JB, trans-ed. *Hermeneutics and the Human Sciences.* London, England: Cambridge University Press; 1981.
13. Ihde D. *Hermeneutic Phenomenology: The Philosophy of Paul Ricoeur.* Evanston, Ill: Northwestern University Press; 1971.
14. Ricoeur P. On interpretation. In: Baynes K, Bohman J, McCarthy T, eds. *After Philosophy: End or Transformation?* Cambridge, Mass: MIT Press; 1987.
15. Ricoeur P. *Freud and Philosophy: An Essay on Interpretation.* New Haven, Conn: Yale University Press; 1970.
16. Ricoeur P; Czerny R, trans-ed. *The Rule of Metaphor.* Toronto, Canada: University of Toronto Press; 1975.
17. Ricoeur P. Structure, word, event. In: Reagan CE, Stewart D, eds. *The Philosophy of Paul Ricoeur: An Anthology of His Work.* Boston, Mass: Beacon Press; 1978.

18. Ricoeur P. What is a text? Explanation and understanding. In: Thompson JB, trans-ed. *Hermeneutics and the Human Sciences*. London, England: Cambridge University Press; 1981.

19. Ricoeur P; McLaughlin K, Pellauer D, trans. *Time and Narrative*. Chicago, Ill: The University of Chicago Press; 1984; 1.

20. Ricoeur P; McLaughlin K, Pellauer D, trans. *Time and Narrative*. Chicago, Ill: The University of Chicago Press; 1985; 2.

21. Ricoeur P; McLaughlin K, Pellauer D, trans. *Time and Narrative*. Chicago, Ill: The University of Chicago Press; 1988; 3.

22. Ricoeur P. Creativity in language. In: Reagan CE, Stewart D, eds. *The Philosophy of Paul Ricoeur: An Anthology of his Work*. Boston, Mass: Beacon Press; 1978.

23. Bernstein R. *Beyond Objectivism and Relativism: Science, Hermeneutics, and Praxis*. Philadelphia, Pa: University of Pennsylvania Press; 1983.

24. Ullman S. *Semantics: An Introduction to the Science of Meaning*. New York, NY: Harper & Row; 1962.

25. Bleicher J. *Contemporary Hermeneutics: Hermeneutics as Method, Philosophy, and Critique*. London, England: Routledge & Kegan Paul; 1980.

26. Frege G. On sense and reference. In: Geach P, Black M, trans-eds. *Translations from the Philosophical Writings of Gottlob Frege*. Oxford, England: Basil Blackwell; 1970.

27. Ricoeur P. The hermeneutical function of distanciation. In: Thompson JB, trans-ed. *Hermeneutics and the Human Sciences*. London, England: Cambridge University Press; 1981.

28. *Diagnostic and Statistical Manual of Mental Disorders*. 3rd ed, rev. Washington, DC: American Psychiatric Association; 1987.

29. *Webster's II New Riverside University Dictionary*. Boston, Mass: Houghton Mifflin; 1984.

30. Ricoeur P. Appropriation. In: Thompson JB, trans-ed. *Hermeneutics and the Human Sciences*. London, England: Cambridge University Press; 1981.

Heuristic Inquiry:
The Experience of Sadness
After Relocation

Maye Thompson, RN, MSN
Doctoral Student
Department of Mental Health Nursing
Oregon Health Sciences University
Portland, Oregon

Mary Waldo, RN, MSN
Doctoral Student
Department of Family Nursing
Oregon Health Sciences University School of Nursing
Portland, Oregon

Betty Ang, RN, MSN, CS
Doctoral Student
Department of Family Nursing
Oregon Health Sciences University School of Nursing
Portland, Oregon

Judy Kendall, RN, PhD
Assistant Professor
Department of Mental Health Nursing
Oregon Health Sciences University School of Nursing
Portland, Oregon

This article describes heuristic inquiry, a phenomenologically oriented research methodology that emphasizes the passionate use of self to access personal knowledge. Less a technique than a way of asking questions, the data in heuristic inquiry may take many forms, and results of a study are presented as an evocative and meaningful depiction of understanding, in the form of a narrative, poem, painting, or performance. The experience of sadness after relocation is used to illustrate the process of heuristic inquiry.

MODES OF INQUIRY are the means by which people seek to know the truth about the way the world works and about the meaning of their lives. The purpose of this article is to introduce nurse clinicians and researchers to one mode of inquiry: heuristic research. Heuristic inquiry involves disciplined, passionate exploration of one's own experience, emphasizing knowing through personal experience. In this way, the researcher becomes the primary research instrument. "Self-search, self-dialogue, and self-discovery"[1(p11)] drive heuristic investigation.

Psychologist Clark Moustakas developed heuristic inquiry as a phenomenological, qualitative research methodology in response to the feelings he experienced during his daughter's serious illness.[2] Observing his own experiences during that time, and those of his daughter and other young patients on the same hospital unit, touched the chords of loneliness. The resonations sounded not only through the experience of illness and difficult treatment decisions, but through his life and his understanding of the human condition. Moustakas began to explore loneliness in all its myriad facets, as they presented themselves in "many moments, conversations, dialogues, and discussions."[2(p104)] His book of essays, *Loneliness,*[3] inspired reams of correspondence to the author by people who found themselves and their own experience mirrored in the book's lyrical and evocative prose.[2]

Other experiences studied by means of heuristic inquiry include feeling angry,[4] growing up in a fatherless home,[5] psychological androgyny,[6] feeling unconditionally loved,[7] being shy,[8] being sensitive,[9] having self-doubt and self-confidence,[10] having ethnic identity,[11] being inspired,[12] and feeling connected to nature.[13]

Our own interest in heuristic research springs from several sources. The first is a long-standing interest in concepts of empathy, the therapeutic use of self, and healing in the nurse–patient relationship as an inward journey.[14] Another source compelling our choice was our recent life experience in relocating from different parts of the country. Our personal encounter and intense feelings surrounding this phenomenon inspired further exploration into heuristic inquiry.

The word *heuristic* as defined by the *Oxford English Dictionary* (1933) means "serving to find out or discover" and comes from the same Greek root as the familiar *eureka.*[15] Educators often use the word *heuristic* to describe the models they use to help students learn and retain materials, such as pictures drawn on the board that relate concepts to one another, often in a schematic or simplified way. Nursing theorist Rosemarie Parse[16] used the word *heuristic* to designate inductively derived descriptions of the structural essence of experience that arise from Heideggerian phenomenological inquiry. In contrast, Moustakas uses the word *heuristic* to designate a way of asking questions, underscoring the unique role of passionate, personal involvement that compels the process of heuristic inquiry from inception to completion.

The passionate use of self to drive inquiry differentiates heuristic inquiry from traditional phenomenological investigation.[15] The norm in the latter is to "bracket" or attempt to detach from one's previous experiences and set the self aside, in order to experience freshly without prejudice the phenomenon of interest. In heuristic inquiry, the investigator immerses his or her self in the experience, connecting with latent or covert meanings and feelings, and gaining a sense of relationship within the experience. This use of self, "the human as instrument," has a long and venerable place in the discipline of anthropology. Lincoln and Guba[17] note that the human instrument brings flexibility, adaptability, and the unique capability to tap tacit knowledge.

Polyani's concept of tacit knowing is the philosophical basis for heuristic research.[1] Such knowing is rooted in the human capacity to sense the unity or whole from individual parts or qualities; to attend simultaneously to both conscious and subliminal information; to integrate that information unconsciously to perform such psychomotor tasks as riding a bicycle, finding our way to a seat in a darkened theater, or playing the piano; and to speculate on alternative scenarios quickly and unconsciously. Intuition, the ability to sense clues or patterns, is another important type of knowing.[1]

This emphasis on tacit knowledge, intuition, and personal involvement brings to mind recent work exploring "women's ways of knowing."[18] Women who were "subjective knowers" relied on "gut feelings," an "inner voice," or "intuition" to decide what was true. They believed that truth was relative and personal: "what may be true for you may not be true for me." Subjective knowers believed understanding or knowing the truth had little value unless it served to prompt action. In general, they found it difficult to identify the source of their knowledge and articulate the process by which they gained access to it. This epistemological stance and mode of thinking have been criticized as antirationalist or "womanly." Nonetheless, recent nursing research has begun to explore this type of knowledge as the basis for expert nursing practice.[19-20] Heuristic inquiry has the potential to do the same in the conduct of nursing research.

The purpose of this article is to describe heuristic inquiry. We will give a brief overview of the heuristic method and then illustrate the process in detail using our own study. Finally, we offer a discussion about the potential contribution of heuristic method to nursing science. We hope to pique the reader's interest in this methodology and recommend Moustakas' book[1] for further insight and information.

PHASES OF HEURISTIC INQUIRY

Moustakas[1] outlined six phases characteristic of heuristic inquiry: (1) engagement, (2) immersion, (3) incubation, (4) illumination, (5) explication, and (6) creative synthesis. These phases are nonlinear; they overlap and may be experienced simultaneously or in a rhythm unique to each researcher. Validation of findings is interwoven throughout the entire process.

The process of heuristic research is predicated on the first phase, engagement. *Engagement* starts with a passionate interest or concern that can arise out of one's personal life, professional interests, or social problems, and can have emotional, intellectual, or spiritual roots. Engagement compels the formulation of the question that drives the research forward.

Immersion is the heart of the exploratory, imaginative, self-directed data collection process in heuristic inquiry. Several techniques may be used to explore the phenomenon. These include systematic observation of active experience; imaginary "dialoguing" with the phenomenon; in-dwelling, a conscious, deliberate, and concentrated introspection; and focusing, a technique described by Gendlin[21] that promotes relaxed, receptive, meditative introspection.[1] The data in heuristic research may take many forms: self-reflective diary or journal entries "about people, places, meetings, readings, nature,"[1(p28)] interviews; stories; even poems, songs, drawings, or paintings.

Another strategy in this phase is seeking accounts of the experiences of others in point and counterpoint with one's own. The openness, trust, self-awareness, and understanding that come with the discovery and refinement of self-knowledge form the base upon which the researcher can "disclose the self as a way of facilitating disclosure from others."[1(p17)] In encouraging others to "express, explore and explicate the meanings that are within his or her experience,"[1(p26)] the researcher can understand the phenomenon more fully, as well as develop a description of the phenomenon that can be conveyed to and understood by others.

It is important to note that heuristic inquiry is not a method *per se,* but rather an approach to gathering and analyzing qualitative data. The boundaries of method in heuristic inquiry are undetermined, and techniques are flexible. Methods of immersion are chosen, developed, or even discovered serendipitously, in accordance with the nature of the phenomenon of interest, the cast of the study question, and each researcher's personality and style.

Once the researcher is immersed in the question, *incubation* may provide a rest from concentrated focus on the problem. Incubation allows the researcher to digest and incorporate all levels of meaning arising from the experiences of immersion. Researchers may find it difficult to justify the time and apparent nonproductivity of this phase, but it is an essential and unavoidable part of the process.

Illumination is the moment when conscious understanding of the multiple meanings, aspects, core themes, and essences of the phenomenon occurs, when understanding becomes tangible. Illumination is the "aha," and is usually accompanied by feelings of discovery and excitement.

After illumination, the researcher *explicates* the meanings discovered by returning to the strategies of the immersion phase, continuing to seek, evaluate, and refine new "angles, textures and features"[1(p31)] of the discovered themes or meanings. Then, the researcher constructs a *creative synthesis* by depicting an understanding of the phenomenon. The depiction may be a written narrative, a poem, or a work of visual art. A sensitive rendering of the depiction in a way that communicates the discovery to others and evokes recognition and confirmation lifts heuristic inquiry beyond mere solipsism "into the world."[22] The end product of phenomenology is a description of the structure of experience. Heuristic inquiry depicts essential meanings and portrays the personal significance of the inquiry; the participants remain visible and whole.[15]

Validation is present throughout the process. The researcher constantly revisits the data to check for accurate and comprehensive capture of meaning, appraise significance, and verify the depiction. Strategies for validation and establishing trustworthiness[17] suitable for qualitative research are appropriate in heuristic research as well.

AN EXAMPLE OF HEURISTIC INQUIRY: THE EXPERIENCE OF SADNESS

Engagement

Our own interest in heuristic research was inspired by an experiential exercise in qualitative methodology, a laboratory assignment in our doctoral-level seminar on research design. The class, using the Oregon Health Project 2000[23] as a guide, chose depression as a substantive phenomenon for study because of its effect on the quality of life of many Oregonians. Our group of three coresearchers had recently relocated and were struggling with feelings of sadness and estrangement in our new surroundings. After some discussion, we decided to focus on sadness, in order not to exclude valuable data by asking only about depression.

We formed a self-selected, purposive sample driven by personal interest in the phenomena of relocation and the need deliberately and systematically to contemplate shared experiences. As the three coresearchers discussed the assignment, we came to believe that knowing each other's stories would trigger understanding of our own in greater depth. We chose each to write the story, a personal narrative, of our recent move as the starting point for our exploration. As we talked and planned, our excitement about the project grew. As we started to write our stories, our passionate involvement intensified.

Mary speaks:

My response to the research question evolved after several days of consideration. My first attempt at heuristic research ended with a one-page list of things I've missed since relocating. I realized that this list didn't meet the requirements of self-search, self-discovery, and self-dialogue. So I talked to my family about what made them sad about moving, and then talked to my coresearchers. I realized I was scratching only the surface. I went back to the literature to try to understand how to create knowledge that was deep and intense enough to meet the requirements of heuristic research.

Betty speaks:

Before writing my own narrative, I reviewed passages in my diary of my first year in Salem as a way to recapture and remember the feelings of that time. I recalled both my excitement and apprehensions about moving, the initial ease of meeting people, and my bitter disappointment in the work setting. In writing my narrative, I was also able to see how things had worked out, how I eventually resolved some conflicts, and how I had changed during those two years.

Maye speaks:

I found myself thinking about the problem not only while consciously focusing on the problem, but also while eating, riding the bus, walking the dog, and bathing; in short, most of the time.

Immersion

Moustakas[1] indicates that self-dialogue is a critical first step in heuristic inquiry. We immersed ourselves in our own experience as we wrote our narratives. The result was pages of understanding.

Mary speaks:

In an attempt to capture the essence of self-dialogue, I again reviewed a memory book that my children and I had created prior to leaving Laramie. This book is full of pictures and names of those that we felt were most important to us. As I went through this book, picture by picture, I tried to capture the emotions I was feeling.

I then looked through my calendar and remembered how I had spent my time and with whom. Again, I tried to capture the emotions that accompanied each memory. With this list of emotions and memories, I examined what was happening here and tried to connect the old and the new.

Maye speaks:

Writing was hard work; I had to face what I had lost in my move and how I felt about it. I tend to avoid feelings and "numb out"; focusing is very difficult work for me. I procrastinated about writing my narrative until the last possible minute. The fearless openness to one's self demanded by heuristic methodology was very difficult for me.

During the immersion phase, the researcher collects data that are used to explore the phenomenon. Below are excerpts from our personal narratives about the experience of sadness after relocation.

The following is from Mary's narrative:

The feelings of sadness did not hit me at first. The weeks prior to relocation were spent in whirlwind activity. Others voiced envy and anticipation of my "adventure"; soon I was calling this move a wonderful adventure also.

No amount of organization could have prepared me for the road detours on the interstate. And the cars!!! There were so many here, and they were going so fast and they were all strangers. These were my first thoughts of sadness. I thought that if we got lost or stuck that there would be no one to call for help. I thought of the people in Wyoming. We knew people who we could count on and whose word we could trust. If we didn't know someone personally, we knew someone who knew someone else, who knew. I thought of the connections that we had developed over the last 30 odd years. We had no connections here. I didn't have a "history" here.

The first few days were spent in unpacking and there wasn't time for sadness or even to be a little homesick. Until the night. Late at night in Wyoming I would go outside and watch the stars. Hundreds and hundreds of stars. On full moon nights I could see the mountains all around me. I could hear the sounds of trees and animals and feel at peace. Neither the stars nor the mountains can be seen here. Even in the early morning the sounds of people and traffic still continue. There is no peace here.

Music used to be peaceful. I used to play my stereo at night. But I haven't lived in an apartment for 11 years. There's people above us and on both sides and you have to be careful not to be too noisy. This area feels very claustrophobic with all the trees and people and houses and cars and stores and roads. What I mean is, there doesn't seem to be room for me, I don't have *my* space yet. There's no place for me, or anyone, to just stretch.

When I needed to stretch at home I'd go for a walk. I used to walk every evening at home, usually two or three miles, sometimes four. Even at night I was safe. I knew everyone on the route. I knew they would help me if trouble occurred. Not here. It's depressing to think that you are surrounded by people and you know no one. My favorite time of the day would be my walks in the evening. I would come home relaxed and ready for the next day. In Oregon nothing's the same. It's too dark to walk in the evening. Trees hover over the paths and it's like walking through a horror house. Sometimes, I come home more tense than I left. And people sounds at night on those paths are more intimidating than comforting.

I used to have wonderful neighbors. We would talk at our boundary—we had an imaginary picket fence to lean on. We watched our kids grow up together. We shared good times and bad. The first week here 14 families moved out and 22 families moved in. I haven't found any stability yet, and no neighbors. Who do I call for emergencies? That line is still blank on my kids' registration forms. That blank line means no friends.

When you don't belong you don't have any power. This lack of power comes from lack of information. A newcomer isn't in the "know." It's a game, you have to hunt for the information until someone decides you've tried hard enough. I guess what bothers me most about this is the lack of control. I ask, but I guess I don't ask the right questions. It's okay most of the time, I'm getting pretty good at this game. But sometimes the information I need is important, when it's for my kids. I just feel sad because it shouldn't have to be this hard. I used to be the person that had the information, but I've lost that. Now I have to wait until someone helps me out.

The following is from Maye's narrative:

Since I have moved, I've felt sad any time I'm not busy. And sometimes even when I am busy, I'm aware of that feeling just below the surface. I find myself sighing, and I'm a lot more irritable and impatient than usual.

Sometimes, when there isn't an immediate task at hand, like going to class or finishing an assignment, I have a hard time getting going; I will isolate myself. I won't return phone calls, or reach out to call local friends whom I have been thinking about.

I've moved a lot in my life, and this has been in many ways the hardest. My feelings about writing my thesis are all caught up in how I think about the move. And the feelings brought up by my failed relationship with my boyfriend are also part of the sadness. Anxiety about school is also in there somewhere. All this besides the usual ugly details of packing, finding a place to live and a job, unpacking, and learning new streets, buses, etc. Because I had no savings and was out of work for about a month, I have money worries. And my current living situation is not all that I would like it to be.

Dealing with my feelings about my boyfriend is very difficult, and I don't feel like I have anyone with whom I can process them. I am only now starting to deal with my feelings of betrayal and disappointment. We did have a comfortable home in a town neither of us was particularly fond of, and I feel sadness at the loss of our cozy home and usually warm companionship. He was a great support to me, especially through the thesis, and I'm wondering how I'm going to do it again, most likely on my own this time.

I worry about school, whether I can handle the workload and whether I will be able to find a group of people with whom I feel emotionally and intellectually comfortable. In

Fresno, my thesis advisor and mentor was a great Teacher and will be hard to replace. School is alternately completely overwhelming and an absolute blast of a good time. I wonder how I will manage my time when papers start coming due. One thing about having finished the thesis; term papers look shorter and easier now.

My current job on call is very difficult. The treatment model is pretty grim, very medical and mechanistic. The staffing is tight and the expectations of on-call staff limiting. I have learned to be satisfied if meds are out on time, charts and other paperwork finished, and I have one or two therapeutic interactions per shift. More difficult is that I have little supervision and virtually no help in processing all I am seeing and feeling and learning. Most of the staff is unwilling to include on-call personnel in the informal support network.

In Fresno, I was a member of an Adult Children of Dysfunctional Families group that met every Tuesday night for almost four years. I have found nothing to substitute for it here. I miss the people and I miss the opportunity to get support and feedback in trying to make sense of my life and do some healing and growing.

The following is from Betty's narrative:

In New Haven, I enjoyed a wealth of professional experiences and opportunities. My work and professional development was most important to me. But upon entering my mid-thirties (which I see as pre-middle age) and I suppose feeling quite competent in my work life, I began to feel that I now needed to attend to other developmental issues such as settling down. I don't mean settling down in the conventional sense of getting married and having children, but settling down in a place where I might want to grow old.

I didn't know if Oregon was exactly the place, but Salem is an eight-hour drive from my family which certainly beat the twelve-hour travel time which was required going from the East Coast to West Coast. Although I didn't know anyone in Oregon, at least I had my dog. And I thought of going out there as an adventure. The state has great natural beauty, was environmentally conscious, and was closer to my folks. I also cautioned myself that it could turn out to be a bad adventure but that did not deter me.

Initially, things went well. I met people during my walks with my dog. Got together with a few people at work. Surprisingly, I was invited to spend Thanksgiving and Christmas with my new friends.

During that first year, I had problems at work. I would remind myself repeatedly that I moved here for personal, not for professional reasons, and if work was so important I should have stayed in New Haven. And then I wondered that perhaps I was one of those individuals who was unable to achieve a satisfactory balance between personal and professional life because of some deficit like lack of creativity or because I was just plain boring. And then after a while, I thought "So what," so maybe I am one of those people who derives most of their sense of personal competence and identity from work which was OK, but was not the way I saw myself as being put together. I mean, it was one thing to intentionally focus my energies towards work, it was another thing to find that was simply the way I was organized.

Salem, Oregon is really different from New Haven and from California (where I grew up) from the perspective of ethnic and cultural diversity. It strikes me as sort of a white bread town with white bread cuisine, with a specialty in franchise cuisine. So I guess you know where my head is at outside of work; I like to eat! I used to enjoy New York City with its sections for Indian, Cuban, Chinese, and Italian cuisine, and great delicatessens. New Haven has the best white clam pizza and calamari pizza—you certainly can't get that here.

Being in Salem as a Chinese-American woman, I always feel slightly foreign, like here I am against a bunch of white people, instead of being amidst pockets of Black people, and pockets of Hispanics, and pockets of Jews, and pockets of Italians, etc. When there is cultural and ethnic diversity, I always feel like it's more acceptable to be different in one's environment.

On occasion when I've mentioned this to some elderly friends, they've told me that "I think of you as White," or "You're just as White as I am." I think they were meaning to be kind, that they don't see me as foreign, yet at the same time, I am somewhat disappointed that they can't appreciate my differences, because being a Chinese-American woman is how I view myself.

So as to the sadness which I have experienced since I've moved, I suppose that the general feeling that I've experienced is a feeling which encompasses loss of a culture and an environment where I felt less strange and more at ease. There was the familiarity of people and places and routines. But I lived in New Haven for eight years after living in California all my life, and now I suddenly remember how horrible my first year in New Haven was. I have also since realized more acutely just how much the time and energy that I seem to like to expend in the area of work affects my personal sense of competence and development or stagnation.

Which explains my being in the doctoral program; I'm just as busy as I used to be in New Haven. Relocating combined with this stage of adult development has certainly forced me to look inward, to ask myself questions as to how to forge a new direction which is invariably dependent on the answers to "Who am I?" and "What kind of woman do I want to be?" and "What kind of life do I want to live?" I don't think those answers can be supplied by other people but not having those answers can sometimes make me feel so alone. I am still seeking the answers to those questions.

Incubation

After the personal narratives were completed, coresearchers shared the written results. A week passed, in which each member of the research team reflected on the experiences of the others.

Illumination

As coresearchers, we had not only to discover the meaning, themes, and essence of our own experience, but also the shared experiences within the phenomenon of relocation. The road taken in this phase was different for each researcher. Further work on our part is needed before we can determine if either route, or perhaps another, would be most illuminating.

Mary speaks:

At this point, I had to not only share this very private paper with others, strangers, but also had to help them understand. I had prepared for this. I had read my interview over and over. Not only so that I would know completely, but also so that I would be immune to the words and emotions. I wanted to be able to look at this objectively, to answer questions and to explain. Maye told me she became paralyzed when we started to code her interview; she didn't notice any such hesitation on my part. I don't think I lost any of the understanding or intensity by preparing in this way; desensitizing almost. I do wonder if I lessened the amount of understanding on the part of the coresearchers.

Maye speaks:

Coding my own narrative was very difficult; my ability to recognize, abstract, and label my own feelings and processes was curiously paralyzed. I found myself unsure about how much of our time I should take, how much detail to offer in explanation to my coresearchers, not so much because I didn't want to share or trust them, but because I didn't want to turn the study into a two-on-one therapy group. My emotional and intellectual paralysis transferred much of the work of coding to my coresearchers. I am not sure about the implications of the fact that I found it so useful to be able to probe and analyze simultaneously, yet felt uncomfortable about my responses to being probed.

Explication

For this study, explication was a constant, comparative process. We attempted to find common meanings within each experience of relocation. Each narrative was coded, codes were clustered, themes were identified, and definitions were created.

As we worked, our roles as researchers and subjects blurred and shifted. Tearing apart the meanings underlying the words of the narrative by probing with questions both gentle and pointed, a form of "member checking" our perceptions and interpretations, became our means of addressing trustworthiness and credibility. Another tactic we used was to compare larger and smaller pieces of the narratives for commonalities and differences both overt and subtle. Our detailed discussion about the nuances and flavor of each of the code definitions reflected our concern with craft. We aspired to the goal of expressing as precisely and evocatively as possible the meaning and emotion of each code as it applied to the data.

In creating definitions for each code, we tried to create the most concise definition for each code and still capture the meaning and emotions. Dictionary definitions were not the most appropriate. For example, the dictionary definition of money (that which is legally established as an exchangeable equivalent for commodities) was rejected for a definition that emphasized the feeling involved (that which is used to pay bills, provide for the roof over your head, the food you eat, and your tuition). Anytime there was discussion regarding a code or definition, we looked to the creator of the narrative and accepted her decision. In this way, we made sure that the essence remained as intended.

Although our process of explication is unfinished, several clusters and themes have emerged in answer to the question, what is our experience of sadness as women who have relocated?

The core theme appears to be the emotions connected with "home." Home represents both the home of the past, which has been lost, and the home of the future. Home is a place of safety, peace, and belonging, as well as the very physical sense of a house, apartment, or room. Home also includes a "hope for the future" with the wanting of "new connections," "new friends," and perhaps most important of all, "personal space" and "belonging."

A large cluster of "connections" to people and places emerged as a theme. This cluster includes those connections before and after relocation. Connections also include the history of the researcher, familiarity of surroundings, availability of support, and old friends. There was a strong sense of "leaving behind" present in all interviews. We included "tying up loose ends" and "saying goodbye" in this cluster. In the end, we finally included all of "leaving behind" in "connections."

Several emotions were identified with relocation. While most of these emotions were clustered under the heading of "emotional reactions to relocation," many emotions were seen to be a part of "changes in social environment." We all felt the effect of changes in our social environment, including being rebuffed, feeling isolation and loneliness, and feeling a lack of trust. The theme of changes in social environment also tentatively includes personal doubt and fear of failure.

"Too much" was identified as a final cluster. This cluster included all those things that were overwhelming to the person who relocated. Too much change in environment both physical and social; losses of people, support, and connections; contributing factors such as jobs, theses, school, and relationships: just too much effort involved.

Creative Synthesis

An end to our heuristic research has not appeared. Nonetheless, the co-researchers agreed that Betty had come closest to a synthesis with which we all resonated:

Our sadness is a flooding of many emotions as we leave our pasts and are hurtled to the unknown of our futures. It is an unknown which is amplified by the strangeness of a new culture, which is both exciting and frightening. We are strangers in a strange land. Our present is still vividly tied to the memories of past alliances, there are no new connections as yet. Different cultures mean different rules and expectations, and so we must begin the uncomfortable process of learning and adapting when not so long ago, there was a routine, and you knew and were known. And you remember how it used to be and the used-to-be is no longer, and you mourn this loss and hopefully will mourn this less when things get better. As a coinvestigator and coresearcher, I would say, "This is what the experience is really like."

Understanding one part of the phenomenon leads to re-examination of another . . . and the cycle continues. While our heuristic inquiry of the experience of sadness in women who have relocated is still unfolding, the initial results offer several implications for nursing care. We suggest that nurses need to be aware of any recent relocation of clients as relocation can have a significant negative impact within a person. The client's perceived social environment also needs to be explored.

Relocation does not affect everyone equally and is best viewed as a small part of an individual's life rather than an acute, isolated event.[24] Nurses need to consider the entire person, including the individual's history, coping strategies, personality, and social support system when attempting to identify the impact of relocation.

•   •   •

Heuristic inquiry is a research process toward understanding human experience in the social world from the initial perspective of the researcher. Phenomena amenable to this inquiry range from socialization of nursing students to burnout in skilled, intensive care unit nurses; from understanding the experience of a normal-term pregnancy to the experience of receiving or providing palliative care in a hospice. Heuristics is an appropriate choice for almost any question regarding human experience that fires the intellectual and emotional passion of the investigator.

Heuristic inquiry's special contribution to knowledge development lies in the acknowledgement by the researcher of passionate, personal involvement in both the subject and the process as a way to access and generate a deep, personal understanding of the phenomenon of interest. This process has the potential to benefit both the researcher and, through evocative, well-crafted, and meaningful depiction, the people with whom the research is shared. In heuristic inquiry, this "knowing" relationship can create opportunities for sharing and generating further understanding and growth.[14] As nurses continue to reclaim our heritage as healers and "wise women,"[25] methods of inquiry and ways of knowing that foster personal growth and healing will become more valued.

The importance and implications of Polyani's idea of tacit knowledge and the value of intuition for nursing practice have become apparent.[19-20] The potential contribution to nursing science of modes of inquiry such as heuristics that focus on these "ways of knowing" is still waiting to be explored.

In its emphasis of use of self, connectedness, and relationship, heuristic inquiry would seem a natural to nurses interested in developing a human science, as has been advocated by several nursing theorists.[14,16,26] The goal of human science is knowledge as understanding, which in and of itself transforms the nurse–client relationship and allows more complete participation in the intersubjective process of becoming.[27] As nurses continue to develop our discipline as a human science, qualitative ways of knowing will foster understanding in service of the transformation of human relationships toward healing and personal growth. Heuristic inquiry is a useful tool in this quest.

REFERENCES

1. Moustakas C. *Heuristic Research: Design, Methodology, and Applications.* Newbury Park, Calif: Sage; 1990.
2. Moustakas C. Heuristic research. In: Bugental JF, ed. *Challenges of Humanistic Psychology.* New York, NY: McGraw-Hill; 1967.
3. Moustakas C. *Loneliness.* Englewood Cliffs, NJ: Prentice Hall; 1961.
4. Blau DS. Through the eyes of the beholder: a phenomenological investigation of anger. *Dissertation Abstracts International.* 1980;41(2):681-B.
5. Cheyne VEB. Growing up in a fatherless home: the female experience. *Dissertation Abstracts International.* 1988;49(12):5,558-B.

6. Clark JB. Duet: the experience of the psychologically androgynous. *Dissertation Abstracts International.* 1987;49(1):235-B.

7. Hawka SM. The experience of feeling unconditionally loved. *Dissertation Abstracts International.* 1985;46(12):4,385-B.

8. MacIntyre MC. The experience of shyness. *Dissertation Abstracts International.* 1982;43(9):3,016-B.

9. McNally C. The experience of being sensitive. *Dissertation Abstracts International.* 1982;43(12):4,156-B.

10. Prefontaine C. Transforming self-doubt into self-confidence. *Dissertation Abstracts International.* 1979;41(1):170-A.

11. Rodriguez AW. A heuristic phenomenological investigation of Mexican American ethnic identity. *Dissertation Abstracts International.* 1984;46(1):313-B.

12. Rourke PG. The experience of being inspired. *Dissertation Abstracts International.* 1983;45(4):1,296-B.

13. Sawyer J. The experience of feeling really connected to nature. *Dissertation Abstracts International.* 1988;49(9):4,025-B.

14. Dossey BM. The nurse as healer: toward the inward journey. In: Dossey BM, Keegan L, Guzzetta CE, Kolkmeier LG, eds. *Holistic Nursing: A Handbook for Practice.* Gaithersburg, Md: Aspen Publishers; 1988.

15. Douglass BG, Moustakas C. Heuristic inquiry: the internal search to know. *Humanistic Psychol.* 1985;25(3):39–55.

16. Parse RR. Human becoming: Parse's theory of nursing. *Nurs Science Q.* 1992;5(1):35–42.

17. Lincoln YS, Guba EG. *Naturalistic Inquiry.* Newbury Park, Calif: Sage; 1985.

18. Belenky MF, Clinchy BM, Goldberger NR, Tarule JM. *Women's Ways of Knowing: The Development of Self-voice, and Mind.* New York, NY: Basic Books; 1986.

19. Benner P. *From Novice to Expert: Excellence and Power in Clinical Nursing Practice.* Menlo Park, Calif: Addison-Wesley; 1984.

20. Benner P, Wrubel J. *The Primacy of Caring: Stress and Coping in Health and Illness.* Menlo Park, Calif: Addison-Wesley; 1989.

21. Gendlin ET. *Focusing.* Toronto, Canada: Bantam; 1978.

22. Moustakas C. The heuristic process in self understanding and discovery of knowledge. 1992. Unpublished manuscript.

23. Skeels MR, ed. *Health Objectives for the Year 2000.* Portland, Ore: Oregon Health Project Team; 1988.

24. Starker JE. Psychosocial aspects of geographical relocation: the development of a new social network. *Am J Health Promotion.* 1990;5(1):52–57.

25. Ehrenreich B, English D. *Witches, Midwives and Nurses: A History of Women Healers.* Old Westbury, NY: Feminist Press; 1973.

26. Watson J. *Nursing: Human Science and Human Care.* Norwalk, Conn: Appleton-Century-Crofts; 1985.

27. Mitchell GJ, Cody WK. Nursing knowledge and human science: ontological and epistemological considerations. *Nurs Science Q.* 1992;5(2):54–61.

Visit: A Method of Existential Inquiry for the Development of Nursing Knowledge

Alice Running, PhD, RN, CS, ANP
Assistant Professor
College of Nursing
Montana State University
Bozeman, Montana

"Visit," a research method created by this author, is presented as an alternative means of developing nursing knowledge. This research method is founded on the belief that all nursing involves relationship, and was created out of the author's desire for a relational research method. Philosophical support for the method is provided by Merleau-Ponty's existentialism, Gadow's existential advocacy, and Watson's human caring theory. Authenticity is proposed as an alternative to the concepts of reliability and validity for judging the scientific merit of the method.

Each person deviates from the ideal construct. Each has experiences that set him/her apart from others and there are no pure types as well we know.

—M.M. Seltzer[1(p6)]

WHEN RESEARCHERS cluster experiential meanings into themes, exhaustive descriptions, or theory believed to embody the essential structure of the phenomenon investigated, typologies are created, and unique individuals are lost. Unique individuals are lost or subsumed within themes, categories, common elements, metaphors, models, or theories that are the end product of much qualitative research. The development of themes, categories, models, or theories is a necessary step in the development of knowledge that is unique to nursing. However useful, they do not serve to illuminate individual descriptions of lived experiences that, in the end, are imperative for the provision of nursing care.

"Visit," a method of relational nursing research, allows and requires that the descriptions of meaningful life experiences be left intact and not extrapolated to give support for a theme or category. The purpose of this article is to explicate a method created by this author called Visit. This relational research method can be used in the development of unique, individual descriptions of any phenomenon under study.

QUALITATIVE RESEARCH

Qualitative research has been concerned with hearing stories in one's own language, understanding contextual meanings, and describing patterns of behavior and processes of interaction, as well as revealing the values and intentionalities that pervade people's experience.[2] Nurse researchers have used grounded theory, ethnography, and phenomenology in an effort to advance nursing knowledge and human science. Still in the process of development, these research methods have been and continue to be extremely useful for nursing scientists. While important as research methods, none conclude with unique, individual perspectives or descriptions in the form of story. Instead, there is the requirement to aggregate similar descriptions or to choose pieces or segments of individual descriptions to support themes or subthemes that emerge from the data. Unique individuals are lost to or subsumed under themes, subthemes, metaphors, models, or theories.

These themes, subthemes, metaphors, models, and theories are thought to represent the phenomenon for all who have experienced it or for some select group responsible for providing the data. Additionally, there does not seem to be a call for the close relationship that may be necessary in order to understand the meaning of a phenomenon or experience—such as health, chronic illness, or death—for another person.

Guided by the belief that the practice of nursing always involves relationship, the method created by this author and described in this article is relational in nature and is called *Visit*. Subjects or participants are referred to as coparticipants and are completely involved in the research process. Because each researcher's view of the phenomenon under study will be uniquely his or hers, these views are openly discussed during the course of the Visit, along with beliefs or views held by others as reported in the literature. Clarification is a necessary part of the research process because the researcher is not the expert. This is very different from the phenomenological process described by Trice, where "care was taken not to attempt clarification as such during the interview so as not to put words into the mouths of the participants."[3(p249)]

Researcher and coparticipant willingly enter into a dialogical conversation, and over the course of months or years, a relationship develops. This relationship provides the researcher, who is both listener and participant, with a new perspective, a better view of the other person's world.

This new perspective calls for the preservation of individual uniqueness as essential for understanding human experience. An enlargement of the vision of the human experience is possible because of a widening of the lens of the researcher as participant until what is viewed or seen as meaningful and necessary to understanding the experience of age or health for a particular individual has been included. Existentialism allows for and requires the return of relationship and interactional dialogue with individuals as foundational to the process of research. Merleau-Ponty's "phenomenology of perception" is proposed as a beginning foundation for Visit as one method of research for the human sciences.

PHILOSOPHICAL FOUNDATIONS FOR VISIT AS METHOD

Merleau-Ponty's Existentialism

Merleau-Ponty's existentialism calls for the return of essence back into existence. For Merleau-Ponty, phenomenology is more of a philosophy than the study of essences: "Looking for the world's essence is not looking for what it is as an idea once it has been reduced to a theme or discourse; it is looking for what it is as a fact for us, before any thematisation."[4(pxv)] Existentialism does not "expect to arrive at an understanding of man and the world apart from any starting point other than that of their 'facticity.' "[4(pvii)] This starting place of perceptual synthesis of a human's understanding of his or her world is an integration of senses, a radical reflection that uncovers the unreflected experience that underlies or makes up each individual's "facticity."

Facticity naturally includes a recognition of each individual's situatedness in a social, cultural, historical drama that is ongoing and open ended. Each person's facticity is reestablished whenever altered situations or experiences require a new view or perspective. Changes in social, cultural, or historical realities are accepted in a world that is always incomplete and open.

Visit as method starts with this situated existence, and through relationship and story illuminates this profoundly dynamic position for others. This illumination is different from absolute knowledge or knowledge developed to describe, create, or support existing theories or models. Instead, there is a reluctance to regard experience as something that can be reduced down to component parts.

Experiential knowledge, or personal knowledge, evolves out of each unique individual's perspective or view of the world. Each perspective will be a reflection or a particular hold on reality that is continually remade by time and always in process. It is this facticity, this individual perspective, this return to the things themselves, that is made possible by research that is relational. Hermeneutical interpretation of the text of each visit by the researcher removes the world that is already there for the participant and replaces it with the world that is there for the researcher.

Existentialism and Visit as method call for the researcher to return to the lived world. Efforts are concentrated on "reachieving a direct and primitive contact with the world."[4(pvii)] This direct and primitive contact with the lived world allows for and requires descriptions.

Neutrality and objectivity, required in analysis, are replaced with relationship and coexistence. People are not observers but participants in relationships with themselves and others. From these relationships, the human situation develops and can be discovered through descriptions or story. Humans already have an acquired world of thoughts, and these thoughts are used as a means of expressing their ongoing dialectic, subjective–objective dialogue with themselves and others. Meanings that emerge are a result of a synthesis of the entire body and the world, including subjectivity and objectivity in dialogue.

For humans, the world is always in process, and the dialectical construction of reality cannot be broken up into fragments. Analysis, or breaking the situations down to their most essential elements, has the potential to remove or alienate humans from their "being in the world."

Existentialism requires instead that any experience is constituted by a dynamic dialogue between a body–subject and that body–subject's position in the world. This dynamic dialogue can provide the researcher with direct descriptions of experience. Experience is believed to be an entity that cannot be separated or analyzed into component parts. Researchers are charged with reporting the descriptions instead of identifying quotations for the development of essences, causal explanations, categories, themes, metaphors, models, or theories.

What is real for a particular individual has already been and continues to be constructed each moment. The world is not ready-made for each individual. Instead, it becomes real or is built up through the ceaseless, dialectic, subject–object dialogue. Dialectic reality, or the movement back and forth among past, present, and future realities, that allows for the emergence of future realities would presuppose ambiguous or changing world shapes. The shapes that the world takes will be different for everyone, and breaking these shapes down into fragments or essences will not make it uniform or consistent. A reality that is being built up or that is unfolding can never be replaced by a reality that is static or theoretical.

Theoretical constructs or prescriptions presuppose a world that is already built, unchanging in its architecture. Unfolding realities are dynamic, where change is inherent in the design. Individual descriptions of this unfolding reality allow it to retain its facticity. Each person's reality presupposes existence, and it is this "existence in the world," this "being in the world," that lends validity to any individual description. This validity is both implicit and vague. According to Merleau-Ponty, "It is always something other than what it is . . . rooted in nature at the very moment that it is transformed by cultural influences, never hermetically sealed and never left behind . . . revealing to us an ambiguous mode of existing."[4(p198)]

Visit as method retains this facticity, accepts ambiguity, and allows each individual to describe his or her reality or perception of reality in that moment. Individuals "have no way of knowing the human body other than that of living it, which means taking upon [their] own account the drama which is being played out."[4(p198)] These individual descriptions of the drama that is being played out are not created in isolation. Coexistence with others is a reality. Visiting with another individual in an effort to understand his or her particular perspective supports coexistence and requires that a relationship be developed.

Existentialism would seem to support Visit as method and call for the development of relationship in order to come to understand another's reality. Existential advocacy as described by Gadow[5] provides additional support for relationship as the ontological foundation for nursing and for Visit as method.

A Foundation in Existential Advocacy

Gadow[5] provides additional support for this method in her discussion of existential advocacy as a philosophical foundation. While Gadow is referring to the practice of nursing in particular, her idea of existential advocacy can be used to support Visit as one method of knowledge development for nursing in particular and the human sciences in general.

Extrapolating from Gadow, the visitor is in the ideal position among researchers to experience the person as a unique human being with individual strengths and complexities. This is a precondition for advocacy and requires a position of mutuality by both researcher and participant. The position of mutuality allows the development of relationship where the participant's description of health is shared with the researcher in its entirety.

Mutuality as a research position requires a relationship between the researcher and the participant that is covenantal, not contractual. Contractual relationships require an agreement beforehand about the process and the product.[6] The relationship to be developed is precisely defined in the terms of the contract, and, if developed correctly, will result in full discharge of the contractual agreement. With an emphasis on mutual advantage, obligations and criteria are clearly specified to avoid a breach of contract. Emotional neutrality allows for withdrawal from the relationship when the contract is no longer pertinent or is terminated.

Covenantal relationships, on the other hand, are spontaneous, developing out of the process of the relationship, each relationship being different. Within covenantal relationships, the two individuals act together to determine whatever the meaning an experience (eg, health, chronic illness, death) is to have in that situation. Individuals are assisted to exercise authentically their freedom of self-determination, which includes as its most profoundly human freedom the right to determine meaning for oneself.[5] Relationships of this kind remove the power of knowledge development (in the case of research) from the researcher. Mutuality, not neutrality, allows for the development by both researcher and participant of descriptions or meanings of each unique individual's understanding of an experience.

Gadow warns of the potential for paternalism in this kind of relationship. Unless there is a caring relationship, the "comprehensiveness, immediacy, and continuity of [the visit] presents an exceptional opportunity for a powerful influence over individuals." [5(p82)]

Many people are trusting and vulnerable, particularly in circumstances where the interview relationship appears to be reciprocal.[2] Unlike paternalism, advocacy is based on the principle that self-determination is the most fundamental human right. Self-determination can only be guaranteed to the participant if the researcher is honest about the purpose of the visit. Advocacy (respect for self-determination) is critical in the course of a visit, allowing and encouraging participants to describe what health or chronic illness is for them. Within the context of the visit, there is the recognition of each person's reality with no intention to influence, convert, or prescribe. The relationships that develop do so because of a sense of mutual trust and a belief that no one reality is the only appropriate reality. According to Von Eckartsberg,

Not only does the subject studied receive valuable feedback from the observer but the observer also obtains valuable clarifying knowledge regarding what he observed from the experiential report of the person studied regarding his own experience. Both the person researched as well as the research person are thus being changed through the existential research method—they change each other.[7(pp75–76)]

Visitors (the two people involved in a visit) are empowered to reflect on and talk about their lives, making a variety of connections with other events in the past, present, and future. Watson's transpersonal caring theory addresses this ability to make connections.

Watson's Human Caring Theory

Watson's human caring theory[8–9] describes the human caring process as a special gift to be cherished, as each visit is a gift to be cherished. Each person involved in the human caring process brings with him or her a unique causal past. Experiential moments become incorporated into the past and help to direct the future. These experiential moments can be further developed or illuminated through Visit as method.

In Watson's theory, the nurse is described as a "co-participant in a process in which the ideal of caring is the human-to-human, subject-to-subject transaction."[9(p220)] Human care can only be effectively demonstrated and practiced interpersonally. It is this interpersonal and intersubjective human process that keeps alive a common sense of humanity, and teaches humanness by the identification of ourselves with others, whereby the humanity of one is reflected in the other.[9]

Additionally, Watson describes relationships that are transpersonal. In relationships that are transpersonal, the nurse enters into the other's experiences, and there is mutual or reciprocal entrance of the other into the nurse's experiences. Both persons are involved, each valuing the other and hoping to discover his or her unique perspectives on the world. It is the transpersonal human process that gives additional form and substance to Visit as a method for developing knowledge about unique human beings.

Foundational to this theory is a high regard and reverence for each unique person, nonpaternalistic values that relate to human autonomy, and freedom of choice. Like Gadow's existential advocacy, Watson's theory holds self-determination in highest esteem and places a high value on the relational process between the nurse and the participant. Each person's subjective life-world is valued. The relational processes between nurse and patient are essential for the full discovery and disclosure of those unique, subjective experiences during the course of a visit.

Oftentimes in research, the subjective experiences of an individual are not seen as essential. Watson views humans as magnificent, spiritual beings who have been "undernourished and reduced to physical, materialistic beings."[9(p224)] Central to her theory is the belief that human experiences may not always be related so much to the external physical world as to each person's inner lived world. Visit as method provides an avenue to the innermost recesses of life, recognizing that the "locus of human existence is experience."[9(p225)] These innermost experiences that are the make-up of the individual can be described through story by each participant during the course of the visit. Knowing the other's reality through his or her stories has been supported in the literature.

STORY: A TOOL FOR DEVELOPING KNOWLEDGE

Authors Outside of Nursing

Sacks[10] first published a book called *Awakenings*. It was his hope and belief that a book containing individual stories about people suffering the aftereffects of encephalitis would have the power to "arouse the sympathetic imagination . . . to awaken an intense and often creative resonance in others."[10(pxxxviii)] Once the stories had been read by others, he believed their view of the postencephalitis world would be different. The ability to imagine someone else's world could have the potential to enlarge the world of the reader.

For Sacks, the individuals who were his patients were also his friends and teachers. As a physician, Sacks felt that the classic, analytic texts on the disease process, while necessary, did not provide the whole picture or tell the whole story. What was needed, he felt, was a book that was more "existential and personal—an empathic entering into patient's experiences and worlds."[10(pxxxvi)] Along with the detailed documentation of neuronal disorders came the need for detailed, nonreductive narratives or stories. The stories that he tells in his book are "exemplars of human predicament and survival"[10(pxxxiv)] in worlds that are almost unimaginable yet inhabited by people just like ourselves.

Likewise, Blythe[11] set out to describe the world of old age, inhabited by people just like ourselves. In his book, Blythe listens to the old talking and contends that "it is the nature of old men and women to become their own confessors, poets, philosophers, apologists, and story-tellers."[11(p29)] Admitting that most of his knowledge about this age group came through the literature of old age, Blythe hoped that by listening to their stories, he would hear what they, as individuals, had to say about aging.

The stories contained in Blythe's book are written in the words of the storytellers. Each storyteller's reality has been reestablished whenever altered situations or experiences have required a new view or perspective. Each story reflects a recognition of the old person's situatedness in a social, cultural, historical drama that is ongoing and open ended. Therefore, the reader should not draw a single conclusion about old age and its inhabitants, rather the stories are given to show that "old age is full of death and full of life. It is a tolerable achievement and it is a disaster."[11(p29)]

Story telling is the foundation for another book written by Coles[12] entitled, *The Call for Stories*. Coles describes his residency as a time when he was encouraged by a certain professor to hear about his clients and their lives, not only about their symptoms. Skilled at taking personal, family, social, and clinical histories, Coles found himself wanting to begin at the beginning again, to have his clients tell him stories of their lives.

Beginning at the beginning was a way for Coles to stop "forcing his patients into theoretical constructs"[12(p14)] or disease processes with predictable outcomes and common treatment modalities. Recognizing that each patient was an individual with different stories to tell, Coles found the theoretical constructs became less critical and at times less usable or even unusable in clinical practice. As a medical student, Coles was encouraged by one of his professors to "tell more stories and less theory . . . to error on the side of each person's particularity."[12(p27)] This same professor is quoted in the book as saying, "Their story, yours, mine—it's what we carry with us on this trip we take, and we owe it to each other to respect our stories and learn from them."[12(p30)]

Nursing's Use of Story

Boykin and Schoenhofer[13] describe story as a link between nursing practice, ontology, and epistemology. For these authors, the content of nursing knowledge should be generated and known through the lived experience of the nursing situation. The nursing situation is brought into existence "for the purpose of promoting the process of being and becoming through caring."[13(p246)] The nursing situation should provide the medium for not only nursing practice but all forms of nursing inquiry.

Through the nursing situation, stories preserve the integrity of nursing knowledge by providing a mode for communicating truth. Additionally, in storytelling there is the incorporation into the story of both or all persons involved in the nursing situation. According to Boykin and Schoenhofer, "Stories call to mind the commonalities of nursing situations as well as the beauty and uniqueness of each."[13(p246)]

If the ontology of nursing is discovered through the study of nursing situations, then the authors of this article present story as the critical element through which the aspects of a nursing situation can be reviewed and understood. Stories are rich data sources for inquiry, and nursing's epistemology can incorporate story as a way of knowing, thereby informing both the practice and theories of nursing.

A note of caution must be added. While stories are rich sources of information, they are unique and constantly in the process of being created. Therefore, when stories are used as a source of information for nursing, it must be remembered that they are momentary. Moving beyond stories to knowledge development in order to define nursing may be more than should be expected.

Narrative approaches in qualitative research are discussed by Sandelowski,[14] who presents narrative as a framework for understanding data in qualitative research. Data or narratives recounting life events are placed in temporal order by the storytellers. The narratives then become the text for scientific interpretation. In other words, it becomes the responsibility of researchers to narrate their version (the researchers' version) of those individual lives in clinical studies, research reports, and scientific treatises.

Narratives are a way of reconstructing individual realities. They provide a means of representing or presenting life at a given moment rather than the entire life itself. In this way, narratives are very different from a theory, for example, the function of which may be to predict what life may or may not be like for someone.

Sandelowski goes on to discuss two types of narrative research. *Descriptive narrative research* aims to describe the nature and function of stories. In this way, "researchers can look for model and variant narrative forms in individuals experiencing common events."[14(p164)] *Explanatory narrative research* is retrospective and retroductive, and the researcher is interested in cause, or in an explanation of an end or outcome. Such explanations are then useful for making predictions, but explanatory narrative research is not so much for the foretelling as the retelling.

Although Sandelowski's approach furthers nursing's knowledge development, it remains dependent on an empirical epistemology. For example, words such as *cause, explanation, outcome,* and *prediction* are seen throughout the article. The importance or value of this interpretation of narrative is significant for nursing. However, allowing narrative or story to remain in its rare, sometimes untidy, form can also can serve as knowledge for nursing.

Gadow[15] proposed that story could render knowing and caring as one. Discussing knowledge development in relation to caring, Gadow notes that we have choices in the way we approach knowledge. As researchers and nurses, we can decide "whether knowing is to accomplish for us distance from the world or engagement."[15(p3)] Scientific distancing techniques require detachment, a safe position from which to order the world or to make sense of it in our own terms, from our own world view. From this (ad)vantage point, it is assumed that the world is finite and can be rendered in the same terms for everyone.

Engagement with the world, on the other hand, calls for a different lens. Instead of assuming the world is finite, the world is seen as inexhaustible and always perspectival for each individual. Therefore, the world will be different for each knower because each person lives in the world knowing it from a different perspective. Although we as individuals can never experience exactly the same world as someone else, our individual worlds can be described to one another.

Comparing exploration for the purpose of developing local or colonial understanding, Gadow makes a case for the importance of local understanding. *Local understanding* requires a regard for local knowledge that is not available from maps. *Colonial understanding* approaches knowledge development as if the land were empty. Requiring definition, colonizers bring with them their own definitions and ways of life in order to rescue the natives from themselves.

Explorers looking for local understanding approach knowledge differently and instead ask how they can best discover what it is like to live in this place. The maps and definitions designed by the colonizers have missed the actual landscape. They have extracted experience out of the way, like a bulldozer can be used to extract those things in its way in order to construct another reality, or hermeneutic interpretation of text can be used to discard those elements of the story that are not necessary for thematic or categorical development.

In effect, these explorers listen to the stories of the natives, the individuals who experience the land daily. According to Gadow, "Only by addressing one another in this way as subject, as authors of experience, can we know others in a way consistent with caring, a way that does not distance them nor reduce them to objects but enlists them in our explorations and joins them in theirs."[15(p15)] It is this relationship that is foundational for the development of Visit as a method of exploring the land of unique individuals:

There are maps that can be studied and the look of the land extrapolated, instead of going there personally. Once there, however, even with maps, even having been there before, the land transcends every schema, every recollection and prediction. It is inexhaustible, different each time. It can be summarized at a distance, but a summary is useless for living there.[15(p10)]

Qualitative studies using phenomenology, ethnography, or grounded theory are map-making studies. Qualitative studies using Visit require the researcher to "go there personally," go to the land of the research coparticipants to hear their stories. Judging the quality or the scientific merit of research such as this requires a broad view of the world and an acceptance of each person's reality.

AUTHENTICITY

Reliability and validity are concepts applicable in a view of the world as orderly, repeatable, predictable, law-like, and measurable. For existential inquiry, other criteria are appropriate. Authenticity is a concept that is philosophically congruent with a method of inquiry based on existential advocacy.

Used as one of the foundations for this methodology, existential advocacy is a philosophy that unifies and enhances the experience of the individuals (both persons in the visit) involved. For humans, understanding is not a matter of forgetting their own horizon of meanings and putting themselves within that of the alien text or society, it means merging or fusing one horizon with another.[16]

Advocacy calls for the researcher's engagement with the participant in determining the unique meaning that the experience of health has for that person.[5] In this way, self-determined descriptions or stories of health are considered authentic.

Gadow[15] describes story as being more than and different from case studies or clinical reports. While case studies or clinical reports are important, they are tools for reducing experience to fact, making experience definable and predictable. In this way, experience can be captured uniformly using common, sometimes technical, language. Instead of creating technical language that will capture an experience uniformly, story allows its creator to use his or her own language to describe his or her experiences.

People become alive through their language and their stories. According to Lopez, "It does not seem to matter greatly what the subject is, as long as the context is intimate and the story is told for its own sake, not forced to serve merely as the vehicle for an idea."[17(p63)] The authenticity of the story comes not so much from the verifiable truth as from an understanding that lying has played no role in the telling of the story. Personal life is inherently transitory. Experiences are continually remade by time, and so attempts at reconstructing individual pasts must be accepted as ambiguous and ongoing.

Sandelowski[14] proposes that narrative truth can be reclaimed from logical positivism. Truth in narrative is different from logical, scientific truths by "its emphasis on the life-like, intelligible, and plausible story."[14(p164)] Stories incorporate past, present, and potential futures into a coherent now. It must be remembered that this coherent now is a fleeting, momentary reality so that an effort to validate the story from an empirical perspective would be inappropriate.

Empirical preoccupations with truth as verifiability are replaced with how the story of an experience is endowed with meaning and significance for the teller of the story. What is significant for the teller of the story may or may not be significant for the audience, but it is not the audience who has lived through the experience. Truthfulness or authenticity is thus subsumed within the stories of each of the participants, who from the first visit are told that they are the experts.

SIGNIFICANCE FOR NURSING

Knowing the Literature But Not the Life

Engagement with the world, and with the participants of this research process, calls for a lens that sees the world as inexhaustible and always perspectival for each individual. The world is different for each knower. In order to understand these different worlds, the inhabitants must be allowed to tell their stories. Although we as individuals can never experience exactly the same world as someone else, our individual worlds can be described to one another.

Within any individual story will be remnants of social, cultural, and historical experiences. Daily influences make understanding of these experiences a fluid, dynamic process. Unique individuals, by virtue of their uniqueness, will have different and changing understandings and descriptions of such things as the meaning of life and chronic illness. While it is true that commonalities run through reports of experience, and that these commonalities are very useful for understanding experience, used alone they do not provide nursing or any other discipline with the whole picture.

The development of mutual, covenantal relationships fosters the authentic exercise of each participant's freedom of self-determination, which includes as its most profoundly human freedom the right to determine meaning for oneself. In this way, the power of knowledge development is removed from the researcher. Visit as method provides an avenue for nurse researchers to develop and disseminate personal knowledge. This personal knowledge can be made available to nursing and others in the same ways that any other knowledge is made available. Documentaries, presentations, publications, textbooks, and other means can be used to disseminate research findings, to disseminate personal knowledge in the form of stories.

What makes the knowledge developed through relational research nursing *knowledge* and not *literature* rests in the perspective of the researcher. To compare knowledge developed using Visit as method to the literary accounts of aging or the information provided in the stories told by Sacks,[10] Blythe,[11] or Coles[12] is to underestimate the importance of covenantal relationship that is foundational to Visit as method but is not foundational to the creation of literary accounts of experience. What may be different about this approach is that after a relationship develops over time, participants are asked to respond to a variety of questions. It is not necessary for participants to be challenged in order to tell their stories. The challenging is not done to intimidate or lead the participant, because for the participants, each of their stories already exists as fact. Instead, it is necessary for the nurse researcher to ask the questions in order to understand the phenomenon from the perspective of a nurse researcher. This open questioning can safeguard against a researcher's narrow or personal interpretation of someone else's experience.

Like the coparticipants in this research method, the people nurses see everyday are experts, living through whatever experience brings them in contact with nursing. Whether the nursing role is one of researcher, practitioner, or educator, listening to each person's story, inexhaustible and uniquely different, provides the basis for the nursing relationship and for the provision of nursing care.

•   •   •

Like the tribal communities in history, the old are the repositories of past life. The tribal elders of old were the libraries, the priests. The nursing clients of today are repositories of their own past, present, and future. With the advent of written language, the tribal elders became less essential to their communities; story lost its significance. Likewise, with the advent of empirical, logical research methodologies, experiential reporting was nonscientific and therefore nonessential. Because of the nonscientific nature of story, it no longer made a significant contribution to the development of predictable, repeatable, law-like knowledge.

Nursing clients, who may have been reduced to physical, materialistic beings, have in their heads, hearts, and spirits volumes of knowledge and wisdom that can be retrieved through the utilization of research methods such as Visit. Visit as method of existential inquiry can provide nursing with a scientific means of reviving the past; of explicating the innermost experiences that are the make-up of any individual and thereby contributing to the development of nursing knowledge.

REFERENCES

1. Seltzer MM. Random and not so random thoughts on becoming and being a statistic: professional and personal musings. *Int J Aging Hum Dev.* 1989;28(1):1-7.
2. Rowels GD, Reinharz S. Qualitative gerontology: themes and challenges. In: Reinharz S, Rowels GD, eds. *Qualitative Gerontology.* New York, NY: Springer; 1989.
3. Trice LB. Meaningful life experience to the elderly. *Image: Journal of Nursing Scholarship.* 1990;22(4):248-251.
4. Merleau-Ponty M; Smith C, trans. *Phenomenology of Perception.* Atlantic Highlands, NJ: Humanities Press; 1989.
5. Gadow S. Existential advocacy: philosophical foundation of nursing. In: Spicker SF, Gadow S, eds. *Nursing: Images and Ideals. Opening Dialogue with the Humanities.* New York, NY: Springer; 1980.
6. Cooper MC. Covenantal relationships: grounding for the nursing ethic. *ANS.* 1988;10(4):48-59.
7. Von Eckartsberg F. On experiential methodology. In: Georti A, Fischer FW, Von Eckartsberg R, eds. *Duquesne Studies in Phenomenological Psychology.* Pittsburgh, Pa: Duquesne University Press/Humanities Press; 1971; 1.
8. Watson J. *Nursing: Human Science and Human Care: A Theory for Nursing.* New York, NY: National League for Nursing; 1985.
9. Watson J. Watson's philosophy and theory of human caring in nursing. In: Riehl-Sisca J, ed. *Conceptual Models for Nursing Practice.* 3rd ed. Norwalk, Conn: Appleton & Lange; 1989.
10. Sacks O. *Awakenings.* New York, NY: Harper Perennial; 1990.
11. Blythe R. *The View in Winter.* New York, NY: Harcourt Brace Jovanovich; 1979.
12. Coles R. *The Call for Stories: Teaching and the Moral Imagination.* Boston, Mass: Houghton Mifflin; 1989.
13. Boykin A, Schoenhofer SO. Story as link between nursing practice, ontology, epistemology. *Image: Journal of Nursing Scholarship.* 1991;23(4):245-248.
14. Sandelowski M. Telling stories: narrative approaches in qualitative research. *Image: Journal of Nursing Scholarship.* 1991;23(3):161-165.
15. Gadow S. Beyond dualism: the dialectic of caring and knowing. Presented at the 12th Annual Conference on the International Association of Human Caring; April 1990; Houston, Tex.
16. Gadamer HG. *Truth and Method.* 2nd ed. New York, NY: The Crossroad; 1990.
17. Lopez B. *Crossing Open Ground.* New York, NY: Macmillan; 1988.

Innovative Approaches to Theory-Based Measurement: Modeling and Role-Modeling Research

Linda S. Baas, PhD, RN, CCRN
Assistant Professor
College of Nursing and Health
University of Cincinnati
Cincinnati, Ohio

Eileen Deges Curl, PhD, RN
Associate Professor
Department of Nursing
Ft. Hays State University
Hays, Kansas

Judith E. Hertz, PhD, RN
Assistant Professor
Department of Nursing
York College of Pennsylvania
York, Pennsyvlania

Karen R. Robinson, PhD, RN
Assistant Chief, Nursing Service
Department of Veterans Affairs Medical Center
Fargo, North Dakota

Despite the recognized need, theory-based and theory-testing research remain infrequent. One reason for this may be the inadequacy of instruments to measure the concepts or the theory. A solution to this dilemma is to apply innovative strategies to the measurement process. This report details how four researchers applied creative approaches to the study of modeling and role modeling (MRM) as proposed by Erickson, Tomlin, and Swain. Specifically, the studies focused on autonomy, hope, denial, and self care. In each instance, the concepts were examined within a framework that was consistent with the theory of MRM, necessitating a critical examination of measurement tools. The creative approach to studying autonomy led to the definition of a new concept, the perceived enactment of autonomy (PEA). A new tool was then developed to measure PEA. In another study, an existing tool measuring hope was reconceptualized to provide theoretical congruence with MRM. In the third study, a tool designed to measure denial was revised based on MRM. Finally, a new tool, the *Self-Care Resource Inventory*, was developed to measure the concepts of self care knowledge and self care resources. These examples illustrate how creative approaches to measurement can strengthen the relationship between theory and research as well as provide implications for practice.

NURSING SCHOLARS have repeatedly appealed for a stronger relationship between theory development and research efforts.[1-3] Despite these arguments for theory-based and theory-testing research, there remains a paucity of work in this area. For example, in Moody and associates'[4] review of 720 nursing research articles published over a decade in 6 journals, only 3% actually tested aspects of theory. Similarly, Silva[5] found that only 9 of 62 research manuscripts reviewed actually reported theory testing.

Difficulties in conducting theory-based and theory-testing research are frequently linked to the lack of instruments for measuring constructs or concepts inherent in specific theories.[6-8] In some instances, instruments may exist that purport to measure theoretically specified concepts, but the instrument may not actually be congruent with the grand nursing theory or paradigm that guides the research question. In seeking a quick solution to the problem, some researchers may opt to use tools that are inadequate for measuring the concept within the context of the theory. Other researchers have opted to select concepts to study based on the availability of tested instruments, rather than to study more theoretically significant concepts, in an attempt to move prematurely ahead with the research. The results of such work do little to build nursing science or guide future research of specific nursing theories.

Faced with these problems, the authors purposefully attempted to test a nursing theory by developing and/or revising research instruments. This resulted in creative and innovative approaches to instrumentation in an effort to provide theoretical congruence between the concepts of concern and the nursing theory. Modeling and role modeling, as proposed by Erickson, Tomlin, and Swain,[9] provided the specific nursing paradigm for the four studies, with the concepts being perceived enactment of autonomy, hope, denial, and self care. The creative methods included reexamination of concepts; reconceptualiziation of existing tools; and development of new, theory-based instruments. Following a brief explanation of modeling and role modeling, each study is presented to demonstrate the innovative approach used to ensure theory-based instrumentation as well as implications for nursing practice.

MODELING AND ROLE MODELING

Modeling and role modeling[9] (MRM) provides a holistic paradigm for nursing practice and research that is based on the integration of a number of theories related to nursing: psychosocial developmental processes,[10] basic and human growth needs,[11] and adaptation to stress.[12] These theories provide the framework for explaining similarities and differences in human responses to illness.

There are four areas that demonstrate similarities in the human experience. First, psychosocial development is an epigenetic process. Second, basic human needs fulfillment is an essential requisite for the human condition; growth needs ascribe to the development of self esteem, with the consummate goal being self-actualization. Third, individuals are holistic. Holism is the dynamic interrelationship of the biophysical, psychological, cognitive, spiritual, and social aspects of the person, recognizing that the whole is greater than the sum of the parts. Fourth, people have the need for affiliated individuation. Affiliation is the need to be dependent on some support system, and individuation is the need to be independent of the same support system. Thus, people are simultaneously dealing with apparently contradictory needs.

MRM also identifies how individuals differ in three major respects. First, there are differences in the inherent endowment of all people. Genetic composition, as well as the specific nature of past health experiences, are unique to each person. Therefore, different biological resources may be helpful to different people.

Second, people differ in their self care knowledge, which is one's personal model of the world. This individualized model is based on perceptions, thus representing the individual's specific reality within the universe of multiple realities. Self care knowledge includes what the person believes caused the illness and what is needed to return to optimal functioning and health.

The final difference is the perceived availability of self care resources. These are the resources that can be mobilized when the person experiences a stressor. Mobilization of resources is needed for coping and effective adaptation to stress.

According to MRM, self care knowledge and self care resources are the determinants of self care actions. The individual experiencing stress relies on personal knowledge of what is needed in recovery as well as mobilization of resources to adapt, thus reducing the effects of the stressor and returning to equilibrium. Nursing assessment focuses on obtaining a model of the person's world, particularly determining self care knowledge and self care resources. Nursing interventions are based on role modeling to facilitate adaptation and health. Based on MRM theory, the authors empirically studied perceived enactment of autonomy, hope, denial, and self care. These studies were conducted in an effort to test the relationship among the four concepts and to facilitate application of the theory in practice. Fig 1 illustrates linkages between MRM concepts and these operational variables.

MEASURING AUTONOMY

In practice, nurses are guided by the ethical imperative to respect client autonomy by supporting self-determination and designing individualized interventions.[13-14] In addition, autonomy has been linked to feelings of well-being.[15-20] Likewise, in MRM theory, nurses are directed to understand the client's world by modeling and then develop individualized interventions to meet the client's perceived needs by role modeling. Through modeling and role modeling, the nurse

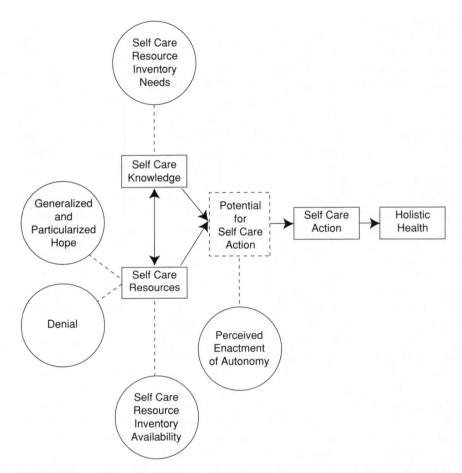

Fig 1. Linkages between the theoretical self care concepts and the operationalized variables.

can therefore respect the client's autonomy and promote and support self care actions that positively influence holistic health.

Most writers infer that to be autonomous, one must be independent. However, Collopy delineated several types of autonomy and inferred that one can act autonomously while simultaneously depending on others for assistance.[15] This notion is congruent with the concept of affiliated-individuation in MRM.[9]

If autonomy is an individual phenomenon, then the individual is the best source of knowledge for determining whether actions are or are not autonomous. In accordance with MRM, the client's perceptions of what actions are needed for self care are most important. Because no extant research instruments were found,[21] the need for methods to investigate the individual's perception of autonomous action in meeting needs for both dependence and independence was identified.

Based on the identified need for new methods to measure autonomy, an extensive concept analysis of autonomy was completed.[22] Three essential components or critical attributes were identified: (1) *voluntariness,* which is freedom from coercion or external constraints; (2) *individuality,* which is self-knowledge of needs and goals; and (3) *self-direction,* which is the ability to guide or control one's own destiny. To focus on the client's perception, the term *perceived enactment of autonomy* (PEA) was coined, and a subjective rather than objective definition was derived. PEA was conceptually defined as "a state of sensing and recognizing the ability to freely choose behaviors and courses of action on one's own behalf and in accordance with one's own needs and goals. This means choosing to act to meet needs for both dependence and independence either separately or simultaneously. This state encompasses perceptions regarding the presence or absence of the attributes of voluntariness, individuality, and self-direction."[21(p15)] This newly developed concept links self care knowledge, resources, and actions in MRM theory.

According to MRM theory, self care actions result from using personal self care knowledge and mobilizing internal and external self care resources to act on one's own behalf.[9] PEA is prerequisite to self care actions; both require using personal knowledge and resources without constraints (implied) to do what is best for oneself. Therefore, PEA is equated to the potential for self care action. Integration of this concept into the grand theory, MRM, expands the theory and facilitates development of a midrange theory of self care with PEA as a central, unifying concept.

Development of the PEA Scale, as a reliable and valid research instrument, proceeded in three phases.[22] Only the first two phases will be described here because they are the most pertinent to the topic of autonomy.

During the first phase, items were developed from a blueprint outlining the components of the definition. Because the target population was older adults, the items were rated by two panels of experts for congruence with the conceptual definition and for applicability for this population. Items were modified based on feedback from the panels. Interrater reliability for agreement about the appropriateness of item content was 100% and 92.2% for each panel. Initial construct, content, and face validity of the scale were established in this phase. The second phase was a pilot study and pretest of the scale. Twenty noninstitutionalized persons, ages 65 to 84 with a mean age of 71.8 years, completed the PEA Scale and were then questioned about the clarity of wording and difficulty or discomfort in responding to selected items. The major purpose was to ensure that the content was pertinent to the clients' life experiences by focusing on their perceptions.

Specific methods for obtaining the clients' perceptions included the following. First, the investigator recorded all comments made during administration of the scale. An interview guide was used to ask the respondents about items that had potentially ambiguous wording, may have been difficult to answer, or could cause discomfort in answering. Subjects defined each of the potentially ambiguous words; these definitions were recorded and then analyzed for general agreement about the word's meaning. A 10-rung Cantril ladder was used to rate difficulty or discomfort in answering selected items. Any items rated greater than 4 on the ladder by more than half of the subjects were to be scrutinized carefully; none was rated as too difficult or causing too much discomfort. Data analysis was done concurrently with data collection to permit wording changes and addition or deletion of items. As a result, the item pool for the scale was reduced to 50 from the original 60 based on the subjects' responses. These procedures contributed to the face and content validity of the PEA Scale for this population.[23]

Development of the PEA Scale, especially in the pilot study, relied predominantly on the client's perceptions about appropriate content for inclusion. This is in accordance with Erickson, Tomlin, and Swain's view of modeling the client's world.[9] Two of the persons in the pilot study actually became tearful while responding to the questions and stated that some of the items were very personal because they were adjusting to life-style changes associated with recently diagnosed health problems. Obviously, the content was meaningful to these individuals.

Nurses may be able to influence PEA by first modeling their clients' worlds and by then intervening to support PEA and each of its defining attributes. For instance, interventions that affect voluntariness and self-direction can be planned by providing more client control especially for those encountering increasing needs for dependency.[9] Values clarification can facilitate clients' abilities to ascertain personal goals and needs,[24] therefore influencing individuality.

In developing new research instruments to test MRM theory, it is not only imperative that investigators maintain the conceptual integrity of the measure but also that they find ways to incorporate the clients' perceptions concerning the appropriateness of content. Utilizing the methods for composing and then pretesting newly developed instruments, as described here, will ensure that both conditions are met.

MEASURING HOPE

MRM theory postulates that hope is an important, internal, self care resource, which influences clients' self care actions and holistic health.[9] The theory conceptualizes hope as a futuristic perspective, including "a projection of the 'self' into the future."[9(p168)] Propositions in the theory relate this futuristic perspective of the self to a sense of trust and to perceived control. In order to have an instrument to test these propositions, a retroductive process was used to reconceptualize an existing instrument.

Retroductive reasoning examines phenomena using deductive logic derived from a grand theory and inductive logic based on research findings.[1,25] In this case, propositions relating hope to a sense of trust and to perceived control, from the grand theory MRM, were compared with findings from a qualitative study by Dufault and Martocchio.[26]

Findings obtained by Dufault and Martocchio[26] suggest that two different phenomena or spheres of hope exist (ie, generalized hope and particularized hope).

Generalized hope is defined as a sense of some future, beneficial, but indeterminate, development. This sphere of hope is perceived as giving life meaning. Particularized hope is concerned with a concrete or abstract hope object that one wants to attain. Inductively linking generalized and particularized hope with deductively derived propositions from MRM suggests that hope is a broad construct comprised of generalized hope (related to a sense of trust) and particularized hope (related to perceived control).

To operationalize these two qualitatively defined types of hope, items on the Nowotny Hope Scale[27] were reconceptualized into two new subscales, based on congruency between the items and the definitions of the two types of hope. For example, generalized hope items encompass spirituality, connectedness to others, and generally looking forward to the future. In contrast, particularized hope items include confidence in facing challenges and setting goals.[28] Content validity of the items in each subscale was evaluated by two judges (Kappa's Cohen = .94).[28]

Construct validity of the subscales was examined by comparing relationships between subscale scores and selected variables. As theorized, significant correlations were found between generalized hope subscale scores ($n = 90$) and frequency of spiritual activities ($r = .59, p < .001$), frequency of contact with family or relatives ($r = .35, p < .001$), and number of support systems ($r = .37, p < .001$). Furthermore, the correlation between generalized hope and favorable trust–mistrust developmental residual was significant ($r = .24, p = .03$).[28]

For the particularized hope subscale, a significant correlation was found between the subscale scores ($n = 90$) and frequency with which one got what was wanted out of life ($r = .33, p < .001$). Also, the correlation between particularized hope and favorable autonomy–shame developmental residual was significant ($r = .57, p < .001$). Convergence between the subscale scores and selected variables supports the construct validity of both subscales.[28] Likewise, reliability of both the subscales was supported (Cronbach's alpha > .82) when evaluated for internal consistency.[28]

To explore whether the two subscales measure different phenomena, subjects' generalized hope scores were compared with their particularized hope scores, because theoretically the paired scores should be different. The significant finding (paired $t = 3.77$, $df = 89$, $n = 90$) provides some evidence that the two subscales measure differing phenomena of hope.[28]

Clinical application of these findings suggests that nurses assess clients' generalized hope as well as particularized hope, rather than looking at hope as only a broad, overall construct. Operationalizing both types of hope also has implications for research (eg, at the situation relating level). Having an instrument to measure both types of hope may facilitate researching the effect of nursing interventions on clients' generalized and particularized hope.

MEASURING DENIAL

Denial is a well-documented phenomenon that may have positive or negative implications. For example, if a person denies the symptom of chest pain, treatment is delayed, and possibly morbidity increases. However, in a person undergoing treatment for the chest pain, denial may be an appropriate coping mechanism.[29]

Recognizing the importance of assessing denial in coronary clients and being unable to locate a self-report instrument that inclusively measured this phenomenon, a self-administered scale entitled the Robinson Self-Appraisal Inventory (RSAI) was developed.[30] Even though the Hackett-Cassem Denial Scale was available for measuring denial, earlier research indicated that the construct denial included factors not measured by the Hackett-Cassem instrument, which was based on clinical judgments derived from interviews; furthermore, it was not a self-report.[31] Two studies were then conducted based on a micro theory of denial. As a result of reexamining the concept, the third and current study focused on developing the Robinson Self-Appraisal Inventory-Form D. This was done in an attempt to measure only the first stage of the grief process: denial. MRM theory provided the framework for the current study.

An assumption in MRM is that all people have a drive toward maximum growth and development across the life span.[9] This drive has at its core instinctive needs that motivate behavior. When needs are met repeatedly, development occurs. Objects that repeatedly meet needs take on a significance for the individuals; thus, an attachment to the object occurs. Loss of the attachment results in the grief response with denial and shock being the first stage of the process.[9,32] Then it becomes necessary for the individual to work through the grief process, reattaching to a new object in order to contend fully with the stressors of everyday life.[9]

The extent of loss a client experiences is directly related to the individual's emotional attachment to the lost object. For example, an acute episode of chest pain for the coronary client may threaten the loss of an attachment object, that is, one's heart function.[29] When an individual is initially confronted with this feeling of loss, denial may provide the necessary time to perceive an adequate, alternative attachment object. Determining a client's level of denial is necessary to understand the client's coping resources. This information is needed before the nurse can develop individualized interventions to facilitate the client's adaptation.

In preparation for the first study, an extensive literature review was conducted, and a concept analysis was prepared for denial. The 31 interview questions on the Hackett-Cassem Denial Scale were studied with 13 of the questions being rewritten so that participants could respond to each of them on a Likert-type scale.[30] Additional items were added to measure the various aspects of the construct that had been identified in concept analysis. Cardiovascular and psychiatric clinical nurse specialists and critical care experts judged the newly developed instrument's content and face validity.

According to the research literature, a relationship between denial and anxiety should exist.[33-34] Therefore, in order to test for construct validity of the 20-item RSAI, two methodological studies were conducted to determine if a relationship existed between denial and state anxiety levels of second hospitalized day myocardial infarction clients. In each of the samples, persons with high denial scores tended to have low state anxiety scores and vice versa. It was concluded that minimal construct validity for the instrument had been established, but further testing was needed.[30,35]

In the first study, the internal consistency of the RSAI was .65 using Cronbach's alpha.[30] An attempt was made to streamline the denial instrument and to increase the reliability by cluster analysis on the original dataset from the 30 subjects.[35] Interitem correlations suggested that the RSAI measured more than one dimension. Cluster analysis identified five subscales. The second study revealed a coefficient alpha of .41; however, the coefficient alpha increased to .62 when the items with a variance greater than 1.05 were removed.[35]

To address the problem of subscales, the current study focused on developing the Robinson Self-Appraisal Inventory-Form D (RSAI-Form D). This was done in an attempt to measure only the first stage of the grief process and to determine how denial changed during the acute phase of illness. Therefore, nine statements on the RSAI-Form D were revised.

In the current study, 130 coronary clients completed the RSAI-Form D on their second and fourth days of hospitalization. A coefficient alpha for the scale was .80 for both points in time, indicating that the 20 items were internally consistent on both days.[36]

Factor analysis in the study indicated that the RSAI-Form D probably is a multidimensional measurement; however, a larger sample is needed to make the final determination. Results of the Day 2 and Day 4 oblique rotations revealed that some items did not load on the same factor, so Day 2 and Day 4 factors were identified and named according to the definition of the items in that particular factor. Based on the literature review, the set of factors identified for Day 2 demonstrated, on a more conceptual basis, the first adaptive phase, denial. However, the Day 4 set of factors appeared to demonstrate a moving away from denial to awareness or a phasing out of denial.

There was a significant decrease in mean RSAI-Form D scores from the second to the fourth hospital day ($t = 5.83$, $p = .001$).[36] This finding is consistent with Cassem and Hackett, who reported that feelings of denial are generally mobilized on Day 2; however, by Day 4, as the individual's condition stabilizes, denial decreases.[37]

Findings of the study did provide preliminary evidence that the RSAI-Form D is a reliable inventory. Four aspects of denial were extracted, thus providing supportive evidence to the nurse that using single specific or global criteria does not provide sufficient data for assessing denial. Based on this finding, the nurse needs to understand the client's world as the client views it. Some individuals may use one type of denial, whereas others may use another type. Individuals instinctively know which type of denial they need to use to recover. Each type of denial has its own purpose for the person and could be denial of secondary consequences, denial of illness and treatment, denial of anxiety, or denial of impact. Therefore, it is beneficial for the nurse to observe and listen closely to clients to understand their perspective as well as determine the type of denial that is being utilized.[36]

The availability of this measurement permits future investigations to increase its reliability and validity as well as increase one's understanding of denial in the coronary client, and enable the nurse to infer the client's ability to mobilize resources needed to contend with the loss. Then, the nurse will be in a better position to develop interventions focused on helping the client address need deficits, establish new attachments, and resolve loss and grief.

MEASURING SELF CARE

Self care has been a part of the lay and nursing literature for several decades.[38-39] However, the self care model in MRM differs from the previous models and offers possibilities for explanatory and predictive, theory-based research. The MRM self care framework includes self care knowledge and self care resources as determinants of self care actions.[9] Self care knowledge includes what the person perceives caused the illness as well as what is needed for recovery. Self care resources are those internal and external factors that can be mobilized to cope with the stress of illness and recovery. Self care actions include coping behaviors that are directed toward promoting health and positive outcomes. The purpose of this study was to examine MRM self care by exploring the relationship among self care knowledge, self care resources, and the outcome of self care actions.

No instruments purport to measure self care knowledge and self care resources from the perspective of MRM. Therefore, the researcher found that it was necessary to develop an instrument to measure self care after reexamining the components of the theory. The result was the development of the Self-Care Resource Inventory (SCRI). Care was taken to identify appropriate items for the instrument as well as a format that would reflect congruence with the theory. A three-phase approach was used to develop the SCRI.[40]

The purpose of Phase 1 was item generation. A thorough review of the MRM self care research literature resulted in the identification of 25 items that could be identified as self care resources.[41-44] These items reflected internal and external resources that were congruent with affiliated individuation. In addition, each item could be viewed as being related to a basic or growth need. Finally, each item reflected an outcome of a stage of human development. These items were reviewed by a panel of 15 experts in MRM. The group reviewed each item for relevance, and a group discussion focused on refinement of the format.[40]

To measure self care resources, subjects were asked to rate how much of each item was available during recovery. To measure self care knowledge, subjects were asked to rate how much each item was needed in recovery. This expert panel preferred the format that listed each item once but had parallel columns so that the subject could first rate the amount needed in recovery and then rate the amount available. The sum of the need column is the Self-Care Resource Inventory Need score (SCRIN), and the sum of the available column is the Self-Care Resource Inventory Availability score (SCRIA). A difference score (SCRID) can be obtained by subtracting the SCRIN from the SCRIA response for each item.

The second phase of tool development focused on further developing content validity. A national panel of eight MRM experts from research, practice, and education were asked to rate each item for relevance to the theory. The overall content validity index was .84, and all but one item exceeded .75. The single low item (.65) was reworded and included in the final version of the tool. At the suggestion of two experts, additional items were added, bringing the total to 32 items.[40]

The third phase of tool development employed reliability and validity testing in a convenience sample of people with cardiovascular disease. Test–retest reliability at a 3-week interval in 55 subjects who had cardiac surgery or a myocardial infarction was .75 and .68 for the SCRIN and SCRIA, respectively. Split half reliabilities were .95 and .88, and Cronbach alphas were .95 and .93, for the respective scores. In addition, construct validity was assessed by correlating the scores of the SCRI with visual analog scales. The results were .60 and .58, respectively.[40]

After the three-phase pilot testing of the SCRI was completed, a study was conducted to examine the MRM self care model. A convenience sample of 84 subjects who had a myocardial infarction in the previous 3 to 6 months was recruited to participate in this study. Subjects were primarily male (69%), married (79%), European-American (90%), with a mean age of 61 years.[40] Life Satisfaction, as measured by the Campbell Index of Well-Being,[45] was determined to be an outcome of self care action and the dependent variable. SCRIN and SCRIA were the predictors variables. SCRIA accounted for 23% of the variance in life satisfaction ($p < .05$). The correlations of SCRIN with SCRIA and life satisfaction were .54 and .06. When SCRIN was added to the regression model, the amount of variance in life satisfaction that was accounted for increased to 28%, demonstrating a suppressor effect. SCRIN was not significantly correlated with life satisfaction; however, there was a moderately strong relationship between SCRIN and SCRIA. SCRIN improved the overall prediction by suppressing the noise in the variable SCRIA. Of interest, use of the SCRID score to predict life satisfaction resulted in a model that only accounted for 15% of the variance.

This study supports the self care model described in MRM. Both self care knowledge and self care resources must be assessed to find the most complete model to examine the outcomes of self care actions. In practice, the nurse can apply this theory by examining both self care knowledge and self care resources with each client. The nurse must look beyond the assessment of the client's perceived availability of resources to examine the situation also in view of the client's assessment of what is needed for recovery. With this holistic approach, the nurse can truly build a complete model of the client's world. From this complete model, the nurse can work with the client to role model interventions to improve health.

•   •   •

The authors have shown how four research programs have begun in an effort to test aspects of MRM theory and contribute to practice. Each researcher had to redefine concepts or instruments to accomplish the goal. The concept of autonomy was reexamined to explicate the new concept of perceived enactment of autonomy; this work led to the development of a tool to measure the new concept. In the study of hope, an existing instrument was reconceptualized and the items restructured to provide conceptual congruence with MRM. A tool measuring denial was revised for congruence with aspects of the grand theory. Finally, self care was examined from the perspective of modeling and role modeling, resulting in the development of a new instrument. These examples demonstrate how creative approaches to theory-based instrumentation can lead to innovative methods that result in a stronger relationship between theory and research.

REFERENCES

1. Chinn PL, Jacobs MK. *Theory and Nursing: A Systematic Approach*. St. Louis, Mo: Mosby; 1987.
2. Fawcett J. The relationship between theory and research: a double helix. *ANS*. 1978;1(1):49-62.
3. Benoliel JQ. The interaction between theory and research. *Nurs Outlook*. 1977;25(2):108-113.
4. Moody LE, Wilson ME, Smyth K, Schwartz R, Tittle M, VanCott ML. Analysis of a decade of nursing practice research: 1977-1986. *Nurs Res*. 1988;37(6):374-379.
5. Silva MC. Research testing nursing theory: state of the art. *ANS*. 1986;9(10):1-11.
6. Meleis AI. *Theoretical Nursing: Development and Progress*. Philadelphia, Pa: Lippincott; 1985.
7. DeVellis RF. *Scale Development*. Newbury Park, Calif: Sage; 1991.
8. Woods NF, Catanzaro M. *Nursing Research: Theory and Practice*. St. Louis, Mo: Mosby; 1988.
9. Erickson HC, Tomlin E, Swain MA. *Modeling and Role-Modeling: A Theory and Paradigm for Nursing*. 2nd printing. Lexington, SC: Pine Press of Lexington; 1988.
10. Erikson E. *Identity, Youth and Crisis*. New York, NY: Norton; 1968.
11. Maslow AH. *Toward a Psychology of Being*. New York, NY: Van Nostrand Reinhold; 1968.
12. Selye H. *Stress Without Distress*. Philadelphia, Pa: Lippincott; 1974.
13. *Code for Nurses with Interpretive Statements*. Kansas City, Mo: American Nurses Association; 1976.
14. *Nursing: A Social Policy Statement*. Kansas City, Mo: American Nurses Association; 1980.
15. Collopy BJ. Autonomy in long term care: some crucial distinctions. *Gerontologist*. 1988;28(suppl):10-17.
16. Evans JG. Prevention of age-associated loss of autonomy: epidemiological approaches. *J Chronic Dis*. 1984;37:353-363.
17. Haug MR, Ory MG. Issues in elderly patient–provider interactions. *Res Aging*. 1987;9:3-44.
18. Lawton MP. The elderly in context: perspectives from environmental psychology and gerontology. *Environment and Behavior*. 1985;17:501-519.
19. Saup W. Lack of autonomy in old-age homes: a stress and coping study. *Journal of Housing for the Elderly*. 1986;4:21-36.
20. Wolk S, Telleen S. Psychological and social correlates of life satisfaction as a function of residential constraint. *J Gerontol*. 1976;31:89-98.
21. Hertz JE. *The Perceived Enactment of Autonomy Scale: Measuring the Potential for Self-care Action in the Elderly*. Ann Arbor, Mich: *Dissertation Abstracts International*. 1992;52(4):1953. University microfilms no. 91-28248.
22. Hertz JE. Perceived enactment of autonomy: concept development. 1993. Unpublished manuscript.

23. Fowler FJ. *Survey Research Methods: Vol 1. Applied Social Research Methods Series.* Rev ed. Newbury Park, Calif: Sage; 1988.

24. Wilberding JZ. Values clarification. In: Bulechek GM, McCloskey JC, eds. *Nursing Interventions: Treatments for Nursing Diagnoses.* Philadelphia, Pa: W.B. Saunders; 1985.

25. Marriner-Tomey A. *Nursing Theorists and Their Work.* St. Louis, Mo: Mosby; 1989.

26. Dufault K, Martocchio BC. Hope: its spheres and dimensions. *Nurs Clin North Am.* 1985;20:379-391.

27. Nowotny ML. Assessment of hope in patients with cancer: development of an instrument. *Oncol Nurs Forum.* 1989;16:57-61.

28. Curl ED. *Hope in the Elderly: Exploring the Relationship between Psychosocial Developmental Residual and Hope.* Ann Arbor, Mich: Dissertation Abstracts International. 1992;53(4):1782 (University Microfilms no. 92-25559).

29. Robinson KR. Denial: an adaptive response. *DCCN.* 1993;12:102-106.

30. Robinson KR. *Denial and Anxiety in Second Day Myocardial Infarction Patients.* Denton, Tex: Texas Woman's University; 1982. Thesis.

31. Hackett TP, Cassem NH. Development of a quantitative rating scale to assess denial. *J Psychosom Res.* 1974;18:93-100.

32. Engel GL. *Psychological Development in Health and Disease.* Philadelphia, Pa: W.B. Saunders; 1962.

33. Bigos KM. Behavioral adaptation during the acute phase of a myocardial infarction. *West J Nurs Res.* 1981;3:150-167.

34. Hackett TP, Cassem NH, Wishnie HA. The coronary care unit: an appraisal of its psychological hazards. *N Engl J Med.* 1968;279:1,365-1,370.

35. Robinson KR. Denial and anxiety in second day myocardial infarction patients. In: Waltz CF, Strickland OK, eds. *Measurement of Nursing Outcomes.* New York, NY: Springer; 1988; 1.

36. Robinson KR. Developing a scale to measure responses of clients with actual or potential myocardial infarctions. *Heart Lung.* 1994;23:36–44.

37. Cassem NH, Hackett TP. Psychiatric consultation in a coronary care unit. *Ann Intern Med.* 1971;75:9–14.

38. Orem D. *Nursing: Concepts of Practice.* New York, NY: McGraw-Hill; 1971.

39. Levine LS, Katz AH, Holst E. *Self-Care Lay Initiatives in Health.* New York, NY: Produst; 1979.

40. Baas LS. *The Relationship Among Self Care Knowledge, Self Care Resources, Activity Level and Life Satisfaction in Persons Three to Six Months After a Myocardial Infarction.* Dissertation. Ann Arbor, Mich: Dissertation Abstracts International. 1992;53(4):1780 (University Microfilms no. 92-25512).

41. Erickson HC, Swain MAP. Mobilizing self-care resources: a nursing intervention for hypertension. *Iss in Men Health.* 1990;11:217-235.

42. Erickson HC, Swain MAP. A model for assessing potential adaptation to stress. *Res Nurs Health.* 1982;5:93-101.

43. Kleinbeck SVM. *Coping States of Stress.* Ann Arbor, Mich: The University of Michigan; 1987. Thesis.

44. Keck VE. *Perceived Social Support, Basic Needs Satisfaction, and Coping Strategies of the Chronically Ill.* Ann Arbor, Mich: The University of Michigan; 1989. Dissertation.

45. Campbell A, Converse PE, Rodgers WL. *The Quality of American Life: Perceptions, Evaluations, and Satisfactions.* New York, NY: Russell Sage Foundation; 1976.

Evidence of Nonlinear Dynamics in Teen Births in Texas: 1964–1990

Patti Hamilton, RN, PhD
Associate Professor
Director of Research
Texas Woman's University
Denton, Texas

Bruce J. West, PhD
Professor and Chair, Physics
University of North Texas
Denton, Texas

H.J. Mackey, PhD
Professor, Physics
University of North Texas
Denton, Texas

Mona Cherri, PhD
Assistant Professor
Mathematics and Computer Science
Texas Woman's University
Denton, Texas

Paul Fisher, PhD
Chair, Computer Science
University of North Texas
Denton, Texas

Traditional methods of analysis have been limited by assumptions of linearity. The irregularity observed in the behavior of complex systems frequently can be traced to intrinsic nonlinearity or Chaos. Such nonlinearities violate linearity assumptions, and, necessitate the application of new methods of analysis. The methods used in this study are based on advanced mathematical, physical and analytical techniques which have been developed for the purpose of understanding nonlinear systems.

The research described here was conducted to describe, the pattern of teen birth in Texas and to evaluate the application of high technology analytic procedures which are now available to nurse scientists.

SEVENTEENTH AND eighteenth century Newtonian science was based on a belief in a universe as regular as clockwork. It was thought that the world and all within it could be understood using simplified representations that smoothed irregularities and omitted disorder. Despite significant scientific revolutions that followed Newton, his models of regularity and order still serve as the bases of most analytical techniques used by nurses today.

Traditional analytic techniques work best when it can be assumed that phenomena are normally distributed within a population; that causal relations, if not linear, could be transformed to fit the assumptions of linear analytic techniques; and that perfect prediction would be possible if the right measurements were made with no error. Few, if any, of these assumptions can be made with confidence when dealing with persons and their health.

Unlike Newton's simplified world, ours is a world far from equilibrium. Changes in future events are unpredictable and punctuated rather than gradual. Therefore, it is crucial to have theories and methods appropriate to describe phenomena that are unstable, irregular, and unpredictable. Until recently, scientists have been handicapped in their ability to study systematically such a complex world.

What follows is an overview of a new science that may enhance our ability to understand an irregular and unpredictable world. The methods derived from this new science have been applied to research concerning the incidence over time of teen births in Texas. This example illustrates the effectiveness of the methods for studying complex nursing problems.

Although the methods will be introduced and illustrated, a fuller understanding of them will require further explanations found in more technical journals in the fields of mathematics and physics. Technical resources are identified and sources of available software are listed for readers who want additional information about the methods.The gap between the mathematical and physical understanding of complex, dynamical processes and the application of that understanding to health problems can be decreased by collaborative studies such as the one described here.

THEORETICAL FRAMEWORK

Nonlinear dynamics is one of a number of emerging methodological and theoretical constructs that make up what is often called *the science of complexity*. The popular name for the "new" science is *chaos theory*. The chaos referred to in the theory is not a lack of organization or order but is instead a complex state in which apparent randomness of a system is really constrained by a type of order that is nonlinear. *Nonlinearity* is a condition in which the output of the system does not match the input; for example, small causes can have large effects.

A number of factors have coalesced to favor the acceptance of a new science of complexity at this particular time in the history of human thought. One factor is today's advanced computing technology. Sophisticated computer hardware and software are now quite accessible to most scientists. New computer technology enables researchers to analyze vast quantities of data and do so rapidly. In addition, one can graphically display data in a variety of forms to assist in the investigation of underlying patterns that are embedded in the data.

Ours is an age in which the stage is set for a science of complexity. The analysis of large datasets and the display of results visually in three or more dimensions have been invaluable heuristic tools for understanding a complex world. There is an increasing interest in accelerated social change in which disorder, instability, diversity, and disequilibrium are coupled with social, economic, and political relationships in which small inputs can trigger large, unexpected consequences.

The aim of chaos theory is a richer description of the complexity of phenomena. Chaos theory lends itself to the exploration of multidimensional interactions within and among individuals, families, and communities. Chaos theory promises to fulfill a portion of our need to understand complexity. What comprises what we are now calling chaos theory? Critical principles of this new science are as follows:

- Most phenomena of interest to physical and social scientists are open systems, exchanging energy and/or matter with their environment.
- Most of reality, instead of being orderly and stable at equilibrium, is seething and bubbling with change, disorder, and process.
- All systems contain subsystems that are continually fluctuating.
- Single fluctuations or a combination of them may become so powerful, as a result of positive feedback, that they shatter the preexisting organization. (This is known as a *bifurcation point.*)
- It is inherently impossible to determine in advance which direction change shall take at a bifurcation.
- Following bifurcation, a system can disintegrate into chaos or leap to a new, more differentiated, higher level of order. (This new order may be called a *dissipative structure* and requires more energy than simpler systems to maintain.)
- In far-from-equilibrium situations, spontaneous reorganization of matter within time and space can take place.

This overview of chaos theory relies heavily on the work of Ilya Prigogine and Isabell Stengers and the reaction to that work by Alvin Toffler.[1]

APPLICATIONS OF CHAOS THEORY TO NURSING

Researchers from many disciplines have found chaos theory helpful in understanding complex phenomena. By employing the principles of chaos theory and the research methods appropriate for nonlinear analysis, nurses could join with economists, educators, biologists, physicists, mathematicians, and sociologists for collaborative investigations of complex human problems affecting health. Another reason chaos theory holds such promise for nursing knowledge development is that other theories have not adequately explained the following:

- Why is the natural history of an illness not the same in "like" cases?
- Why can we not make reliable predictions about the future even when we have accurate information about the past?
- How is it that crisis can be a positive experience?
- How do we understand wholeness?

- Why is seemingly random or chaotic functioning in body systems healthy and optimal functioning?

Chaos theory, operationalized through nonlinear dynamical analysis, offers new ways to address these difficult questions. The aim of this new science is richer description of the complexity of phenomena, not prediction and control in the usual sense. Nonlinear dynamics allows researchers to depict complex patterns of behavior within a system over time in ways that reveal the limits of the behavior but still preserve the variation within those limits. Chaos theory challenges researchers' ability to predict future events. This challenge is based on the principles of *nonlinearity* and *sensitivity to initial conditions,* which hold that a nonlinear dynamical equation can have solutions that are irregular. The irregularity results in small changes being amplified by the nonlinear nature of the system. This means that if the initial state of a nonlinear system is changed only slightly, we cannot predict the difference in how each system would evolve over time. One often-cited example of the effects of nonlinearity and sensitivity to initial conditions was given by the meteorologist, Ed Lorenz. Lorenz[2] explained, mathematically, why predicting the weather with precision will be impossible. He demonstrated that two virtually identical weather systems will behave differently over time due to their complex, nonlinear nature and due to inputs from the environment that are infinitely small. He suggested, somewhat tongue-in-cheek, that even the flapping wings of a butterfly could result in a tornado because of nonlinear processes at work even with the smallest factors causing the weather.

West and Goldberger[3] startled the medical community in 1987 when they reported that the beat-to-beat variation in the human heart is neither regular nor random but, instead, may be chaotic. Complex, chaotic systems often appear random, but when analyzed using methods of nonlinear analysis, the apparent randomness is found to be deterministic. This chaos or constrained randomness is not necessarily pathologic but can aid the heart in its efforts to meet the constantly fluctuating needs of the body. There is acceptance across disciplines of the idea of chaos as healthy in complex systems.[4-8] This notion has led to greater application of nonlinear analysis to a variety of research questions.

The importance of nonlinearity in analysis of human systems rests on two assumptions regarding linearity. First, if a system is linear, outputs of that system will be in proportion to inputs. Second, if a system is linear, two trajectories initiated at nearby points in phase space would evolve in close proximity. Said another way, at any point in the future, the two trajectories (or states of the system) would be near one another.

Few systems with which nurses work could truly be called linear. Whether researching physiologic responses of individuals or researching health problems of whole communities, nurses are faced with understanding apparently nonlinear systems in which very small inputs can result in disproportionately large outputs. In addition, research challenges nurses to describe and explain phenomena that seem to evolve very differently in apparently similar systems. In other words, we ask, "Why would a health care intervention for two essentially equivalent patients result in such different outcomes?" or "Why is a particular type of service effective in one community and ineffective in another when the two seem to be demographically indistinguishable?"

PURPOSE AND RATIONALE OF THE STUDY

The complexity of the phenomena of interest in nursing research requires that the most sophisticated means available be brought to bear on our research questions. Determining factors that contribute to teen births are but one example of the complex problems facing nurses and other biomedical researchers today. There is increasing interest in more technologically advanced procedures for nonlinear analysis in biomedical research, but, to date, the necessary technology has been inaccessible to disciplines such as nursing.

The new methods of nonlinear analysis were used for the purpose of identifying patterns in the daily occurrence of births to teens in Texas from 1964 to 1990. While the rise and fall of birth rates to teens over this period had been well documented, it was hypothesized that there were many more rich complexities of the data that had not, heretofore, been described.

Traditional research of teen births in a population over time had been conceptualized to answer research questions such as, "which time intervals or periods are characterized by high frequencies of teen births?" or "can a regression equation be derived that is predictive of future rates of teen births?" With nonlinear dynamical analyses, these questions can be addressed, and a researcher can determine the overall patterns of change in teen births across time. Further analysis of the embedding dimensions of the overall pattern can yield the number of parameters at work determining the changes within the process over time. The goal of this type of analysis is richer description and deeper understanding, not prediction of specific events, as in the case of past research.

BACKGROUND AND SIGNIFICANCE

In 1992, Schlitt,[9] the coordinator for the Southern Center for Adolescent Pregnancy Prevention, drew a comparison between predicting the deadly path of destruction of a hurricane and predicting the potential tragedy of adolescent pregnancy. Schlitt lamented the need for patterns and predictors of early parenthood. When public agencies can become better forecasters, writes Schlitt, they can "better identify children and adolescents at greatest risk for early parenthood and . . . provide early interventions which might positively impact adolescent decision-making."[9]

Attempts to discern patterns in teen pregnancy must contend with the irregularity and nonlinearity that Lorenz observed in his weather patterns. The term *pattern* is used to describe the features of change in phenomena—in this case, births to teens. However, rather than thinking of pattern as being regular, stable, and predictable, knowledge of the "real" world necessitates we think of pattern instead as being a representation of the features of a complex, changing phenomenon over time. In the case of this study, pattern is not synonymous with regularity, stability, and predictability. Rather, it is a description of the dynamics of an evolutionary process. Pattern in the science of complexity is associated with the intrinsic dynamics of a process. These dynamics can be irregular, unstable, and predictable only for a relatively short time interval.

The goal for this study was not precise prediction but, rather, rich and detailed description of the process.

In Texas, teen pregnancy has become a serious public health concern. The following are excerpts from the Texas Teen Fact Sheet prepared by the Texas Department of Human Services in June 1992.[10] The most current data indicate the following:

- Texas had more births to mothers under the age of 15 than any other state.
- Texas ranked second in the number of births to mothers under the age of 14.
- Texas had more births to mothers under 20 than any state except California.
- Texas ranked second in the nation (behind New Mexico) in the percentage of mothers under 20 who received inadequate prenatal care.
- In Texas in Fiscal Year 1991, over $215 million were spent on 131,804 Medicaid-paid deliveries. Approximately 29% of these deliveries were to teenage mothers.

Jones et al[11] estimate that in the United States, 43% of all female adolescents and 63% of black adolescents will give birth before their 20th birthday. Births to teens are the result of individual decisions. However, individual decisions are influenced by complex interactions of factors, which include characteristics of the young woman, her partner, her peers, and her family, as well as the social, political, and economic influences of her community.[12]

The relatively unequal distribution of income, lack of openness about sex, less sex education, and limited distribution of contraception appear to account for a very different pattern of teen births in the United States than in other developed countries.[11] Norr asserts that there appear to be three patterns of adolescent pregnancy and birth within the United States. The Southern states, Alaska, and some Western states appear to reflect "a continuation of a preindustrial pattern of early family formation. Higher rates of adolescent childbearing are associated with higher levels of religiosity, especially fundamentalism, social and sexual conservatism and a pattern of early marriage and low education. . . ."[12(p180)] In the Northeast, the Midwest, and California, the pattern is more European. There are relatively liberal attitudes toward sexuality, higher rates of sexual activity, more unintended pregnancy often due to lack of contraception (not choice), and there is a more frequent use of abortion. A third pattern of adolescent childbearing may be "a response to community disorganization and the inability to control youth activities plus a lack of perceived opportunities that would reward delayed childbearing."[12(p180)]

Norr further suggests that there should be three areas of research of the factors influencing teen pregnancy in the United States:[12(p176)]

1. comparative analyses of vital statistics,
2. investigation of individual and community characteristics of the phenomenon, and
3. evaluation of existing program interventions.

LIMITATIONS OF TRADITIONAL METHODS OF PATTERN RECOGNITION AND FORECASTING

Predicting teen births is immensely difficult, in part because of the problems in understanding the abundant, ragged ups and downs that characterize this and many other changes in natural populations.[13-16] In Fig 1, you can see the jagged appearance of the teen birth data. It looks very much like a plot of static or noise in a radio signal. High frequencies appear to be interspersed randomly with low frequencies. However, there has been great progress made in analysis of nonlinear dynamics leading to findings that suggest even the noisiest variation may have its origin in simple, deterministic mechanisms.[17] Only recently have advanced methods for nonlinear analyses been developed that can distinguish between chaos and noise.

There is a traditional assumption that causal factors at work in the pattern of a changing phenomenon exert their influence in a uniform, or stationary, way. The nonstationary nature of birth data has been a persistent problem for current methods of modeling. Texas teen birth data are no exception; they exemplify a process that is markedly nonstationary.[18]

Distribution of age and race as well as patterns of sexual behavior of the population changed dramatically in Texas between 1964 and 1990. There has been a dramatic upward shift in the age distribution of Texas females over the last 20 years, most of which is due to the maturation of the post-World War II baby boomers. For example, in 1970, women aged 15 to 19 years comprised 9.5% of all females in Texas, whereas those aged 30 to 34 years accounted for only 5.8%. By 1990, women aged 15 to 19 years had fallen to 7.4% of the female population; those aged 30 to 34 had risen to a full 9% of the total.[19]

In addition to the shift in age distribution, there has been behavioral change among women of reproductive age. Assuming that Texas women have been following the national trend, there has been a marked increase in the percentage of older women who have not yet given birth. However, the first-birth rate for women aged 15 to 19 years consistently has been about twice as high for blacks and Hispanics as it has for whites.

The breakdown in ethnicity indicates the increasingly multicultural character of the state. Compared to 1987, the number of white births in 1991 decreased by 6.6%, and those for Hispanics increased by 24.6%, others (primarily Asians) by 20.8%, and blacks by 2.2%. Among blacks and Hispanics, fertility rates rise quickly between the ages of 15 and 24 and then begin to decrease. Among whites and others, however, fertility peaks and tapers off slowly in the 25 to 29 group.[19]

RATIONALE FOR USE OF NONLINEAR DYNAMICAL ANALYSIS METHODS

The research team thought that the application of nonlinear analyses to the data might yield new insights for understanding teen births. If our analysis indicated that the phenomenon conformed to the behavior of a nonlinear or chaotic system, then further nonlinear analyses would be conducted. This preliminary step was not aimed at explanation of factors contributing to teen births but, instead, was aimed at description of the change in this apparently complex phenomenon over time. Detailed description is necessary prior to any explanatory research.

Nonlinear dynamical analysis techniques were considered promising methods to employ due to the complexity of the pattern of teen births in Texas. This complexity was marked by ragged ups and downs in the process over time and by constantly changing (nonstationary) background features of the population. The research was conducted to answer the following two questions:

1. What are the patterns of occurrence in births to teens in Texas from 1964 to 1990?
2. Is change in the phenomenon of teen births in Texas a nonlinear process?

ANALYSIS

The data were extracted from birth certificates at the Texas Department of Health. Data included dates and frequency of births to women 10 to 19 years old on each day from January 1, 1964, to December 31, 1990. Preliminary analysis revealed that the average number of births to teens in Texas each month over the 26-year period was 3,984. The average daily incidence was 126 with a standard deviation of 17.2. The number of babies born to teens during the study period was in excess of 1,200,000. No data regarding abortions or repeat pregnancies were analyzed in this study. Analysis of more detailed data is planned for subsequent studies.

The total number of young women ages 10 to 19 during each year of the study period was obtained. The birth data were normalized by dividing frequencies of births in a given year by the number of young women in that age group in the same year. This normalization offset the effect of changes in age distributions during the 26-year period.

Traditional time-series analyses, including spectral density analysis (PSD), were used to display the data. The time-series plot of the data is shown in Fig 1. Visual inspection of the data indicated an apparently random, noisy process. In fact, the histogram shown in Fig 2 indicates a good fit of the fluctuations to a normal distribution as shown by the solid curve. Normality is evidence of random or noisy distribution of the frequencies.

The PSD of the time series is shown in Fig 3. The PSD is used to expose the periodic components in the data (indicated by the sharp peaks) and determine the

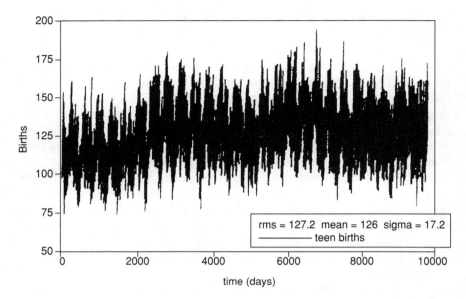

Fig 1. The number of births to young women 10 to 19 in Texas during the period 1964 to 1990.

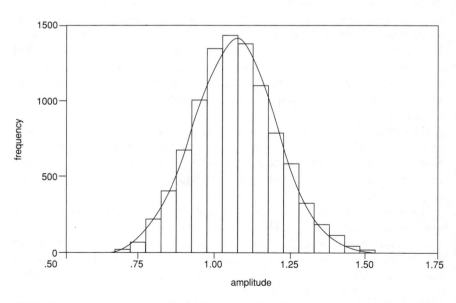

Fig 2. A histogram representing the frequency distribution of the daily birth occurrences. The amplitudes are in normalized units.

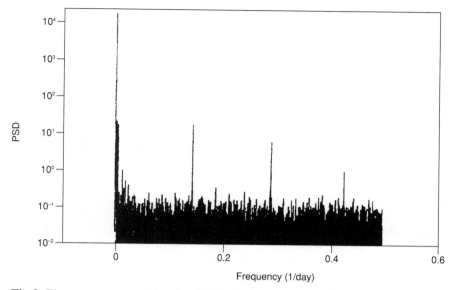

Fig 3. The power spectral density (PSD) for the teen birth time series plotted as a function of frequency (t) in units of l/day.

amount of variance attributable to the background fluctuations. Very large effects were found at periods of 7, 182, and 372 days.

These results are consistent with two quite different interpretations. The first one is the most familiar. This interpretation suggests that the process is a deterministic, linear process embedded in random process. The peaks in the spectrum would in this case correspond to the deterministic linear process and the noise would correspond to random occurrences.

The second interpretation is that of a nonlinear, deterministic process, in which case, the noise would actually be chaos, and the peaks would correspond to strong correlations in the dynamical system. One method of deciding between these two interpretations is that of *singular value decomposition* (SVD). Using SVD, the dominant variables in the system can be isolated, that is, separated from the noise.[20] To accomplish this, the daily incidence of teen births were plotted as points in a multidimensional phase space.

Imagine that you are taking the pulse, blood pressure, and temperature of a patient every hour, and you want to graph the relationships among all three vital signs as they change over time. You could construct a graph that was marked at the center by the intersection of three axes, one for each of the vital signs. (See Fig 4.) Connecting these points in temporal sequence forms a trajectory. In nonlinear dynamical analysis, this trajectory is referred to as an attractor.

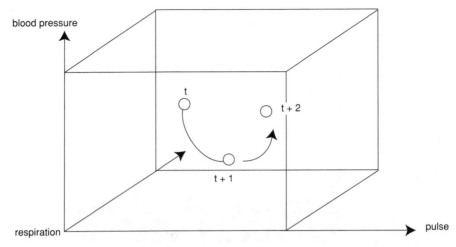

Fig 4. Graph of change in relations among three variables in phase space.

In our teen birth example, there were not three separate variables to be plotted. Instead, the daily incidence of teen births was graphed as a continuous series of three values of the single variable as it changed over time at (t, t +1, t +2). This represents a major innovation in graphing change in a system as a series of measures of only one of the variables in the system. Gleick calls this method "one of the most enduring practical contributions to the progress of chaos."[21(p265)] The method is based on the assumption that a single variable from within a chaotic system has been influenced by all the other variables within the system. Therefore, knowledge of the entire system can be deduced from knowledge of a single variable as it evolves.[21]

By examination of the dimensional characteristics of an attractor, knowledge of the evolving pattern system can be determined. This pattern describes the process as it evolves as a whole. Fig 5 shows the attractor formed from the teen birth data. The spacing between data points along each axis in the phase space is denoted by τ (tau). Tau simply refers to the number of days that separate any two data points. One can construct time-series and trajectory analyses using a variety of values of tau in order to examine patterns with different time-dependent features.

In Fig 6, the singular values (depicted as eigenvalues) are plotted against the singular value index. The two curves indicate a time separation of $t = 1$ and $t = 7$. This process is suggestive of factor analysis. In the SVD analysis, the eigenvalues indicate the degree of relationship among points occurring in phase space over time. Just as in a scree plot, the singular values above the floor, or leveling-off point, indicate the number of dominant deterministic variables in the process. The SVD illustrates that for $t = 1$, perhaps six variables are dominant, but for $t = 7$, only three variables are dominant. This would suggest that a three-variable model of

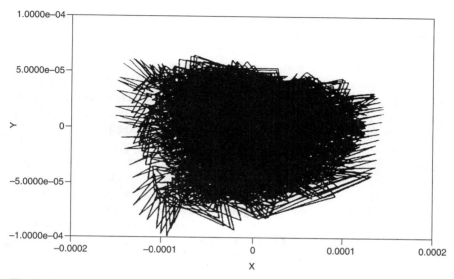

Fig 5. The attractor reconstruction technique is used to plot the time series X(t), X(t-tau), X(t-2tau) as the three axes. The teen births form the ball in phase space.

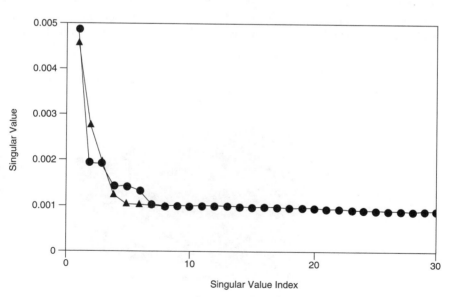

Fig 6. The singular values (eigenvalues) plotted against the singular value index. The two curves indicate a time separation of $t = 1$ for the • and $t = 7$ for the ▲. Singular values above the "floor" indicate dominant deterministic variables in the process.

the process would provide an adequate description of the dynamics of this very complex process of teen births.

The nonlinear interpretation of the teen birth process is further supported by means of what is called a *return map*. If one were to "slice" the attractor (Fig 7) on which the trajectories evolve by inserting a plane transverse to the attractor, one could see how closely related the points on the attractor were as they crossed the plane. If the points are closely related, they form a return map. This return-map function indicates a low-dimensional attractor exists for the process. A low-dimensional attractor is indicative of a process dependent on few variables for the pattern of its change over time. When very complex systems appear random but can be modeled by a low-dimensional attractor, they are said to be chaotic.

In Fig 8, we see some indication of the existence of a return-map function relating successive values of the data. The diagonal cluster of closely spaced points suggests the existence of a low-dimensional attractor. For an uncorrelated, random time series, this mapping function would be a random spray of points. Additional analyses of the data are required to determine the detailed structure of this function.

CONCLUSION

Evidence indicates a substantial nonlinear component to the data. Visual inspection of the time series and the frequency histogram reveals a data pattern that is noisy and shows superficial signs of randomness. However, when more advanced, nonlinear methods of analysis were applied, there seemed to be a complex, but

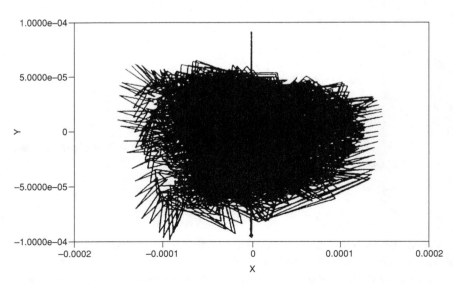

Fig 7. The intersection of the attractor with a transverse plane in phase space.

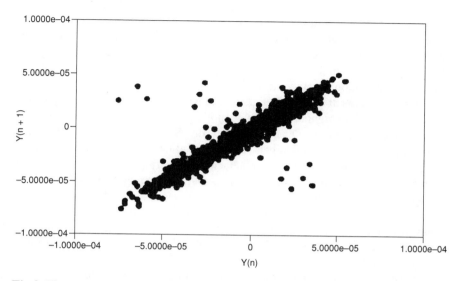

Fig 8. The return map function obtained by recording the intersection of the trajectory constructed from the teen birth data with a transverse plane in the phase space. The dots represent the trajectories of the data as they cross the plane in a positive direction.

deterministic, process at work. Ironically, one property of low-dimensional, non-linear processes is that their pattern of change can often be reconstructed using very few parameters (here, only three would be needed). Therefore, it was concluded that the "noise" was chaos, and the peaks correspond to strong correlations in the dynamical system. In other words, what had at first appeared random was constrained by a deterministic process still to be identified.

The analysis of the effects of ethnicity, culture, economy, and other variables thought to contribute to teen pregnancy and birth will be augmented by a more accurate description of the dynamic process reflected in the data over time. According to Schaffer and Kot, "The time is past for models that are only caricatures of the data."[13(p349)] Advanced computer technology and theory from physics and mathematics have provided the foundation for more sophisticated modeling of teen births. Through this study, it was hoped that linear, stationary representations of the data might be replaced with richer descriptions of the patterns modeling the complexity with which the process actually occurs. Through more detailed and rich descriptions of patterns, the study may enhance research efforts in all three areas of teen birth research suggested by Norr.[12]

The findings of this study shall become the foundation for a long-term program of research that shall compare patterns of teen births across ages, races, and sociodemographic conditions in various states and regions of the United States. These very detailed comparisons may provide more precise analysis of the influence of individual and community characteristics on births to teens. The findings also may provide a much more sensitive epidemiologic measure for the community-wide evaluation of interventions.

A long-range result of improved pattern identification would be the identification of patterns that might become epidemiological "markers" for the influence of specific factors on the incidence of teen births. Such markers could be used to identify particular times and targets for intensified interventions.

The research described here was conducted to describe, in detail, the pattern of teen births in Texas and to demonstrate and evaluate the application of high-technology, analytic procedures derived from mathematics and physics, which are now available to nurse scientists. The methods presented may greatly enhance analysis of the complex changes in natality in Texas during the period under investigation. The methods can address the "problem" of nonstationarity of the data and can describe the complexity of the orbit of the dynamic process through phase space. These methods of analysis are appropriate for data gathered at equal time intervals. The amount of data required is dependent on the dynamics of the process. The more complex the process (or the more variables or parameters it takes to reproduce the attractor), the more data are required.

Examples of the types of data that might lend themselves to nonlinear analysis and that are of interest to nurse researchers would include repeated measures of heart beats, respiration, blood pressure, temperature, blood gases, or other indicators of physiological function in individuals. At the community level of analysis, data might include population changes, incidence of disease, resource utilization, immunization levels, or mortality rates.

Traditional methods of analysis of such problems have been limited by their often implicit assumptions of normality of attribute distribution in populations and of an underlying linearity of causal processes. It is now recognized that the irregularity so often observed in the behavior of complex systems or processes frequently can be traced to intrinsic nonlinearity or chaos. The existence of such nonlinearities not only violates the linearity assumptions, but more importantly, necessitates the application of new methods of analysis. The methods used in this study are based on advanced mathematical, physical, and analytical techniques that have been developed in the last decade for the purpose of understanding nonlinear systems.

Advanced mathematics and nonlinear analysis have been proposed as possible tools appropriate for nursing analysis.[5-6,22] The use of nonlinear dynamics has been suggested specifically for research involving nursing at the community level.[7-8] The investigation of phenomena at the community level and the development of appropriate analytic techniques with which to do that are among the priorities for research identified by the Association of Community Health Nursing Educators in 1991.[23]

RESOURCES FOR FURTHER INVESTIGATION OF METHODS OF NONLINEAR DYNAMICAL ANALYSIS

Gleick's book, *Chaos: Making a New Science,*[21] provides a general overview of chaos theory and some of the methods mentioned above. *Chaos: The Software* is also available through *Autodesk* in Bothell, Washington. This software program will allow the user to explore principles of chaos theory by interactively manipulating the excellent color graphics. However, more complex programs are required for actually analyzing data. One such program is *Dynamical Software,* which is available in basic and advanced versions from *Aerial Press* in Santa Cruz, California. Both versions are designed for teaching and research but are more expensive and less user friendly than *Chaos: The Software.*

One book that illustrates the concepts of chaos in deterministic systems and describes explicit techniques for detecting each of these concepts is *Global Bifurcations and Chaos: Analytical Methods* by Wiggins. A more recent collection of methodological articles can be found in the June 1992 issue of *IEEE Engineering in Medicine and Biology.* The computer programs used in the analyses conducted in our study were developed by the research team and incorporated new technical information as it became available. Many of the articles referenced above also provide more technical information about the methods.

•   •   •

This new science is evolving quickly and is dependent on technical expertise from mathematics, physics, and computer science, so it is unlikely nurses will be using these methods independently in the near future. Interdisciplinary research teams seem far more likely to be successful in applying the methods to nursing research problems. A nurse researcher will contribute vital insight to such studies. The nurse researcher is expert in identification of appropriate research questions and available and appropriate data for analysis using these methods. Interpretation of the findings is also dependent on the nurse's knowledge of the substantive variables and systems involved.

REFERENCES

1. Toffler A. *Science and Change (Foreword) in Order out of Chaos by Prigogine, I: Stengers, I.* New York, NY: Bantam Books; 1984.
2. Lorenz E. Deterministic nonperiodic flon. *Journal of Atmospheric.* 1963;20:130.
3. West B, Goldberger A. Physiology in fractal dimensions. *American Scientist.* July/August 1987: 354–365.
4. Pool R. Is it chaos or is it just noise? *Science.* 1989;243:25.
5. Davidson AW, Ray M. Studying the human-environment phenomenon using the science of complexity. *ANS.* 1991;14(2):73–87.

6. Phillips J. Chaos in nursing research. *Nurs Sci Q.* Fall 1991;4(3):96–97.
7. Vicenzi A, Hamilton P. Concerning partnerships between theoretical physics, mathematics and community health nursing. In: Chambers B, ed. *State of the Art of Community Health Nursing Education, Research and Practice.* Lexington, Ky: Association of Community Health Nursing Educators; 1990.
8. Vicenzi A, Hamilton P. Chaos, Fractals and Strange Attractors. *Notes on Nursing Science.* Spring 1990: 3–4.
9. Schlitt J. *Primary Prevention of Adolescent Pregnancy Among High-Risk Youth.* Washington, DC: Southern Center for Adolescent Pregnancy Prevention; 1992.
10. Texas Department of Human Services, Client Self-Support Services. *Adolescent Pregnancy Prevention Report.* Presented to the 72nd Legislature; 1992.
11. Jones E, Forrest J, Goldman N, et al. Teenage pregnancy in developed countries: determinants and policy implications. *Fam Plann Perspect.* 1985;17(2):53–63.
12. Norr K. Community-based primary prevention of adolescent pregnancy. In: S. Humanick & N. Wilkerson, eds. *Adolescent Pregnancy: Nursing Perspectives on Prevention.* White Plains, NY: March of Dimes; 1991.
13. Schaffer W, Kot M. Do strange attractors govern ecological systems? *BioScience.* 1985;35(6):342–350.
14. Catalano R, Serxner S. Time series designs of potential interest to epidemiologists. *Am J Epidemiol.* 1987;126:724–731.
15. Joyce TA. Time series analysis of unemployment and health: the case of birth outcomes in New York City. *J Health Economics.* 1989;8:419–436.
16. Heckman J, Walker J. Forecasting aggregate period-specific birth rates: the time series properties of a microdynamic neoclassical model of fertility. *Journal of American Statistical Association.* 1989;48(408):958–965.
17. West B. *Fractal Physiology and Chaos in Medicine.* River Edge, NJ: World Scientific; 1990.
18. Gilliam S. Time series analysis and application. Denton, Tex: Texas Woman's University; 1992. Unpublished manuscript.
19. Texas Department of Human Services, Client Self-Support Services. *Adolescent Pregnancy Prevention: A Progress Report.* Presented to the 72nd Legislature; 1992.
20. Broomhead DS, King GP. Extracting qualitative dynamic from experienced data. *Physica D.* 1987;20:217.
21. Gleick J. *Chaos: Making a New Science.* New York, NY: Viking; 1987.
22. Coppa D. Chaos theory suggests a new paradigm for nursing science. *J Adv Nurs.* 1993;18:985–991.
23. Concerning partnerships between theoretical physics, mathematics and community health nursing. In: Bianca Chamber, ed. *State of the Art of Community Health Nursing Education, Research and Practice.* Lexington, Ky: 1990.

Describing Cognitive Structures Using Multidimensional Scaling

Julia Fisco Houfek, PhD, RN
Assistant Professor
College of Nursing
University of Nebraska Medical Center
Omaha, Nebraska

Describing cognitive structures may help nurses better understand individuals' health-related experiences. Multidimensional scaling (MDS), a multivariate technique, can be used to portray dimensional models of cognitive structures. MDS displays the structure of proximity data as spatial "maps." The maps show the interrelations among a group of stimuli, with each stimulus portrayed as a point in the multidimensional space. From the positions of the stimuli, inferences can be made about their underlying dimensions. MDS can quantify cognitive structures without imposing dimensions *a priori* and can help determine how perceptions influence behavior.

UNDERSTANDING THE WAYS individuals interpret their health-related experiences is an important area of inquiry for nursing.[1] One approach to investigating the meaning of experiences for individuals is to describe their perceptions of the events, objects, or people involved. Perception is an active process that involves both attending to and interpreting stimuli.[2] As part of the perceptual process, a person's organized mental representations of prior experiences are assumed to guide interpretation. These mental representations are also known as *cognitive structures* or *schemas*.[3-4] Schemas exist in dynamic interchange with the environment. They develop from repeated participation in situations and reflect the regularities of these experiences.[2] Schemas are believed to regulate an individual's perceptions and behaviors and, in turn, to be modified by new experiences.[5] A person stores in memory many types of schemas, such as schemas of situations, persons, and the physical environment, at varying levels of complexity.[2,6] Schemas operate at both the conscious and unconscious levels of awareness.[7]

Leventhal, Diefenbach, and Leventhal proposed that people respond to illness and other threats to health by attending to stimuli in their internal and external environments, interpreting this information according to their health-related schemas, and using these interpretations to select coping mechanisms.[8] The role that cognitive structures or schemas play in the process of coping with illness and threats to health make them an essential part of understanding individuals' health and illness experiences.[9] Furthermore, the potential for new experiences to alter existing structures makes the assessment of cognitive schemas an important aspect of studies that investigate the effects of nursing interventions on individuals' thoughts and behaviors.

Cognitive schemas can be inferred from individuals' judgments about their relevant domains,[3] and structural features can be described in terms of the underlying attributes or dimensions.[4] This article discusses the use of multidimensional scaling (MDS), a descriptive, multivariate statistical technique, to construct dimensional models of individuals' organized mental representations or schemas. A brief introduction to MDS, the data used in MDS analyses, and the types of MDS are presented. To illustrate the use of MDS, an analysis of adult surgical patients' representations of routine nursing care situations is explained.[10] Implications for the use of MDS in the development of nursing knowledge also are discussed.

ANALYZING DATA WITH MDS

MDS refers to a family of data analysis methods that represent the structure of data as spatial "maps."[11] The maps show the interrelationships among a group of stimuli, with each stimulus portrayed as a point in a multidimensional space. Davison defined MDS as "a set of multivariate statistical methods for estimating the parameters in and assessing the fit of various spatial distance models for proximity data."[12(p2)] In the spatial maps, stimuli are arranged so that the distances between them have the strongest possible relation to the similarities between the pairs of stimuli.[13] Positioning stimuli close together reflects much similarity, whereas placing stimuli far apart reflects much dissimilarity. From the positions of the stimuli in the MDS configuration, inferences can be made about their underlying attributes or dimensions. Typically, the MDS configuration is displayed in Euclidean space, the space used in everyday experience. Because people intuitively understand the characteristics of Euclidean space, the configuration is often easy to interpret, even by those unfamiliar with the principle of MDS.[11] The spatial representation of data structure is the essential feature of all MDS methods.[11]

MDS is well suited for studying complex stimuli whose psychological dimensions are not known or not well understood. MDS does not require that investigators possess prior knowledge of either the attributes to be scaled[14] or the dimensionality of the stimuli. During data collection, researchers need not specify the attributes subjects are to consider. Rather, subjects are frequently free to choose the attributes on which they base judgments about the stimuli. In effect, MDS often helps researchers "discover" the attributes of a group of stimuli that are relevant to subjects.

Proximity Data for MDS

Data used in MDS studies are measures of proximity between pairs of stimuli. A proximity is a number that indicates how similar or dissimilar two stimuli are or are perceived to be.[15] Davison classified proximity data as direct or derived.[16] For direct proximity data, subjects judge the similarity or dissimilarity of a group of stimuli. Proximity data are called similarities when large numbers indicate that stimuli are much alike and dissimilarities when large numbers indicate that stimuli are very different. A common method for obtaining direct proximity data requires subjects to judge the similarity (or dissimilarity) of all possible pairs of the stimuli using category or graphic rating scales. Other typical data collection tasks include sorting stimuli into groups according to their similarity or ranking stimuli based on their similarity to a stimulus serving as a standard.[14] Derived proximity data are computed from other suitable measurements. For example, correlations that are computed from measurements on pairs of variables are derived proximities.

In preparation for an MDS analysis, the proximities are arranged in a square matrix, stimulus × stimulus, in which the numbers of columns and rows are equal and refer to only one set of stimuli. Because it is usually assumed that the proximity measure of a stimulus pair would be the same regardless of which stimulus in the pair is presented first, the matrix is frequently symmetric. For symmetric matrices, the lower triangle of the matrix is sufficient input for an MDS analysis.

Levels of Measurement and MDS

An MDS analysis can be performed using metric or nonmetric MDS procedures. The distinction between metric and nonmetric MDS refers to assumptions about the level of measurement of the proximity data used in the analysis.[14] Metric MDS assumes that the data are at least interval level and attempts to fit the data to the distances of stimuli in the MDS configuration. Metric MDS maintains a linear relationship between the distances and the proximities. The distances are computed to be as much like the proximity data as possible, commonly using the method of least squares.[13] Nonmetric MDS assumes that the data are ordinal and monotonically related to the distances (ie, as x increases (decreases), y either increases (decreases) or remains the same). In nonmetric MDS, an unknown monotonic function, which is estimated by the computer program, fits the rank order of the proximities to the rank order of the distances.[14,16] Because nonmetric MDS preserves only the rank order relationships between the data and the distances, it provides configurations with a better fit to the data in low dimensionalities than metric MDS.[14] The development of nonmetric MDS, with its less restrictive assumptions, popularized the use of MDS as a data analysis technique.[11]

Types of MDS for Proximity Data

MDS procedures can be classified according to the number of data matrices used in the analysis and whether the MDS model used to construct the configuration of the stimuli employs weights to show the emphasis that is placed on the dimensions.[11,14] This classification scheme yields three types of MDS for proximity data: (1) classical MDS (CMDS), using one matrix and an unweighted model; (2) replicated MDS (RMDS), multiple matrices, unweighted model; and (3) weighted MDS (WMDS), multiple matrices, weighted model.[13] The matrices used in an MDS analysis usually represent subjects, but they can also represent occasions, settings, or treatment conditions. The major output for each type of MDS consists of a matrix of coordinates for the stimuli in the multidimensional space and a geometric picture that displays the spatial representation of the coordinates, which is known as the stimulus space.[14] Additionally, the output for WMDS includes a set of weights, one weight per dimension, for each data matrix. Because the weights indicate the importance or salience of the dimensions for each data matrix, WMDS enables researchers to separate information specific to each data matrix from information common to the group.[14] Readers interested in additional information on the types of MDS can consult Schiffman, Reynolds, and Young[14] or Young.[11]

A STUDY OF PATIENTS' REPRESENTATIONS OF NURSING CARE EPISODES

To illustrate the application of MDS to nursing phenomena, excerpts from a study of patients' representations of nursing care episodes are presented. The purpose of this exploratory study was to describe the dimensions of 17 nursing care episodes as perceived by adult surgical patients. To ensure that subjects were familiar with the stimuli to be scaled, the episodes were limited to nurse–patient interactions that subjects were likely to encounter more than once during the postoperative period (eg, vital signs, deep breathing, and assessment of the operative site). Only the research design, the data analysis, and the interpretation of the MDS solution are discussed. The complete study, which also included nurses' representations of the episodes, is reported in Houfek.[10]

Symbolic Interactionism and the Study of Episodes

Symbolic interactionism served as the conceptual basis of the study. A basic premise of symbolic interactionism and other social interaction theories is that individuals organize their perceptions about their experiences into cognitive structures or schemas.[3-4,17-18] In accord with the tenets of symbolic interactionism, patients were viewed as active participants in their care who internalized nurse–patient interactions and organized these memories into implicit knowledge structures. It was further assumed that patients used these knowledge structures to guide their behavior in future nurse–patient situations. Forgas noted that a symbolic interactionist conceptualization of interpersonal episodes or situations has two distinct aspects: (1) episodes as structural units that have culturally based, consensual meaning for individuals; and (2) episodes as processes, the continuous creation of meanings as individuals interact in actual situations.[18] This study focused on nursing care episodes as structural units rather than as processes. Specifically, the structure of the episodes can be classified as a semantic schema,[2] which contains attributes to help people characterize and give meaning to their experiences. Because MDS does not require that researchers define the attributes of the group of stimuli to be scaled *a priori,* these methods are well suited for describing semantic schemas, which are implicit knowledge structures.[2] In future studies, the relationships between subjects' semantic schemas and their interactions during actual nursing care situations can be explored.

Stimuli Selection and Data Collection Tasks

A convenience sample of 17 nursing care episodes was chosen from a domain of 45 episodes that depicted recurrent nurse–patient interactions in the postoperative period. The domain was developed by the investigator using the nursing literature and descriptions of postoperative nursing care situations provided by nine registered nurses (RNs). Each episode was written to express a single idea. As suggested by Forgas,[4] episodes were described in general terms; details were not specified. Examples of the episodes are "Having the nurse help you walk after surgery," "Talking with the nurse about your discomfort or pain," and "Having the nurse take your blood pressure." For convenience, the episodes were given brief labels, which appear in Fig 1 and Fig 2.

The episodes were arranged into a categorical rating task that contained all possible pairs of the episodes (ie, 136 pairs) plus 10 replicated pairs to estimate test–retest reliability. (See Fig 3 for an example of the categorical rating task.) The Ross matrix,[19] which is a pattern for determining the optimal order of paired comparisons in a dataset, was used to sequence the stimulus pairs for data collection. Using the Ross matrix ensured that the order of the stimuli was balanced for space effects (whether a stimulus is presented first or second in the ordered pair) and time effects (whether the appearance of a stimulus is spaced evenly throughout the rating task).[12,19] Data collection time for subjects was minimized by use of an incomplete design, in which the set of stimulus pairs is divided into subsets, and each subject judges the pairs in one of the subsets.[12] Specifically, the categorical rating task was divided into three parts, each part consisting of 48 or 49 episode pairs. Subjects, who were assigned one of the three subsets, were asked to judge the dissimilarity of the stimulus pairs using a rating scale of "the episodes were exactly the same" (0) to "the episodes were highly dissimilar" (9). Subjects were instructed to use any criteria they wished when making their judgments. To estimate the consistency of subjects' judgments, the replicated stimulus pairs were used to calculate the test–retest reliability for the proximity data, which was .77.

The investigator also chose 10 adjectives or descriptive phrases that were plausible attributes of the episodes. The adjectives or phrases were chosen from the nursing literature and suggestions made by RNs and patients. These attributes, which are listed in Table 1, were used to interpret the dimensions of the episodes objectively. For this rating task, subjects rated each of the 17 episodes on the 10 attributes using an 8-point scale that ranged from "the attribute does not characterize the episode" (0) to "the attribute very much characterizes the episode" (7). A table of random numbers was used to determine the order of presentation of both the episodes and the attributes in the rating task. Content representativeness for

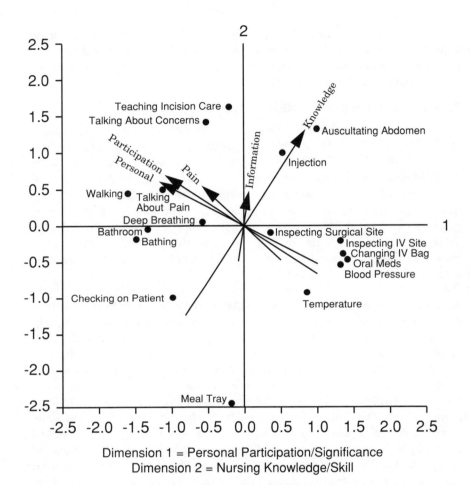

Fig 1. Dimensions 1 and 2 of RMDS configuration of patients' representations of nursing care episodes with rating scale regression vectors.

both the episodes and the attributes was judged by six adult surgical patients and six nurses with master's degrees in nursing, and is reported elsewhere.[10,20]

Subject Selection

Based on guidelines suggested by Davison, a minimum of 30 subjects were needed to judge one third of the total number of stimulus pairs (ie, 48 or 49 pairs).[12] This sample size ensured that there were at least 20 proximity judgments to estimate each stimulus coordinate for the episodes up to four dimensions. A convenience sample of 35 subjects made usable proximity judgments about the

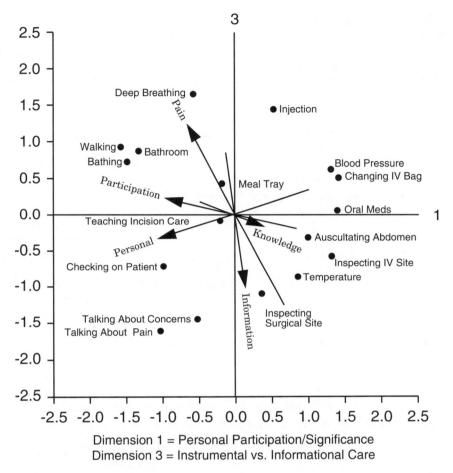

Dimension 1 = Personal Participation/Significance
Dimension 3 = Instrumental vs. Informational Care

Fig 2. Dimensions 1 and 3 of RMDS configuration of patients' representations of nursing care episodes with rating scale regression vectors.

episodes. These subjects, 29 females and 6 males, ranged in age from 22 to 60 years (mean = 38.71 and SD = 10.28) and had an average of 14.33 years of education (SD = 1.93). The median number of previous hospitalizations for the sample was 3. All subjects had experienced abdominal surgery, were recovering normally, and were hospitalized at least 72 hours. Data were collected on or after the third postoperative day.

In addition, a separate convenience sample of 14 abdominal surgery patients who also met the subject-selection criteria rated each of the 17 episodes on the 10 attribute scales. Because the attribute ratings were used only as an aid to interpret

Directions: Please circle the number that in your judgment best indicates the amount of difference for each pair of nursing care situations.

1. A. Having the nurse assist you to deep breathe.
   B. Talking with the nurse about your discomfort or pain.

EXACT   MOST
SAME   DIFFERENT
  0   1   2   3   4   5   6   7   8   9

2. A. Receiving an injection (shot) from the nurse.
   B. Having the nurse take your temperature.

EXACT   MOST
SAME   DIFFERENT
  0   1   2   3   4   5   6   7   8   9

Fig 3. Sample of categorical rating scales to collect direct proximity data.

Table 1. Results for multiple regression of the attribute ratings on the dimensions of the RMDS configuration of the nursing care episodes.

Attributes	R	Standardized regression coefficients on each dimension		
		1	2	3
Reassuring	.50	0.213	0.418	−0.183
Important	.49	0.201	0.467	−0.032
Personal	.76*	−0.616	0.328	−0.233
Causes me concern	.53	−0.280	0.392	−0.181
Gives me information	.77*	0.094	0.430	−0.603
Helpful to my recovery	.50	0.146	0.486	0.170
Involves discomfort/pain	.84*	−0.426	0.332	0.619
Requires my participation	.74*	−0.587	0.380	0.125
Requires nursing knowledge/skill	.79*	0.383	0.676	−0.189
Routine	.63	0.624	0.170	0.150

*$p < .01$

the dimensions of the episodes objectively, background data for subjects who made the attribute ratings were not considered relevant and were not collected. The use of a different sample to make these ratings ensured that the proximity judgments and attribute ratings were independent of one another.

DATA ANALYSIS

Subjects' proximity data were analyzed using PROC ALSCAL (*Alternating Least Squares SCALing Algorithm*), an MDS computer program in the *Statistical Analysis System* (SAS), Version 5.[21-22] PROC ALSCAL was used to perform nonmetric RMDS. RMDS analyzed the 35 data matrices simultaneously and produced one solution, known as the group stimulus space,[14] which represented the collective representation of the subjects. RMDS accommodated individual response styles (ie, the different ways subjects used the response scale) by allowing separate data transformations for each matrix. In RMDS, the distances of the stimuli in the MDS configuration were determined to be simultaneously like all the data matrices.[13]

In the nonmetric analysis, the proximity data were assumed to be ordinal and themselves monotonically related. The goal of the nonmetric MDS analysis was to fit the rank order of the dissimilarity data to the rank order of the distances of the episodes in the MDS configuration.[14] Because the dimensionality of the episodes was not known, MDS solutions in Dimensions 2 through 5 were obtained. From these, the one configuration that best represented the data was chosen based on two criteria: (1) fit of the model to the data and (2) intuitive interpretability of the configuration. Once selected, this configuration was also interpreted objectively to give empirical support for the identification of the dimensions of subjects' mental representations of the episodes. The overall goal of the data analysis was to construct a dimensional model that described subjects' semantic schema of the nursing care episodes.

Evaluation of Goodness of Fit

Stress, a descriptive statistic, was used to measure the fit of the model to the data. Stress indicates the degree to which the rank order of the estimated distances of the stimuli in the geometric solution achieves a one-to-one correspondence with the rank order of the proximity data. Stress is scaled to range between 0 and 1. Low stress values indicate little discrepancy between the distances and the data.

ALSCAL computes two stress statistics: (1) squared stress (SSTRESS), which is the statistic optimized by ALSCAL;[23] and (2) overall stress (STRESS), which is an average of the stress values for several matrices.[21] ALSCAL strives to minimize stress. The SSTRESS and STRESS values for Dimensions 2 through 5 were compared to values expected for random data. The values for subjects' data were lower than values for random data, indicating a degree of structure in the data. For the two-dimensional configuration, values of SSTRESS and STRESS were .40

and .18, respectively. For the three-dimensional configuration, SSTRESS = .32 and STRESS = .13, which indicated that the three-dimensional configuration provided a better fit to the data than did the two-dimensional solution.

Intuitive Interpretation

Initially, the MDS configurations were interpreted intuitively by inspecting the placement of stimuli along the coordinate axes for changes that indicate plausible attributes used by the subjects. The process of interpreting the dimensions of an MDS configuration intuitively can be compared with the process of naming factors in factor analysis.[24] Both the two- and three-dimensional configurations were subjectively interpretable. The four- and five-dimensional configurations were not readily interpretable. Because the three-dimensional solution was intuitively interpretable and had relatively low stress values, it was selected for further analysis using an objective approach. Intuitively, the three dimensions were named: (1) Patient Participation, (2) Nursing Knowledge/Skill, and (3) Technical versus Psychosocial Nursing Care. The three-dimensional MDS configuration, plotted two dimensions at a time, is displayed in Fig 1 and Fig 2.

Objective Interpretation

Linear multiple regression was then used to identify the three dimensions of the MDS configuration objectively. To use multiple regression, investigators need either ratings on plausible attributes of the stimuli or measurements of the physical properties of the stimuli. In the multiple-regression equation, the attribute ratings or physical measurements function as the criterion variable, one at a time, and the coordinates for each dimension serve as the predictor variables. The goal of the multiple-regression analysis is to find, for each attribute variable, a weighted combination of the stimulus coordinates in the MDS configuration that explains or accounts for the attribute. If the multiple correlation coefficient is high (ie, $\geq$ .70),[15] then it is likely that subjects used this attribute or a similar one when making proximity judgments. In addition, the multiple correlation between the attribute and the stimulus coordinates must have a significance level of at least .01[15] because the stimulus coordinates are not independent of one another, and the significance levels can be inflated.[14] Finally, the attribute must have a high regression coefficient on the dimension it is used to interpret.[15]

Table 1 shows the results of regressing the mean attribute ratings over the three-dimensional configuration. Five attributes (Personal, Gives Me Information, Involves Discomfort/Pain, Requires My Participation, and Requires Nursing Knowledge/Skill) were significantly correlated with the configuration and could be used to interpret the configuration objectively. The attributes were drawn into the MDS configuration as vectors, two dimensions at a time, using procedures suggested by Schiffman, Reynolds, and Young.[14]

Fig 1 and Fig 2 show that the vectors representing the attributes Personal and Participation are positioned close together and lie closest to Dimension 1. Table 1 indicates that these attributes have a high multiple correlation with the configuration. These attributes also have high regression coefficients for Dimension 1, and their vectors run in similar directions. The objective interpretation suggests that the episodes that require active participation also have a psychosocial component that represents the personal significance of the episodes for patients. In both Fig 1 and Fig 2, episodes on the left side of Dimension 1 include activities of daily living that patients performed independently prior to surgery and require participation postoperatively. Also located at this end of the dimension are psychosocial episodes that require some degree of self-disclosure (eg, talking with the nurse about concerns). For patients, performing activities of daily living after surgery may be interpreted as a sign of recovery that is personally significant as well as indicative of participation in care. Also, expressing thoughts and feelings to the nurse may help patients reflect on their experiences and may be personally meaningful to them.

In the middle of Dimension 1 are episodes that involve technical nursing care requiring the nurse to expose and touch parts of the patient's body that socially are considered personal or private. These episodes, however, also typically require some participation or cooperation by the patient (eg, receiving an injection). On the right side of Dimension 1 are episodes requiring technical nursing care that involve touching more publicly exposed parts of the patient's body (eg, having the nurse take the patient's blood pressure or change an IV bag) as well as less patient activity. To incorporate the idea of personal significance of the episodes for patients into the interpretation of Dimension 1, the initial label Patient Participation was changed to Personal Participation/Significance.

Dimension 2, which was intuitively named Nursing Knowledge/Skill, appears in Fig 1. Episodes requiring much nursing knowledge or skill (eg, teaching incision care) are located at one end of Dimension 2, toward the top of the figure. At the opposite end, toward the bottom of Fig 1, are episodes that can be perceived as requiring much less nursing knowledge or skill, such as having the nurse check on the patient and having the nurse pick up the patient's meal tray. Episodes involving activities of daily living (eg, walking or bathing) and nursing activities that can be viewed as requiring a moderate amount of nursing knowledge or skill appear in the middle of the dimension.

Fig 1 shows that the vectors representing the attributes Information and Nursing Knowledge/Skill are positioned close to Dimension 2. Table 1 indicates that the attribute Nursing Knowledge/Skill has a high regression weight on Dimension 2, whereas the attribute information has a smaller regression weight on this dimension. The lengths of the vectors in Fig 1 show that the attribute Information accounts for less of the variance of the episodes in the two-dimensional space than the attribute Nursing Knowledge/Skill. The high correlation of the attribute Nursing Knowledge/Skill with the configuration and the high regression coefficient on Dimension 2 give support for the interpretation of Dimension 2 as patients' perceptions of the degree to which knowledge or skill is needed by the nurse in the episode. Accordingly, the label Nursing Knowledge/Skill was retained for Dimension 2.

Dimension 3 is depicted in Fig 2. Episodes involving technical nursing care (eg, receiving an injection and deep breathing) are anchored at one end of this dimension, at the top of the figure. Episodes pertaining to psychosocial care (eg, talking with the nurse about concerns) anchor the opposite end of Dimension 3. In addition, episodes involving nursing assessment, such as inspecting the surgical site, appear at the same end of Dimension 3. These assessment episodes typically involve interpersonal interaction between the patient and the nurse, such as an explanation of the assessment and findings. Tentatively, Dimension 3 was labeled Technical versus Psychosocial Nursing Care.

The vectors representing the attributes Pain/Discomfort and Information are most closely aligned with Dimension 3 (see Fig 2). These vectors run in opposite directions. The placement of the vectors suggests that the episodes located at the top of Fig 2 (eg, deep breathing and receiving an injection) involve pain or discomfort. Episodes that are low in the amount of pain or discomfort involved but focus on providing the nurse and patient with information occur at the opposite end of the dimension, at the bottom of Fig 2. The alignment of the vectors for Pain/Discomfort and Information with Dimension 3 suggests that important attributes of Dimension 3 are whether the episode involves pain or discomfort and whether nurses provide patients with information. Although the attribute Pain/Discomfort had a higher correlation with the MDS configuration than did the attribute Information, both correlations were significant, and both attributes had high regression coefficients on Dimension 3. Therefore, it was decided that both attributes helped define Dimension 3. To reflect the activity aspect of the episodes involving pain or discomfort as well as the informational aspect of the episodes involving assessment or psychosocial care, the label for Dimension 3 was changed to "Instrumental versus Informational Nursing Care."

The three-dimensional MDS model suggested that subjects' mental representations of the nursing care episodes can be described using the following attributes:
- the amount of participation expected in the episodes and the personal significance of the nursing care activities,
- the nursing knowledge/skill needed in the episodes, and
- whether the episodes involved pain/discomfort or provided patients with information.

USING MDS TO DEVELOP NURSING KNOWLEDGE

The proximity judgment tasks used to collect data for an MDS analysis offer advantages over predetermined attribute scales for describing individuals' perceptions of their health-related experiences. Because MDS does not require investigators to specify the dimensions to be scaled in advance, these methods may uncover attributes that are more salient to subjects than those chosen by an investigator.[14] In addition, during data collection, subjects do not need to identify the criteria they are using to make the proximity judgments. Consequently, MDS may capture attributes that subjects cannot readily articulate or those that are less easily addressed by direct measures, such as rating scales or interviews.[25]

The output from an MDS analysis also offers advantages in interpreting individuals' perceptions. MDS can scale stimuli on two or more attributes simultaneously. The spatial representation of the episodes provides a visual picture of their location on the dimensions or attributes. The dimensions have the same metric and use a common origin, enabling investigators to compare stimuli on a number of attributes easily. For example, Fig 1 and Fig 2 show that the episode "Receiving an injection from the nurse" requires a moderate amount of participation and has a degree of personal significance for subjects. Fig 1 and Fig 2 also simultaneously show that subjects judged that an injection requires a high level of nursing knowledge and involves technical nursing care and pain or discomfort.

As the study of nursing care episodes illustrates, MDS can be used as an exploratory technique to model relevant psychological attributes of a group of stimuli.[26] With models of these tacit knowledge structures, researchers and clinicians may better understand the processes that people use to cope with their health and illness experiences. For example, Dimension 2 for the episodes, Nursing Knowledge/Skill, suggests that subjects have an organized structure about nurses' work and provides nurses with information about subjects' understanding of the knowledge and skill needed for nursing care. On Dimension 2, the position of the episode "Inspecting Surgical Site" indicates that subjects viewed this episode as requiring less nursing knowledge/skill than receiving an injection or listening to the abdomen with a stethoscope. In actuality, however, inspecting a surgical site is a complex activity, requiring that the nurse apply knowledge of wound healing and the skill of inspection in the situation.

Because social interaction theories assume that cognitive structures mediate interpersonal behaviors, dimensional models of individuals' representations of stimuli can be used to test the hypothesized role of cognitive structures in interpersonal interactions.[17,25] For example, it can be hypothesized that patients may use Dimension 2, in part, to judge the competency of the nurses who care for them. When a nurse expertly performs a nursing activity that patients perceive as requiring much knowledge and skill, such as teaching about incision care, patients' estimation of the nurse's competency may be higher than if the nurse expertly performs an activity that patients judge as requiring less knowledge or skill, such as taking the patient's temperature. Because MDS is able to quantify the attributes possessed by a group of stimuli, dimensional models of cognitive structures can also be used in statistical procedures to describe the relationships between individuals' mental representations of their experiences and their actual or expected behaviors. For example, Bishop explored the relationships between the cognitive representations of physical symptoms and individuals' expected self-care activities.[27] Finally, the relationships between individuals' cognitive structures and measures of functional status, such as actual health or quality of life, can be described.

In the realm of nursing intervention studies, MDS can be used to determine differences in cognitive structures over time or between groups. In effect, MDS techniques can provide investigators with pictures of individuals' perceptions at various points in time or among various treatments or settings.[14] The more sophisticated WMDS procedures enable researchers to determine both the dimensions of stimuli that are common to a group of subjects as well as subgroup differences in the emphasis placed on the dimensions. The use of WMDS presupposes that subjects differ not in the attributes used to interpret their experiences but in the emphasis they place on the dimensions. If the stress values for individual matrices indicate a poor fit of the model to the data, then the subgroups can be analyzed separately using CMDS or RMDS to determine if different dimensions emerge during the MDS analysis.[28] Thus, as a part of intervention studies, MDS techniques can be used to determine the effects of nursing interventions on individuals' cognitive structures. Such knowledge, in turn, can lead to the development of theories about the relationships among nursing interventions, cognitive structures, and health-related behaviors.

•   •   •

MDS methods can be used to construct dimensional models of individuals' cognitive structures. Because MDS methods quantify cognitive structures, they can be used to test the relationships between cognitive structures and behaviors. Testing these relationships can lead to the development of useful theories that consider the contribution of cognitive structures to individuals' interpretations of their experiences and their health-related behaviors.

REFERENCES

1. Kasch CR. Toward a theory of nursing action: skills and competency in nurse–patient interaction. *Nurs Res.* 1986;35:226–230.
2. Landau RJ, Goldfried MR. The assessment of schemata: a unifying framework for cognitive, behavioral, and traditional assessment. In: Kendall PC, Hollon SD, eds. *Assessment Strategies for Cognitive–Behavioral Interventions.* New York, NY: Academic Press; 1981.
3. Wegner DM, Vallacher RR. *Implicit Psychology.* New York, NY: Oxford University Press; 1977.
4. Forgas JP. Episode cognition: internal representations of interaction routines. *Adv Exp Soc Psychol.* 1982;15:59–101.
5. Markus H. The self in thought and memory. In: Wegner DM, Vallacher RR, eds. *The Self in Social Psychology.* New York, NY: Oxford University Press; 1980.
6. Horowitz MJ, ed. *Person Schemas and Maladaptive Interpersonal Patterns.* Chicago, Ill: The University of Chicago Press; 1991.

7. Singer JL, Salovey P. Organized knowledge structures and personality: person schemas, self schemas, prototypes, and scripts. In: Horowitz MJ, ed. *Person Schemas and Maladaptive Interpersonal Patterns.* Chicago, Ill: The University of Chicago Press; 1991.

8. Leventhal H, Diefenbach M, Leventhal EA. Illness cognition: using common sense to understand treatment adherence and affect cognition interactions. *Cognitive Therapy and Research.* 1992;16:143–163.

9. Bishop GD. Understanding the understanding of illness: lay disease representations. In: Skelton JA, Croyle RT, eds. *Mental Representations in Health and Illness.* New York, NY: Springer-Verlag; 1991.

10. Houfek JF. *A Multidimensional Scaling Analysis of Nursing Care Episodes as Perceived by Adult Surgical Patients and Professional Nurses.* Austin, Tex: The University of Texas at Austin; 1989. Dissertation.

11. Young F. *Multidimensional Scaling: History, Theory, and Applications.* Hillsdale, NJ: Erlbaum; 1987.

12. Davison ML. *Multidimensional Scaling.* New York, NY: Wiley; 1983.

13. Young F. Multidimensional scaling. In: Kotz S, Johnson NL, eds. *Encyclopedia of Statistical Sciences.* New York, NY: Wiley; 1985;5:649–659.

14. Schiffman S, Reynolds ML, Young FW. *Introduction to Multidimensional Scaling: Theory, Methods, and Applications.* New York, NY: Academic Press; 1981.

15. Kruskal JB, Wish M. *Multidimensional Scaling.* Newbury Park, Calif: Sage; 1978.

16. Davison ML. Introduction to multidimensional scaling and its applications. *Applied Psychological Measurements.* 1983;7(4):373–379.

17. Jones LE. Multidimensional models of social perception, cognition, and behavior. *Applied Psychological Measurements.* 1983;7(4):451–472.

18. Forgas JP. *Social Episodes: The Study of Interaction Routines.* London, England: Academic Press; 1979.

19. Ross RT. Optimal orders in the method of paired comparisons. *J Exp Psychol.* 1939;25:414–424.

20. Houfek JF. Nurses' perceptions of the dimensions of nursing care episodes. *Nurs Res.* 1992;41:280–285.

21. Young FW, Lewyckyj R. *ALSCAL-4 User's Guide.* Chapel Hill, NC: Data Analysis and Theory Associates; 1979.

22. *SUGI Supplemental Library User's Guide.* Version 5 ed. Cary, NC: SAS Institute, Inc; 1986.

23. MacCallum R. Evaluating goodness of fit in nonmetric multidimensional scaling by ALSCAL. *Applied Psychological Measurements.* 1981;5(3):377–382.

24. Forgas JP. Multidimensional scaling: a discovery method in social psychology. In: Ginsberg GP, ed. *Emerging Strategies in Social Psychological Research.* New York, NY: Wiley; 1979.

25. Jones LE. Construal of social environments: multidimensional models of interpersonal perception and attraction. In: Hirschberg N, Humphreys LG, eds. *Multivariate Applications in the Social Sciences.* Hillsdale, NJ: Erlbaum; 1982.

26. McLaughlin FE, Marascuilo LA. *Advanced Nursing and Health Care Research: Quantification Approaches.* Philadelphia, Pa: W.B. Saunders; 1990.

27. Bishop GD. Lay conceptions of physical symptoms. *Journal of Applied Social Psychology.* 1987;17(2):127–146.

28. Rudy TE, Merluzzi TV. Recovering social–cognitive schemata: descriptions and applications of multidimensional scaling for clinical research. *Advances in Cognitive–Behavioral Research and Therapy.* 1984;3:61–102.

Index

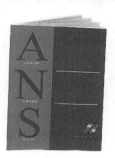